American Culture through Religion and Sport

Also Available from Bloomsbury:

The Bloomsbury Reader in Cultural Approaches to the Study of Religion, edited by Sarah J. Bloesch and M. Cooper Minister

The Body in Religion, by Yudit Kornberg Greenberg

Race and New Religious Movements in the USA, edited by Emily Suzanne Clark and Brad Stoddard

American Culture through Religion and Sport

Annie Blazer

BLOOMSBURY ACADEMIC
LONDON • NEW YORK • OXFORD • NEW DELHI • SYDNEY

Bloomsbury Academic
Bloomsbury Publishing Plc, 50 Bedford Square, London, WC1B 3DP, UK
Bloomsbury Publishing Inc, 1359 Broadway, New York, NY 10018, USA
Bloomsbury Publishing Ireland, 29 Earlsfort Terrace, Dublin 2, D02 AY28, Ireland

BLOOMSBURY, BLOOMSBURY ACADEMIC and the Diana logo are
trademarks of Bloomsbury Publishing Plc

First published in Great Britain 2026

Copyright © Annie Blazer, 2026

Annie Blazer has asserted her right under the Copyright, Designs and
Patents Act, 1988, to be identified as Author of this work.

For legal purposes, the Acknowledgments on pp. ix–x constitute an
extension of this copyright page.

Cover design by Jade Barnett
Cover image © Jena Ardell / Getty Images

All rights reserved. No part of this publication may be: i) reproduced or transmitted in any form, electronic or mechanical, including photocopying, recording or by means of any information storage or retrieval system without prior permission in writing from the publishers; or ii) used or reproduced in any way for the training, development or operation of artificial intelligence (AI) technologies, including generative AI technologies. The rights holders expressly reserve this publication from the text and data mining exception as per Article 4(3) of the Digital Single Market Directive (EU) 2019/790.

Bloomsbury Publishing Plc does not have any control over, or responsibility for, any third-party websites referred to or in this book. All internet addresses given in this book were correct at the time of going to press. The author and publisher regret any inconvenience caused if addresses have changed or sites have ceased to exist but can accept no responsibility for any such changes.

A catalogue record for this book is available from the British Library.

A catalog record for this book is available from the Library of Congress.

ISBN: HB: 978-1-3501-9707-7
       PB: 978-1-3501-9708-4
       ePDF: 978-1-3501-9710-7
       eBook: 978-1-3501-9711-4

Typeset by Integra Software Services Pvt. Ltd.
Printed and bound in Great Britain

For product-safety–related questions, contact productsafety@bloomsbury.com.

To find out more about our authors and books, visit www.bloomsbury.com
and sign up for our newsletters.

for Jesse

Contents

Acknowledgments ix
Preface: Notes for Educators xi

Introduction

1   Is Sport a Religion? 1

Part 1: Sports in Religious Communities

2   Muscular Christianity 19
3   Jewish Immigration and Antisemitism 37
4   Sports Ministry 54
5   Muhammad Ali 71
6   Asian Martial Arts 88
7   Muslim Athletes 106

Part 2: American Christianity and Social Issues in Sport

8   Sex and Gender 125
9   Youth Sports 143
10 Native American Mascots 160

11	Doping	**178**
12	College Sports	**195**

Notes	**212**
Selected Bibliography	**238**
Index	**247**

Acknowledgments

Writing a book is never a solitary endeavor, and I am grateful for the professional and personal support that I have had throughout the process. I began imagining this book in 2018, and through discussions with many interlocutors, my ideas evolved to become this manuscript. Lalle Pursglove and Seb Claas at Bloomsbury were instrumental in bringing this project to fruition. I'm very grateful to Lalle for encouraging my vision and for believing in this project's success at all stages of its development. My deepest thanks to the many people who took time to make this book better; the remaining imperfections are my own.

I am grateful to the people who allowed me to interview them for this book. I learned a tremendous amount from our conversations, and this book is better for the inclusion of your voices and perspectives. Thank you to the sports ministers who took time to help me understand current challenges in ministries for college athletes and the Muslim athletes who shared their stories, adding a richness to my chapter on Muslim American athletes that would have been impossible without your voices. I would also like to thank the individuals and institutions who assisted me in acquiring the images and primary sources that are included in this book; thank you for your generosity of time and labor.

When this book was still a germ in my head, colleagues in the subfield of religion and sport encouraged me and shared resources with me. I'm grateful to Art Remillard, M. Cooper Harriss, Jeremy Sabella, Jeff Scholes, Cody Musselman, Rebecca Alpert, and Tracy Trothen for sharing syllabi for their courses on religion and sports. Paul Putz, Eric Bain-Selbo, Terry Shoemaker, Brian Bolt, Doug Cowan, and Zachary T. Smith were also valuable discussion partners. I'm grateful to the leadership of the Religion, Sport, and Play program unit for the American Academy of Religion for continuing to push the subfield in nuanced and complex directions.

I had several opportunities to receive peer feedback on my ideas through publications in edited volumes and in the journal *Religions*. I would like to thank my anonymous peer reviewers for those publications, and for this one, for pushing me to clarify my positions and perspectives. In particular, I am grateful for the editorial feedback from Jeffrey Scholes and Randall Balmer (coeditors of *Religion and Sports in North America: Critical Essays for the Twenty-First Century*); Zachary T. Smith, Dennis J. Frost, and Steven G. Covell (coeditors of *Religion and Sport in Japan*); David Torevell, Clive Palmer, and Paul Rowan (coeditors of *Training the Body: Perspectives from Religion, Physical Culture and Sport*); and Jenna Gray-Hildenbrand, Beverley McGuire, and Hussein Rashid (coeditors of *Teaching Critical Religious Studies*).

My colleagues in the department of religious studies at William & Mary—Alex Angelov, Patton Burchett, Kevin Vose, Andrew Tobolowsky, Randi Rashkover, Rahel Fischbach, Michael Daise, Maggie Kirsh, Joanna Homrighausen, Mark McLaughlin, and Faraz Sheikh—have supported me and this project tirelessly for many years. William & Mary provided valuable financial assistance for this project in the form of three faculty research grants and the Plumeri Award (funded generously by Joe Plumeri). Students at William & Mary have helped this book in numerous ways. The students enrolled in "Religion and Sports in the US" and in "Theory and Method in the Study of Religion" read drafts of my chapters and provided feedback on what I was leaving out and what I could communicate better. In addition, student assistants provided valuable source research for multiple chapters. Thank you, Abby Comey, Madison Cleavinger, Taylor Slaven, Audrey Courcier, and Alayna Barrios for your excellent work.

During the years that I worked on this book, I was diagnosed with breast cancer (and beat it), the world shut down for the COVID-19 pandemic (and reopened), I fell in love (and got married), and through all that, I have had a tremendously supportive network of family and friends. My parents, siblings, siblings-in-law, and extended family provided a bedrock of love and support that helped me weather challenges and gave me confidence to persevere. My friends near and far continue to teach me the joys of curiosity, kindness, and bravery through the many ways they inspire and support me and each other. Special thank you to Brice McGowen for sharing your artistic expertise and for being a stalwart friend; to Jessica Delgado, Nicole Kirk, Kathryn Gin, and Judith Weisenfeld for personal and professional support; to my band, Jojo and the Kick Its (Jordan McDonald, Erin Lingo, Ty Phelps, Andrea Wright, and Jonathan Tallert) for providing much needed entertainment and collaboration; to my Dungeons and Dragons crew (Sarah Schriber, Chris Williamson, Mary Williamson, and Allen Bristow—can we level up yet?) for encouraging my creativity and imagination; to my women's circle for lighting so many candles for so many moons and listening so well; and to the rest of my amazing community in Richmond (Tyler Brown, Lizzie Garrett, Fabricio Prado, Hannah Buckley, Monica Seger, Clint Studdard, Jamie Lynn Haskins, Claire Hope, Eric Han, Scott Sliauzis, Robbie Mackey, Jessie Gaynor, Dan Young, Tina Giancola, and Kevin Davis) for making and strengthening the bonds that make daily life a pleasure.

Sharing my life with Jesse Tolj has made every part of it better. Our lives began to intertwine just as my ideas for this book were percolating, and its process and completion feels deeply connected to the selfless love, ongoing curiosity, gratitude, and celebration that you have always brought to our relationship and to my work. This book is dedicated to you; I can't imagine it any other way.

Preface

Notes for Educators

I began teaching on the intersections of religions and sports in graduate school while working on my dissertation on evangelical sports ministries in the United States. Since then, I have taught courses on religions and sports at three different institutions and for nearly two decades. When I cobbled together that first syllabus, I had no idea these courses would become the mainstay of my teaching career. This book is the book I wish had existed when I was designing my first courses. It is the culmination of version after version of course revisions, conversations with colleagues who teach regularly on these topics, and feedback from students on what they know, what they don't know, and what they don't know that they don't know. This preface is an overview for the organizational choices for the book and what each chapter provides, as well as the holes in this book with recommendations for sources that could further flesh out a course on this topic. This book is for you: please take what you like and disregard the rest.

I organized this book the way I construct my courses. Opening with an introduction to religious studies via an exploration of whether sport is a religion or not, this debate gives students access to competing definitions of religion and helps them understand that definitions are not neutral and have consequences. Part I of the book, "Sports in Religious Communities," proceeds chronologically through six chapters that address specific religious traditions and sports. Muscular Christianity sets the stage for much of sporting life in the United States, and students are often fascinated to learn that muscular Christians popularized the idea of "character building" and invented the sport of basketball. These white Protestants were reacting to major demographic changes in the United States as is further explored in the next chapter on Jewish immigration and antisemitism. Following American Jews through the decades of high immigration through the end of World War II showcases immigrant experiences of using sport to showcase cultural belonging.

Whereas the first two chapters of Part I focus on a bounded historical period, the remaining four chapters trace a story across time to the present day. Post–World War II, evangelical Christians began to focus on sports and develop special programming and institutions for Christian athletes. Chapter 4 on sports ministry traces these evangelical innovations from their invention in the 1950s and 1960s to today, focusing on issues of capitalism and sexuality. Chapter 5 on Muhammad Ali's life and career tells the story of the Nation of Islam, the Vietnam War, and race relations in the United States from the 1960s. Chapter 6 on Asian martial arts harkens back to muscular Christianity to show early adoption of martial arts by American elites and continues through time to offer a complex historical tapestry of Japanese internment, American occupation of Japan, and the kung fu movie industry. The final chapter of Part I attends to Muslim athletes in the United States, focusing on the challenges of modest clothing and fasting for Ramadan as obstacles to full participation in sports.

As more and more young people grow up nonreligious, I have noticed a decline in overall religious literacy among the students in my classroom. To address this, the chapters in Part I include broad overviews of the religious traditions covered. Recognizing that two or three paragraphs can never do justice to the long, complicated histories of religions, I nevertheless want to provide baseline knowledge. If this is the only religious studies course a student takes over a college career, perhaps it can foster curiosity about religious diversity even if my descriptions of religions are broad and introductory.

Part II of the book, "American Christianity and Social Issues in Sport," offers five in-depth, thematic investigations on the ways in which Christianity in America informs some social issues of sport. I chose the topics of sex/gender, youth sports, Native American mascots, doping, and college sports because these topics work together to raise the question: what is the point of sports? In thinking about why sports are segregated by gender, what young people learn from sports participation, why Native American mascots were once common, how performance-enhancing drugs became against the rules, and who benefits from the economics of college sports, students can flex their critical thinking skills, bolstered by the historical knowledge they developed through Part I. Bringing American Christianity into these conversations can reveal the roots of our cultural assumptions and offer reflection points that can enhance nuance and complexity.

Each chapter of the book includes an excerpt from a primary source, providing a firsthand account of the topic under consideration. Primary sources emerge from a particular time and place and allow us to imagine the context and thought processes that give rise to its perspective. I provide context and discussion questions for each primary source in hopes of spurring engaging classroom discussion. Each chapter also provides resources for further study that include media, an online archive, and readings.

This book is not comprehensive. Intersections of religions and sports are numerous and ongoing. I offer here some suggestions for addressing holes in this book's coverage. European Catholics immigrated to the United States along the same timeline as European Jews and used sports in much the same manner. Several great resources exist that offer windows onto American Catholicism and sports. For an overview, see Gerald Gem's article "Sport and the Assimilation of American Catholics," and for a case study, Julie Byrne's *O God of Players: The Story of the Immaculata Mighty Macs* provides an insightful treatment of how Philadelphian Catholic women dominated college basketball in the mid-twentieth century.[1] I have assigned the film *The Mighty Macs* alongside Byrne's work, and this generated classroom discussion on portrayals of American Catholics and the tendency for sport films to create underdog stories even if that narrative does not match the historical record.² Mormons also sought cultural belonging in the twentieth century much the same as Jews and Catholics. For an analysis of how Mormons used Brigham Young University's (BYU) football program to position themselves as mainstream Americans, see Hunter Hampton's "Saints Embrace Savagery: BYU Football and the Making of Modern Mormonism."³

This book uses the story of Muhammad Ali to tell the story of the Nation of Islam, the African American civil rights movement, and reactions to the Vietnam War. Some resources exist that move beyond this story to address the role of sports for Black Christians in the United States. Paul Putz's work on sports ministry specifically addresses racial divides in his chapter "Jesse Jackson Has Reason to Be Concerned" in *The Spirit of the Game: American Christianity and Big-Time Sports*.⁴ An important case study on Black men's religion and basketball is *Black Gods of the Asphalt: Religion, Hip-Hop, and Street Basketball* by Onaje Woodbine.⁵

Chapter 6 of this book explores Asian martial arts in the United States, but further investigation of Asian religious traditions and sports may be of interest. Richard Light and Louise Kinnaird's article "Appeasing the Gods: Shinto, Sumo, and 'true' Japanese Spirit" provides an introduction to the relationship between Shinto and sumo wrestling.⁶ This pairs nicely with the film *Sumo East and West*, which explores the popularity of sumo wrestling in Hawaii.⁷ Although scholarly analyses of American Hindus and sports have yet to be produced, resources on American Hinduism and physical culture are available, largely focusing on yoga. Andrea Jain's *Selling Yoga: From Counterculture to Pop Culture* is a highly teachable source that traces the evolution of yoga in the United States from margin to mainstream.⁸ Beyond the United States, Joseph Alter's book on Hindu wrestling in India, *The Wrestler's Body: Identity and Ideology in North India*, shows how institutions and participants in Indian wrestling incorporated Hindu beliefs and practices.⁹

Chapter 10 addresses the use of Native American mascots in American sports but does not address Native American participation in sport or Native American religions. For sources on these topics, see Philip P. Arnold's overview text, *The Gift of Sports: Indigenous Ceremonial Dimensions of the Games We Love*, and Thomas Vennum's case study of lacrosse, *American Indian Lacrosse: Little Brother of War*.¹⁰ For further resources on religion and sport in the United States and beyond, Rebecca Alpert's *Religion and Sports: An Introduction and Case Studies* provides succinct overviews, discussions questions, and sample classroom activities for a range of historical examples.¹¹

Over the past decade, several edited volumes on religion and sports have appeared, offering a range of approaches, topics, geographical focus, and historical period. Rebecca Alpert and Arthur Remillard's *Gods, Games, and Globalization: New Perspectives on Religion and Sport* and David Torevell, Clive Palmer, and Paul Rowan's *Training the Body: Perspectives from Religion, Physical Culture and Sport* focus on religious experiences in sports globally, both offering analyses of multiple sports and religious traditions.¹² More geographically focused, Jeffrey Scholes and Randall Balmer's *Religion and Sport in North*

America: Critical Essays for the Twenty-First Century takes on sport as a site for debates over gender, race, capitalism, media, and civil religion.[13] Forthcoming in 2026, Rebecca Alpert, Afe Adogame, and James Deming will offer the *Routledge Handbook on Religion and Sport*, which includes a range of scholarship on intersections of religions and sports.[14] In addition, the *International Journal of Sports and Religion* publishes new scholarship quarterly.

Students drawn to courses on religion and sports are often athletes or sports fans and bring their own lived experiences into the classroom. These passions can prove valuable classroom assets, and I have been lucky to learn from my students about their range of sports experiences. If this book helps you develop a course or a unit, contributes to your existing teaching, or fosters curiosity about teaching religion and sports, I welcome your questions, comments, and feedback.

Chapter 1

Is Sport a Religion?

In September 2024, I took a trip to Charlotte, North Carolina, to see a comedian perform at a venue downtown. Unbeknownst to me (and to the comedian), the weekend of this performance coincided with the 2024 Duke's Mayo Classic college football game between North Carolina State University and University of Tennessee-Knoxville at the Bank of American Stadium, which the North Carolina Panthers use. Attendance at the game that day was 72,730.

Making my way downtown to have dinner before the show, the streets and the light rail were packed with people of all ages wearing bright orange for Tennessee or bright red for NC State. I watched as perfect strangers fell into easy conversation facilitated only by the color of their clothing. The sense of camaraderie between the oranges and the reds was palpable as they traveled on the same sidewalk or train car to the stadium district to participate in the rituals of college football fandom. The city of Charlotte, host for these out-of-town fans, transformed from an orderly, shiny city of banks to an overgrown mass of pop-up tents, parking lot picnics, and overflowing bars as the reds and the oranges spilled over the streets of downtown. I felt as though I was interloping on a pilgrimage as the sea of people in orange and red seethed through the city streets good-humoredly teasing fans of the opposing team or making new friends with fellow fans.

It is fairly common to hear sports reporters and members of the public compare big-time sports to religion. It is easy to see why: sport involves sacred spaces (stadiums, arenas) with larger-than-life figures (athletes, coaches); special clothing, special foods, and special chants that only happen on the special day of the game; community boundaries drawn between insiders and outsiders; taboos, superstitions, and unshakable faiths on display. And for many fans, athletes, and coaches, their sport provides meaning, community, and structure to their lives. Gameday puts these attributes on full display, as I witnessed in Charlotte, and it is no wonder that even some religious studies scholars have raised the question: is sport a religion?

For example, Eric Bain-Selbo and D. Gregory Sapp's book, *Understanding Sport as a Religious Phenomenon*, makes the following claim:

> What we are arguing is that the human drives and needs that compel some to be a part of a particular religion are the same drives and needs that compel some to be part of

sport in some way.... We are saying that sport can be religious for some in the same way that participating in the activities of a mosque, temple, or church can be religious. Sport can function like a religion in that it meets the same needs and desires satisfied or promised by formal religions.[1]

Bain-Selbo and Sapp argue that the function of religion is to satisfy humans' desire for ethical structures and to provide models for human perfection. When we think about the question of whether sport can be considered a religion, we have to investigate what religion really is.

For a concept that Americans reference all the time, "religion" is very difficult to define. As a classroom exercise, I ask my students to brainstorm a list of characteristics of religion. I write on the board as they call out things: rituals, community, sacred texts, belief in a superhuman power, traditions, holidays, sacred spaces, moral guidance, and rules for everyday living. Although this list seems to encapsulate quite a lot, it is still difficult to get this list to hold the things we call religion while excluding the things we do not. For example, most Buddhists and some Jews do not ascribe to belief in a superhuman power, but most commonsense definitions of religion would want to include Buddhism and Judaism as religions. For another example, many African and Native American religious traditions do not rely on sacred texts as essential to their religions' practices, but we would want any definition of religion to include these groups. However, if we were to get rid of the components of belief in a superhuman power and the use of sacred texts, we might find that things that we do not normally think of as religious (like fraternities and sororities, like Swifties, like the Duke's Mayo Classic college football game) would fit in the category of religion.

So, what do we do with this difficulty of defining religion? This book is about religion, but what even *is* religion? Unfortunately, that question has no easy answer, but by exploring different approaches to defining religion, we can learn quite a bit about why defining religion matters and the consequences of different kinds of definitions. Definitions are arguments. By this, I mean definitions make claims based on evidence, and different definitions arise depending on what sorts of evidence the definition uses. By examining different definitions of religion, we can explore how sport might fall into the category of religion and how it might trouble the category of religion.

How You Define Religion Will Influence How You Study It

Religious studies scholar Paul Myhre argues in his *Introduction to Religious Studies* chapter, "What Is Religion?," that humans tend to demonstrate something that we would call religion regardless of their historical period or cultural context. He writes, "Consider the history of any people and you will find numerous examples of religious beliefs and practices playing a part in wars, leadership succession, human relationships, purity codes, legal documents, social and environmental ethics, and so on."[2] Because of religion's ubiquity, Myhre points out that it is not surprising that scholars disagree on what religion is and how to study it. He notes that "how you define religion will directly influence how you study it."[3] Definitions are ways of seeing—a definition reveals some things and obscures others.

Let's compare different methods of defining religion and consider for each definition whether sport could be included in the category. Three main approaches to defining religion are functional definitions (what does religion do?), formal definitions (what does religion look like?), and substantive definitions (what is the essence of religion?). A functional definition will assert what religion accomplishes, and therefore anything that accomplishes that thing belongs in the category of religion; a formal definition will describe the necessary components of a religion, and therefore anything that shares those components belongs in the category of religion; and a substantive definition of religion will identify an essential core to religion, and therefore anything in the category of religion must share that same essence. Using these sorts of definitions, scholars have argued for and against including sport in the category of religion.

Functional definitions of religion lend themselves to comparison with sport. Social theorist Emile Durkheim argued that religions function to orient persons in sacred time and sacred space, allowing believers to separate the sacred and the profane. In *Elementary Forms of the Religious Life*, published in 1912, Durkheim argued that the separation of the world into the sacred and the profane allows people to experience "effervescence," an exciting sensation of power only accessible through the sacred.

> In one world [the religious person] languidly carries on his daily life; the other is one that he cannot enter without abruptly entering into relations with extraordinary powers that excite him to the point of frenzy. The first is the profane world and the second, the world of sacred things.[4]

According to Durkheim, effervescence is the overwhelming feeling of belonging to something greater than oneself. He argues that this feeling is only possible socially, not individually. Effervescence gives religion emotional meaning and therefore ensures the continuation of religious institutions.

Durkheim's emphasis on sacred space and its ability to inspire a feeling of effervescence might remind you of a crowd cheering together in a sports stadium. Religious studies scholar David Chidester has described baseball in terms strikingly similar to Durkheim, emphasizing the function of baseball in the lives of fans: the season serves to delineate sacred times and sacred spaces.

> [Baseball] is a religious institution that maintains the continuity, uniformity, sacred time, and sacred space of American life. As the "faith of fifty million people," baseball does everything that we conventionally understand the institution of the church to do.[5]

In a similar argument, scholar of religion and sports Joseph Price maintains that big-time sports in America form a sacred calendar with football, basketball, and baseball elevating

Image 1.1 The Paint Crew is the student section at Purdue Boilermakers' Mackey Arena in West Lafayette, Indiana. The three thousand students who buy access to the Paint Crew commit to wearing the same clothing. In this photo, the Paint Crew cheers during a game against the Michigan State Spartans on March 2, 2024. *Getty Images/Icon Sportswire.*

and distinguishing sacred times and spaces.[6] Price goes so far as to argue that the Super Bowl "functions as a major religious festival for American culture" by invoking myths of American origin and dominance. As a "contemporary enactment of America's frontier spirit," Price argues that the Super Bowl reaffirms the myth of American manifest destiny as well as revels in the violence of conquest.[7] For Price, the Super Bowl being set apart spatially (in the stadium) and temporally (occurring only once a year) allows it to achieve this religious outcome. If the function of religion is to delineate special times and places and to produce ecstatic communal feelings, then sport (especially big-time, spectator sport) might fit the category of religion.

Religious studies scholar Catherine Albanese employs a formal approach to defining religion, identifying four features of a religious system: creed ("explanations about the meaning of human life"), code ("rules that govern everyday behavior"), cultuses ("rituals to act out the insights and understandings that are expressed in creeds and codes"), and communities ("groups of people either formally or informally bound together by the creed, code, and cultus they share").[8] Using this formal explanation of religion, we might argue that sporting communities constitute religious communities; and indeed, Albanese has made this argument, noting that sport constitutes an "American code of living." She writes,

> [Sports and deliberate religious rituals] both are examples of dramatic actions in which people take on assigned roles, often wearing special symbolic clothing to distinguish them from non-participants… Through their performances, [these activities] create an "other" world of meaning, complete with its own rules and boundaries, dangers and successes.[9]

Albanese argues that both religious rituals and sports create meaning through specialized activity, and this meaning can impact life beyond the boundary of the activity.

Michael Novak, Catholic theologian and scholar, took the argument that sports are formally religion even further in his work. He wrote,

> Sports flow outward into action from a deep natural impulse that is radically religious: an impulse of freedom, respect for ritual limits, a zest for symbolic meaning, and a longing for perfection… Sports are religious in the sense that they are organized institutions, disciplines, and liturgies; and also in the sense that they teach religious qualities of heart and soul.[10]

Novak's claim that sport is a religion relies on understanding religion as an organized community bound together by rules, rituals, and a shared understanding of human perfection. Due to these formal similarities between religion and sport, both Albanese and Novak treat sport as a religion.

Rather than thinking about what religion accomplishes (functional) or what religion looks like from the outside (formal), substantive definitions of religion seek to identify the internal qualities that make something undeniably religious. For example, Rudolph Otto, a German philosopher writing in the early twentieth century, argued that the concept of "the holy" contains an "overplus of meaning," which he named "the numinous." According to Otto, the numinous quality of religion can stir in people a feeling of powerlessness and holy dread in the face of absolute power.[11] This was an attempt to name an integral aspect of religion. For Otto, if something does not invoke this sensation, it is not religion.

A second example of a substantive definition of religion would be theologian Paul Tillich's assertion that what makes something a religion is the quality of "ultimate concern." For Tillich, religions provide a person with a sense of meaning that infuses their life and decision-making. An ultimate concern demands surrender from the believer and takes priority over all other concerns. For Tillich, everyone has a religion because everyone has an ultimate concern.[12]

Although some have argued that sport can inspire holy dread or serve as an ultimate concern, other scholars have used substantive definitions of religion to challenge the idea that sport is a religion. For example, Joan Chandler's article "Sport Is Not a Religion" argues that religion raises questions of ultimate meaning and provides followers with answers based on the supernatural. She writes, "While sport may provide us with examples of belief, ritual, sacrifice, and transcendence, all of them take place in a context designed wittingly and specifically by human beings, for the delight of human beings."[13] For Chandler, sport is explicitly void of supernatural content and cannot be considered a religion.

In his opening chapter, "Religion: Some Basics," in *Religion: The Basics*, Malory Nye addresses the problem of how to define religion. Before presenting and assessing definitions, Nye emphasizes that we should think of religion as something humans do. The study of religion is the study of humans acting in the world. Using this basic foundation for religion, he argues that religion is "nearly always *both* a set of ideas and beliefs that people engage with (to some extent or other), *and* also the framework of their lived experiences and daily practices."[14] Nye uses the example of Sigmund Freud. He points out that Freud defined religion as a misguided, unhealthy impulse arising from failed attempts to work through one's relationship with their father. Nye points out that Freud assumed that all religions were similar to Christianity and Judaism in their inclusion of a father figure deity. This example is useful because it shows that Freud's cultural context constrained his impressions of religion; he was more familiar with some religious traditions than others. Given this, we might think about how our own familiarity/unfamiliarity with religious traditions might inform our impressions of what makes a religion.

Religion Is a Legal Category

In the United States, religion is a special category protected under the U.S. Constitution. Its First Amendment contains these clauses: "Congress shall make no law respecting an establishment of religion, or prohibiting the free exercise thereof." These are known as the "establishment clause" and the "free exercise clause" and constitute two contradictory impulses in our governance. Court cases that test the establishment clause attempt to show that certain ordinances or laws favor one religious tradition and/or discriminate against another. Court cases that test the free exercise clause claim that a certain group deserves exemption to laws that substantially burden their ability to practice their religion. However, if the courts grant an exemption for one religious group, this could be construed as favoring that group and would therefore contradict the establishment clause.[15] This is an inherent contradiction built into the way the U.S. legal system treats religion.

Scholars such as Jonathan Z. Smith have argued that paying attention to what kinds of definitions of religion our legal system uses can help us understand the context and motivation for including and excluding things from the category of religion. In his essay "God Save this Honourable Court: Religion and Civic Discourse," he analyzed the use of religious categorization in American courtrooms. Because the U.S. tax code allows for tax exemption for religious organizations, the Internal Revenue Service (IRS) must delineate which organizations are religious and which are not. We know that how one defines religion has consequences.

If you had to guess, would you say that the IRS uses a functional, formal, or substantive definition of religion? Well, whatever you guessed, you would be wrong. The IRS defines religion based on a Christian prototype. A prototype is an example of a thing that other things are measured against and then, based on how closely they resemble the prototype, categorized as the same or different than it. According to the IRS, a religious organization is that which is "organized and operated exclusively for religious purposes" and these organizations, which the IRS refers to as "churches," do not have to submit statements of activities or an informational tax return as other nonprofit organizations are required to do. Let's turn to Jonathan Z. Smith's analysis of identifying a church legally:

> In the Department of the Treasury Regulation 1.511-2(a)(3)(ii), "church" for the purpose of this rule, is defined as the following: "The term 'church' includes a religious order or a religious organization if such order or organization is (a) an internal part of a church, and (b) is engaged in carrying out the functions of a church."... At first glance, what we read appears to be a set of tautologies masked as definitions in violation of the first rule of lexicography, "a word may not be defined in terms of itself." Surely, it is singularly uninformative to assert with the Internal Revenue Service that a religious organization must be organized for religious purposes or that a church must be part of a church or engaged in carrying out the functions of a church![16]

Smith notes that these tautological definitions show that the IRS is quite wary of defining religion and prefers to rely on the prototype of Christianity, a religion already recognized by the U.S. government, to measure others' claims for tax exemption. Although Smith published this analysis in 2004, not much had changed by 2024 when the IRS offered this list of characteristics of a "church":

> distinct legal existence, recognized creed and form of worship, definite and distinct ecclesiastical government, formal code of doctrine and discipline, distinct religious history, membership not associated with any other church or denomination, organization of ordained ministers, ordained ministers selected after completing prescribed courses of study, literature of its own, established places of worship, regular congregations, regular religious services, Sunday schools for the religious instruction of the young, schools for the preparation of its members.[17]

The IRS does not require that all characteristics are met for an institution to qualify as a "church." The use of the term "church" as well as terms such as "ministers" and "Sunday school" lets us know that a Christian prototype is in place. The use of a Christian prototype in U.S. law reveals the privileged place of Christianity in our culture as well as a tendency to marginalize or discount other religious traditions.

It is interesting to test whether sporting organizations fit the IRS's definition. Were the Green Bay Packers formed and operated exclusively for religious purposes? Is Wimbledon an internal part of a church? Could we argue that the National Hockey League carries out the functions of a church? Given that the IRS uses a Christian prototype to define religion, it is difficult to imagine the IRS granting tax-exempt status to any professional sports organization, especially because all tax-exempt nonprofit organizations must show the IRS that no individuals are benefiting financially from their organization.

Religious studies scholar Craig Martin makes the case that "how [religion] is defined, as well as what's included or excluded in the definition, depends on the interests of those making up the definition."[18] To illustrate this, Martin turns to a case study questioning whether yoga is religious. He notes that yoga studios became tax exempt in Missouri by claiming that yoga is religious, whereas in California, yoga teachers and enthusiasts argued that yoga was not religious and could therefore be included in public-school physical education classes. He writes, "Thus, rather than ask ourselves 'What is religion?,' it would be better to ask, 'Why does this group define religion this way rather than that way, what do they hope to accomplish, and how does the definition serve their interests?'"[19] Because religion in the United States is a legal category, it is useful to remember that Christianity is the religion that benefits the most from the use of a Christian prototype in legal definitions of religion.

Religion Is a Word That Changes Meaning over Time

The term "religion" has a particular history. Premodern languages had no word for "religion," and scholars have warned against using the concept to analyze premodern societies. Craig Martin writes, "When we translate premodern terms as 'religion,' we are actually projecting our own, contemporary ideas back into the past."[20] The idea that things can be categorized as either religious or secular did not exist in the ancient world. In sixteenth-century Europe, reform movements emerged that challenged the dominance of the Catholic Church. The civil unrest that these movements generated led to the European Wars of Religion that raged over the course of the sixteenth, seventeenth, and early eighteenth centuries. These wars were not only violent but also disrupted trade and political endeavors. The violence that emerged after the Protestant Reformation led to the first usage of "religion" that contains some components we associate with religion today—namely, that religion is a private choice beyond the bounds of politics and the state.

The European fight over which version of Christianity was true became a global question for Europeans as colonists and missionaries brought back information about the peoples of the Americas and Africa. Europeans interpreted what they encountered using their own experiences of sectarian conflict and projected their ideas about what is and is not religion onto the groups they sought to understand. Historian Brent Nongbri notes,

> This projection provided the basis for the framework of World Religions that currently dominates both academic and popular discussions of religion: the world is divided among people of different and often competing beliefs about how to attain salvation, and these beliefs should ideally, according to influential figures like Locke, be privately held, spiritual, and nonpolitical. It was only with this particular set of circumstances in the sixteenth and seventeenth centuries that the concept of religion as we know it began to coalesce.[21]

The idea that religion is an internal, private set of beliefs related to salvation (and unrelated to economics or politics) became the dominant understanding of religion in Europe.

In the seventeenth century, as European missionaries and colonists strove to understand the variety of foreign peoples they encountered in their global explorations, Europeans began to consider non-European cultural traditions as potentially religions. In general, their concern in studying these other religions was to show that Christianity was the true religion and others such as Judaism or Islam were false religions. During the era of colonial expansion as Europeans differentiated true and false religions, they began to apply an evolutionary framework to religions—primitive religions could eventually evolve into advanced religions like Christianity. This mind-set succeeded in painting Christianity as the pinnacle of human development and justified colonial missionary work, settlement, exploitation of and war against non-Europeans. As Martin notes, "Presenting 'primitives' as evolutionarily backward was useful for justifying colonialism and slavery."[22] In this way, definitions can be tools of war and colonialism; definitions can have deadly consequences.

"Religion" is not a neutral or universal idea; it is an idea that emerged from a particular period in European history, and its use has reinforced systems of colonial domination. The definitions of religion explored in this chapter are all inheritors of the history of the concept of "religion"; and it is worthwhile to note that tendencies to position some practices as "religious" and others as "superstitious" or "magical" reflect colonial judgments that often positioned the worldviews of Native Americans, Africans, and other indigenous peoples as invalid or primitive.

Does "sport" have a similar historical trajectory? Did Europeans use the concept of sport to evaluate the cultural sophistication of other groups of people? Sort of. For much of human history, physical activities not necessary for survival were predominantly ritual practices for acting out symbolic meanings. During the European enlightenment in the eighteenth century, sport activities began to look like modern sports today; but rather than serving a ritual function, Europeans tended to treat these activities as diversions, as secular forms of entertainment and fun. Some Europeans, such as the Puritans who came to North America, frowned on all forms of diversion and saw games and physical contests as not only frivolous but dangerous to the human soul. Because of the European affiliation of games and physical contests with either fun or danger, Europeans tended to judge other cultures that used games or physical contests as forms of symbolic expression as inferior or barbaric.

For example, the modern sport of lacrosse originated as a Native American athletic contest in northeastern North America. Multiple tribes in the region played variations of a game of moving a ball to a goal using sticks. Historian Donald Fisher has noted that the game served multiple purposes: physical fitness prepared men for war; intertribal competitions served as diplomacy to avoid violent conflict; tribal religious leaders called for games to heal the sick, alter the weather, or honor the dead; and gambling on the game's outcome allowed for wealth redistribution.²³ The carving of sticks for play was a specialized activity in a tribe, and tribes treated the sticks as sacred objects. Jesuit missionaries were the first to refer to the game as "crosse" and, although the missionaries worried that playing distracted Indians from learning about Christianity, they tolerated the sport.

In the mid-nineteenth century, Canadians organized lacrosse games between white men and Native Americans. George Beers was a Canadian enthusiast of the game and thought that with standardization, the sport would grow in popularity and could become Canada's national sport. One change that he advocated was the shortening of the field. Native Americans would play on fields as long as one mile, and white men could not compete with the running style of play that the Indians used. Beers saw the Native American game as a savage holdover and saw his role as modernizing the game to make it "civilized." Beers's project was largely successful; the sport grew in popularity, and Canada organized a tour to England to showcase whites and Indians playing lacrosse. The exposition organizers intended to showcase the differences between "gentlemen" and "savage" players to cultivate an image of Canada that would inspire immigration from

Image 1.2 Game of Lacrosse between Canadians and Iroquois in Belfast, United Kingdom, on May 10, 1876. This engraving by William Ralston was originally published in *The Graphic*, an illustrated weekly newspaper in the United Kingdom. The accompanying article described the game: "twelve Canadian gentleman played against twelve real live Iroquois Indians, each with an unpronounceable name."²⁴ *Getty Images/Duncan, 1890.*

England.[25] In this example, we can see how the trajectory of the concepts of "religion" and "sport" are intertwined with colonial and imperial understandings of civilization and savagery.

Primary Source

Primary sources provide firsthand accounts of the topic under consideration. They emerge from particular times and places and allow us to imagine the context and thought processes that give rise to a perspective.

"The Super Bowl as Religious Festival," by Joseph Price, abridged.
Copyright by the Christian Century Foundation and used with permission.

Context:

- This article first appeared in *The Christian Century* on February 22, 1984, following Super Bowl XVIII held in Tampa, Florida, on January 22, 1984.
- The halftime show was sponsored by the Walt Disney Company and titled "Salute to Superstars of the Silver Screen." It featured choreographed dances to Hollywood standards such as "Puttin' on the Ritz."

Discussion Questions:

- Have you watched a Super Bowl? If so, what do you like about it? What do you dislike about it? What parts of the event strike you as religious, ritualistic, or nationalistic?
- Why do you think the Super Bowl resonates with most Americans? Do you agree with Price's assertions that the Super Bowl fulfills a mythic function in American culture? Why or why not?
- How does the most recent Super Bowl compare to Price's description of the 1984 Super Bowl? What values did you see reflected in the most recent halftime show?

The Super Bowl as Religious Festival
There is a remarkable sense in which the Super Bowl functions as a major religious festival for American culture, for the event signals a convergence of sports, politics and myth. Like festivals in ancient societies, which made no distinctions regarding the religious, political and sporting character of certain events, the Super Bowl succeeds in reuniting these now disparate dimensions of social life. Two dominant myths support the festivity and are perpetuated by it. One recalls the founding of

the nation and the other projects the fantasies or hopes of the nation. Both myths indicate the American identity.

The first concerns the ritual action of the game itself. The object of the game is the conquest of territory. The football team invades foreign land, traverses it completely, and completes the conquest by settling in the end zone. The goal is to carry the ritual object, the football, into the most hallowed area belonging to the opponent, his inmost sanctuary. There, and only there, can the ritual object touch the earth without incurring some sort of penalty, such as the stoppage of play or the loss of yardage.

This act of possession is itself reflective of cosmogonic myths. Conquering a territory and bringing order to it is an act equivalent to consecration, making the space itself sacred by means of recalling and rehearsing the primordial act of creation. The specifically American character of the mythology has to do with the violent nature of the game. Not only does it dramatize the myth of creation, it also plays out the myth of American origins with its violent invasion of regions and their settlement. To a certain extent, football is a contemporary enactment of the American frontier spirit.

Amidst the ritual of the forceful quest, there is the extended "time out" of halftime, a time of turning from the aggressions of the game to the fantasies of the spirit. During the halftime show, the second dominant American cultural myth is manifest. It revolves around the theme of innocence. The peculiarly American quality about this myth is that even in our nation's history of subjugation, a sense of manifest destiny was often associated with extending the nation's boundaries. Indeed, the idea that a divine mandate had authorized the people to move into a place to which they had no claim indicates that the people did not think they bore final responsibility for the displacement of natives. In other words, the assignment to God of the responsibility for territorial expansion was an attempt to maintain the illusion of blamelessness among those who forcibly took alien lands.

In this year's Super Bowl [1984], the theme of righteousness was acted out in a three-ring circus which featured 2,100 performers from Walt Disney Productions. Although acts took place in the outer rings, which were colored blue, attention was focused on the largest center ring, which was white. In this area, most of the performers wore white or pastel shades of yellow. The visual effect was an overwhelming sensation of cleanliness and purity.

The overall effect was one of feigned innocence and the naïve hope often exemplified for Americans by Walt Disney's vision. Finally, the transition from this scenario was accomplished by the explosion, of fireworks along the perimeter of the field. The fantasy and violence of exploding Roman candles shifted the scene back to the play of the American frontier, simultaneously reviving intimations of the festival's patriotic character. Fireworks are the hallmark of the Fourth of July, and evoke the national anthem lyrics' imagery—"the rockets' red glare, the bombs bursting in air."

> As a sporting event, the Super Bowl represents the season's culmination of a major American game. As a popular spectacle, it encourages endorsement by politicians and incorporates elements of nationalism. And as a cultural festival, it commands vast allegiance while dramatizing and reinforcing the religious myths of national innocence and apotheosis.

Religion and Sports Shape American Culture

Jay Coakley, a foundational scholar in sociology of sport, has identified a pervasive and unshakable American belief in what he calls the "great sport myth." Coakley describes this as three interrelated, unsubstantiated claims: 1) sport is inherently good and pure, 2) the purity and goodness of sport is transmitted to those who play or consume it, and 3)

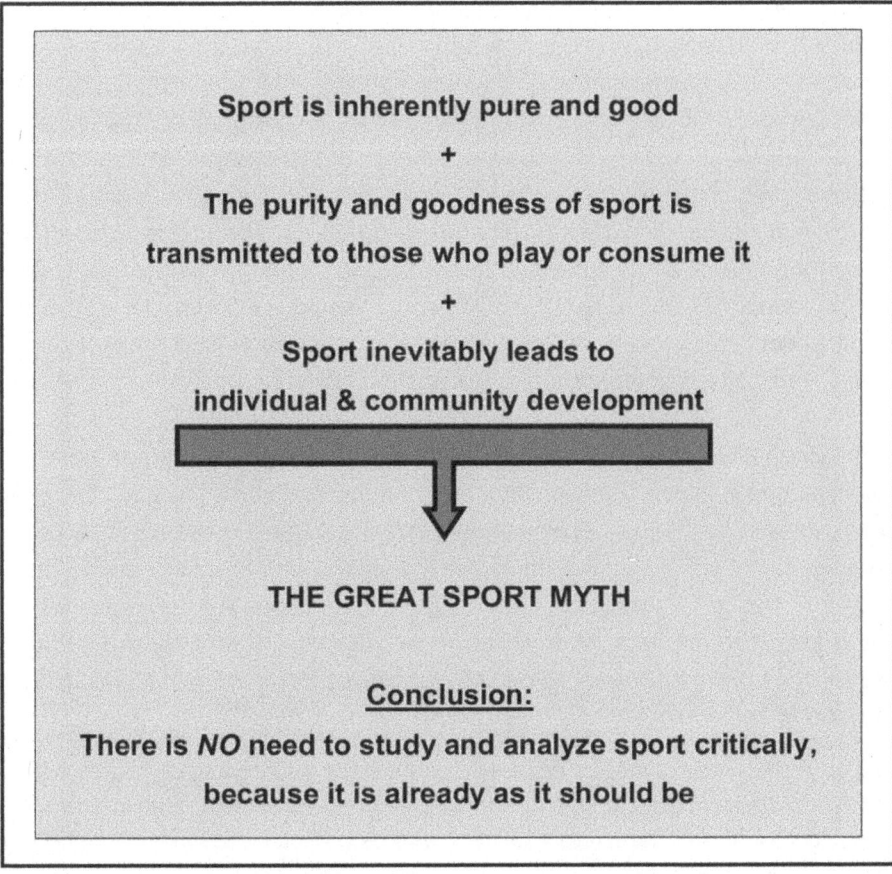

Figure 1.1 The great sport myth. Sociologist Jay Coakley argues that American culture treats sport as inherently good and pure; therefore, it is both difficult and necessary to bring critical attention to sports. *Courtesy of Sage Publications.*

sport inevitably leads to individual and community development. Coakley argues that for those under the spell of the great sport myth, "They already know the truth about sport and their faith in that truth is much like religious faith—isolated from empirical reality and regularly expressed through unquestioned support of policies and programs in which sport is the focus."[26] Coakley notes that the great sport myth blinds people to the idea that sport may have systemic flaws that can lead to dubious moral actions. Instead, when unethical conduct occurs, media and institutions tend to blame individuals for tainting the pureness of sport with their own greed.

The great sport myth lies behind the huge economic investment in sports at every level across society. Because Americans tend to see sport as good, they are willing to pay (with their own money and with their tax dollars) to support the enterprises of sport. Large-scale sporting events such as the FIFA World Cup and the Olympic Games do not necessarily have positive consequences for the host nations, but these events are shielded from critique by the power of the great sport myth. The communities and rituals of sport can seem natural and organic, and it is useful to remember that both sports and religions are cultural constructions; they are codes and practices developed over time that people use to organize their relationships and their world.

Religious studies scholars Megan Goodwin and Ilyse Morgenstein Fuerst use the example of baseball fandom in Boston to show that, like religion, sports fandom can have real consequences for individuals whether or not they pay attention to baseball. In Boston, baseball has a sacred space (Fenway Park); baseball structures time and space by making opening day a cultural event and controlling the flows of traffic and people on game days; baseball rituals include clothing, cheers, and collective emotional responses to the Red Sox winning or losing. One summer day, while in graduate school in Boston, Ilyse walked out of her house wearing a Yankees cap. She was on her way to a market and oblivious to the cultural sin that was the ball cap on her head. A man yelled at her on the T, the Boston subway, because in her words, Ilyse "had broken the first commandment of Boston: thou shalt not fly enemy colors."[27] In a town where fans shouted "Yankees suck!" after the Patriots won the 2002 Super Bowl (a championship for football, not baseball), wearing a Yankees cap was tantamount to sacrilege.

"Red Sox Nation," like religion, is a cultural construction, but that does not mean that it is imaginary or fake. Men yelling at women on the subway goes badly for women all the time; consequences can be dangerous for ignoring or flaunting cultural constructions.

> Like baseball, religion provides occasions and spaces to bring people together for a common purpose and a shared understanding of the world and our place in it. And like those Red Sox fans on the T, religion also draws lines between who's in—which is to say who's safe, who's included, who's protected—and who's out.[28]

Red Sox Nation is a community that, like a religious community, establishes insiders and outsiders using rituals. And like the real-world consequences of belonging or not belonging, religions and sports fandom can have negative outcomes for those deemed outsiders.

Conclusions: Is Religion a Sport?

It is worthwhile to question why far fewer people claim that religion is a sport than those that claim that sport is a religion. If religion and sport have so much in common, why aren't scholars and journalists interested in making the comparison in the other direction? If some definitions of religion allow for the inclusion of sport in that category, do definitions of sport allow for the inclusion of religion?

Just as scholars of religion have struggled and refined definitions of religion over time, scholars of sport have also debated and contested the boundaries of the category of sport. Is chess a sport? What about professional wrestling? What about rock climbing? In an attempt to determine the limits to the category of sport, sociologists of sport have emphasized that sport has the following features: "sports are institutionalized competitive activities that involve rigorous physical exertion or the use of relatively complex physical skills by participants motivated by personal enjoyment and external rewards."[29] Using this definition, sociologists can distinguish sports from mental competitions such as chess or spelling bees, from noncompetitive activities such as yoga or hiking, from informal noninstitutionalized activities such as children playing tag, and from activities done solely for personal enjoyment (play) or solely for external reward (dramatic spectacle).

One could argue that institutionalization, personal enjoyment, and external reward are also important characteristics of most religions, but scholars and adherents would likely be uncomfortable applying the features of competition, rigorous physical exertion or complex physical skills to religions. It feels like a stretch to include embodied activities such as prayer or meditation in the same category as competitive sprinting or golf. When commentators call sport a religion, they often want to draw attention to the specialness of sport and to the importance that fans and athletes ascribe to sporting competition and activity. On the other hand, if we were to call religion a sport, it would draw attention to aspects of religion that are rule-oriented, exclusive, and provide personal satisfaction. As we have seen, this would not be the whole picture of religion; and vice versa, we need to recognize that calling sport a religion is not the whole picture of sport.

Resources for Further Study

Media

Megan Goodwin and Ilyse Morgenstein Fuerst, "INCORRECT: Sports," *Keeping It 101: A Killjoy's Introduction to Religion.* Podcast. https://www.buzzsprout.com/810974/episodes/11937163-incorrect-sports.

Online Archive

Religion of Sports, a production company based in Los Angeles, California, makes videos that treat sports competitions and athletes as sacred figures. They describe their subject as, "Larger than life heroes playing in grand cathedrals, succumbing to agonizing curses, conjuring awe-inspiring miracles."[30] https://www.religionofsports.com.

Reading

Eric Bain-Selbo, "Conclusion: Sport as Religion? A Summary and Final Assessment." In *Game Day and God: Football, Faith, and Politics in the American South* (Macon, GA: Mercer University Press, 2009), 213–39.

Joan M. Chandler, "Sport Is Not a Religion," in *Sport and Religion*, ed. Shirl Hoffman (Champaign, IL: Human Kinetics, 1992), 55–62.

Jay Coakley, "Assessing the Sociology of Sport: On Cultural Sensibilities and the Great Sport Myth," *International Review for the Sociology of Sport* 50 (2015): 402–6.

Part I

Sports in Religious Communities

The six chapters of this part of the book explore how different religious communities have used sports to bolster their sense of religious identity and belonging in America. Beginning with late-nineteenth-century white Protestants, we can see how the social movement of muscular Christianity laid the groundwork for much of our cultural assumptions about the value of sporting participation. Muscular Christians saw sport both as morally valuable and as an important tool for training boys in proper masculinity. The influence of this movement is evident as we turn to Jewish immigrant communities and their use of sport for demonstrating assimilation to American culture. Jewish immigrants turned to sport to combat antisemitic stereotypes of Jews as weak as well as for communal experiences such as cheering on Jewish athletes and teams.

Evangelical Christians, Black Muslims, Asian Americans, and Muslim Americans have also engaged sports in ways that meshed with their beliefs and practices while at the same time showcasing belonging in America. Evangelicals sought celebrity athletes as spokespeople for their tradition and worked within the systems of sports to find opportunities to share their theological message. Turning to the life and times of Muhammad Ali helps us consider the religious movement of the Nation of Islam in the context of the African American civil rights movement. Exploring the American adoption of Asian martial arts as sports helps to reveal an interrelated narrative of Asian immigration, U.S. military involvement overseas, and the kung fu movie industry. Today's Muslim American athletes face specific challenges to uniting sports and their religion when it comes to wearing a hijab and fasting for Ramadan. Learning more about these challenges can help us understand how athletes negotiate sports when American cultural norms conflict with religious commitments.

Part I shows that sports matter for a variety of religious communities. These communities have sought ways to play, watch, and organize sports that adhere to their values amid larger American cultural understandings of sport that form the background for their participation.

Chapter 2

Muscular Christianity

The period from the mid-nineteenth century to the 1920s was a time of rapid demographic change in the United States. Immigration and internal migration contributed to unprecedented growth of cities, and industrial factories replaced agriculture as the focus of American economic labor. According to historian of sports William Baker, as industry replaced agricultural labor as the defining force in men's lives, "another kind of male dominance, athletic prowess, became a central feature in the definition of manliness."[1] Muscular Christianity, a Protestant commitment to health and manliness, emerged in Britain in the 1850s and spread to America. Muscular Christianity promoted a religious manliness that relied on improving the body as well as the soul. As muscular Christianity took hold in America, it became commonplace to describe health and vigor as key manly virtues. Moses Coit Tyler, author of the fictional epitome of a muscular Christian village, Brawnville, summed up the ideology: "It is as truly man's moral duty to have a good digestion, and sweet breath, and strong arms, and stalwart legs, and an erect bearing as it is to read his Bible, or say his prayers, or love his neighbor as himself."[2] Muscular Christianity set in motion the now commonplace assumption that sport builds character; in fact, the phrase "character building" emerged during this time. By examining the institutions and values of muscular Christianity, we can see that this influential movement was not neutral but carried with it assumptions about gender, race, and class.

A brief explanation of Christianity is in order. Christianity is a global religion centered on the story of two miraculous events set around two thousand years ago: Jesus Christ, a semidivine child, is born to a virgin and, as an adult, is killed and comes back to life. The two miracles of Jesus's virgin birth and resurrection, showcased in the Christian holy text, the Bible, form the basis for Christianity's beliefs and practices. The major holidays of Christmas and Easter celebrate the birth and resurrection of Christ respectively. Over time, Christianity experienced several major schisms, usually over debates about doctrine. The first major schism was between Roman Catholicism and Orthodox Christianity in the Middle Ages over roughly 1000 to 1200 CE. These two groups disagreed on whether Christianity should be centralized (the Roman Catholic position) or decentralized (the Orthodox position) and on the doctrinal issue of whether the divine power of the Holy Spirit stemmed from both God and Jesus (the Roman Catholic position) or from God alone (the Orthodox position). This split largely followed geographic lines: western Europe adhered to Roman Catholicism; and Greece, eastern Europe, and central Asia adhered to Orthodoxy.

A second major schism emerged in sixteenth-century Europe between Catholicism and Protestantism. This split was also driven by a disagreement about power and authority. The Roman Catholic Church centralized power in the figurehead of the pope, and statements of correct belief and correct practice disseminated from the pope to the church. The Protestant movement offered a new perspective on religious authority claiming two central tenets: scripture alone (the Bible and not the pope was the final authority on Christianity) and priesthood of all believers (every believer has the same relationship with God; priests do not have a special or more powerful connection to God). A significant problem with putting Protestant tenets into practice was that oftentimes the text of the Bible is not straightforward and requires interpretation, leading to a variety of understandings of what Christianity is and should be. Similarly, if every believer has equal authority, these varieties of understanding scripture can lead to competing factions that offer differing priorities and practices. This is exactly what happened: almost immediately Protestantism fragmented into multiple factions called denominations. Today, these number more than one hundred.

The first European settlers in North America were Protestant, and partly due to the expansion of European settlements across the continent, forms of Protestantism proliferated across the land. By the time we get to the mid-nineteenth century and the beginnings of muscular Christianity, American Protestantism had reached a crossroads. In the decades leading up to the Civil War (1861–1865), Protestants disagreed with each other on the morality of slavery and largely split North (antislavery) versus South (pro-slavery). Following the Civil War and abolition of slavery, American Protestantism underwent a reorganization with two main branches emerging: mainline Protestantism (popular in the North) and evangelical Protestantism (popular in the South). Mainline and evangelical Protestants disagree on the priorities of human work in the world. Most mainline Protestants hold to a doctrine of "social gospel," the idea that Christians have an ethical obligation to address human suffering in the world by combating poverty, inequality, and vices such as alcohol and gambling. Although most evangelical Protestants agree that human suffering deserves attention, their priority is helping as many people as possible convert to Christianity. This is because evangelicals believe that God is in full control of humanity's destiny, so the best thing that Christians can do is focus on the salvation of human souls, not the living conditions of human beings.

Muscular Christianity was largely a mainline Protestant project, headquartered in American cities. Muscular Christians saw their mission as twofold: showcasing the manliness of (mostly white) Protestant men in the face of waves of immigration (of non-Protestants) and migration (of rural white and Black folks) and overseeing the activities of boys to ensure that they would develop the morals, personality, and authority to carry on Protestantism.

Changing Demographics and White Protestantism in Crisis

Waves of immigration impacted the demographic makeup of the United States from the mid-nineteenth century until the passage of a highly restrictive immigration law in 1924. In addition to the continuation of white Protestant immigration from Europe, the United States saw three major streams of immigration: Chinese immigration to the West Coast; Catholic immigration to the northeast from Ireland, eastern, and southern Europe; and Jewish immigration to the Northeast from eastern Europe. From the 1850s until Congress passed the Chinese Exclusion Act of 1882, approximately 322,000 Chinese immigrants came to the West Coast to work jobs related to the gold rush and the expansion of railroads. From 1860 to 1890, the Chinese-born population of California was around 10 percent of the total population; this was by far the largest sector of the foreign-born population of California. In 1850, Catholics made up only 5 percent of the total U.S. population, but by 1906, they made up 17 percent and were the single largest religious denomination in the country. The famine in Ireland combined with changing agricultural practices across Europe led many poor Europeans to seek a way out of poverty by immigrating to the United States. In addition, antisemitism in eastern Europe led many Jews to seek a new life in the United States. Two and half million Jews immigrated between 1881 and 1924 and mostly settled in northeastern cities. In 1830, the percentage of foreign-born immigrants in the United States was 1.6 percent; by 1930 it was 13.6 percent, the highest it has ever been.

At the same time that immigration was impacting the demographics of the United States, the country was experiencing the greatest internal migration of a people to ever occur. Known as the "great migration," six million African Americans migrated from the rural South to cities to the West, Midwest, and Northeast from the 1910s to the 1970s. Following train routes, African Americans from the Texas/Arkansas/Louisiana area tended to head west to cities such as Los Angeles and San Francisco; African Americans from the Mississippi/Alabama/Tennessee/Kentucky area tended to head north to cities such as St. Louis, Chicago, and Detroit; and African Americans from the southern East Coast states tended to head north to cities such as Washington, D.C., New York City, Philadelphia, and Baltimore.

About five million rural white Southerners also relocated as the promise of factory work drew them to cities. Lower crop prices made farming a more difficult living, and the promise of industrial jobs made moving to the city appealing. Although factory conditions before labor laws were unhealthy to say the least, factory employment offered several advantages over farming. Rather than one's income depending on good weather and a big harvest, the reliable wages of factory jobs gave families some financial security.

For immigrants and migrants, push and pull factors led to their decision to relocate. Push factors included poverty and discrimination; pull factors included the promise of economic security and human rights. For the white Protestant majority in cities, the

Table 2.1 Population Growth of Cities, 1860–1920[3]

	1860	1880	1900	1920
New York City	813,669	1,206,299	3,437,202	5,620,048
Philadelphia	565,529	847,170	1,293,697	1,823,779
Baltimore	212,418	332,313	508,957	733,826
Boston	177,841	362,839	560,892	748,060
Cincinnati	161,044	255,139	325,902	401,247
St. Louis	190,524	350,518	575,238	772,897
Chicago	109,260	503,185	1,698,575	2,701,705

arrival of immigrants and migrants caused significant anxiety as cities teemed with new languages, a physically strong workforce engaged in factory labor, and a wider variety of religious practices. Two ways that this anxiety manifested was through increased diagnoses of a disease called "neurasthenia" and attention to a condition in boys and men called "over-civilization."

Neurasthenia, a disease first diagnosed in 1869, became a prominent fear as doctors increasingly diagnosed men and women with the disease. Symptoms included depression, lethargy, anxiety, pain, insomnia, as well as digestive complications, sexual disfunction, and weight loss. Historian David Schuster argues that these symptoms were due to men and women realizing that they could not live up to the gendered ideals of the time: some men found themselves unable to provide financially in an era of changing employment norms, and some women found themselves unable to provide moral anchoring for their families and achieve the ideals of an orderly home.[4]

Relying on records from the Cooper Medical Center free clinic in 1880s San Francisco, Schuster shows that men with economic anxieties sought treatment for neurasthenia. For men in particular, loss of employment meant both a failure to provide economically and a loss of social identity and community respect. Men's neurasthenic symptoms of sexual disfunction such as premature ejaculation, nocturnal emissions, and impotence "were downright crippling to their sense of pride and manly confidence… and had the appearance of being entirely personal and unrelated to outside factors or influence, which made it easier for men to place guilt for it squarely on themselves."[5] These neurasthenic men perceived the cause of their disease to be personal failing.

A well-documented representative case of a male neurasthenic is Theodore Dreiser (1871–1945), a novelist who suffered from neurasthenia following the commercial flop of his first novel, *Sister Carrie*, in 1900.[6] Dreiser's symptoms included insomnia, mental disorganization, decision paralysis, weight loss, and general hopelessness. Dreiser's older brother, Paul, paid for him to go to a sanatorium in White Plains, New York, that specialized in male neurasthenia. William Muldoon, a former champion wrestler, ran the facility and forced the men there to engage in rough physical activity under a steady stream of verbal abuse. Muldoon controlled the minutia of everyday activities for his charges. Schuster summarizes Muldoon's philosophy of care:

> By dictating what time patients awoke, what time they slept, how much they ate, how hard they exercised, and even the way they bathed, Muldoon sought to lift the burdens of thought and decision-making from neurasthenic men overwhelmed by their lives and responsibilities.[7]

Muldoon intended his hypermasculine activities to force men's minds to rest by taking over all their daily decisions. Treatment for male neurasthenics emphasized that the disease was an individual problem and that individuals could resolve it through dedication to increased manliness.

Muldoon's masculine work cure did not appear in treatment for female neurasthenics. S. Weir Mitchell developed a rest cure for women with neurasthenia that was nearly opposite Muldoon's approach. According to psychiatrist Diana Martin's description of Mitchell's treatment,

> The patient was instructed to lie in bed for twenty-four hours each day, sometimes for months at a time, with a special nurse who would sleep on a cot in the room, feed her, and keep her mind from morbid thoughts by reading aloud or discussing soothing topics. Visits from family and friends were forbidden. The day was punctuated by electrotherapy and massage, sponge baths with a "rough rub" using wet sheets, and frequent feedings.[8]

Women diagnosed with neurasthenia were more likely to attribute the disease to flawed gender roles that constrained them to tedium and second-class status. Some women such as the author Charlotte Perkins Gilman vehemently opposed Mitchell's rest cure and sought pathways for increased intellectual stimulation and meaningful work for women as treatments for the disease.[9]

By the turn of the century, the threat of neurasthenia was well integrated into American culture, and Americans attempted to develop strategies that would prevent the disease, not merely treat it. Fears of neurasthenia and over-civilization coupled with urban overcrowding due to immigration and migration led to Protestant institutional responses meant to hone Christian manliness and train boys in masculine expectations. We turn now to institutions formed with these objectives in mind: the Young Men's Christian Association (YMCA) and organizations for boys.

Young Men's Christian Association

The YMCA was founded in England in 1844 by George Edwards. Originally, the organization provided Bible study and prayer as alternatives to urban pleasures for men who had recently relocated to cities for work. In 1851, the YMCA came to the United States and served roughly the same purpose. Beginning in the early nineteenth century, single men from rural areas began to flock to cities in large numbers. The apprenticeship system that had offered one-on-one tutelage to instill skills and values disintegrated after the Civil War with the onset of mass industrialization. Without the apprenticeship system, commercial leaders worried that the newly arrived rural, single men would fail to develop proper morals. City life was far different from the slow-moving, tightly knit agrarian backgrounds of these men, and with few respectable and affordable entertainment options for young men, new arrivals tended to frequent saloons and disreputable establishments. Saloons adapted to this new clientele and began to offer such services as free lunches, a savings bank, and employment services, making these social centers for young men in cities.

Against this backdrop, Protestant businessmen grew concerned about the survival of their ethics and values. The YMCA seemed a solution to this concern; and in 1865, New York City's YMCA elected a new board of directors comprising prominent businessmen. This new board proposed a building in the heart of the city with features that would attract young men. On December 2, 1869, the New York YMCA opened its new headquarters at the corner of Fourth Avenue and 23rd Street in lower Manhattan. The New York YMCA was the first modern YMCA featuring a revival hall, gymnasium, library, employment office, social parlor, and classrooms all under one roof. It became a model for YMCA buildings constructed across the country in the late nineteenth century.

The YMCA saw a need to develop a competitive game that could be played indoors during the winter months, noting that between football and baseball seasons was a glaring lack of competitive sport for physical education. At the YMCA training facility in Springfield, Massachusetts, director of physical education Luther Gulick assigned the task of creating an indoor winter sport to James Naismith. Basketball was the result. According to Naismith, by the 1890s,

> [Football, baseball, and track] had been firmly established, and many of the more active students took part in them. When the men engaged in these sports went to the city to enter business and found that they had leisure time, it was only natural that they should look for some kind of athletic diversion.[10]

These men were "frankly discontented" with winter gymnastics compared to the action of football. "What this new generation wanted was pleasure and thrill rather than physical benefits."[11] And so basketball in its early form integrated thrilling competition with values of teamwork and fair play.

After experimenting with versions of indoor rugby and football, often resulting in injury, Naismith elevated goals to emphasize accuracy over brute strength. The initial rules of basketball allowed the ball to move up and down the court only by passing, emphasizing teamwork and cooperation.[12] Naismith believed that simply playing the game could provide moral education.

Basketball was inexpensive to implement. As opposed to baseball or football, which required special fields and equipment, basketball could be played in any gymnasium

Image 2.1 James Naismith, the inventor of basketball, poses for a photoshoot in 1900 with a basketball and a peach basket representing the original basket that became the namesake of the sport. *Getty Images/Bettman.*

with relatively little equipment. This economic factor helped basketball spread quickly throughout American school systems. High schools implemented the sport soon after its invention, and by 1905 colleges recognized it as an official winter sport.[13] Social workers turned to basketball as an activity for bringing immigrant children into larger American culture, and the sport became dominant in many urban immigrant communities. Because the game discouraged rough physical contact, the YMCA saw it as an appropriate sport for women, and women began to play the game a year after its invention.

Set hours for the workday meant that workers had leisure time in their nonworking hours. Factory owners sponsored competitive team sports for their employees to partake during their leisure time. Team sports held at least two significant benefits for factory owners: First, sport taught the value of self-sacrifice for the benefit of the team just as factory workers sacrificed their time and their health for the financial benefit of their families. And second, sport socialized obedience to authority that factory owners hoped would prevent unionization and challenges to workplace conditions.

Whereas agrarian work life demanded labor from men and women for revenue generation and sustenance, factory work shifted revenue almost entirely to men's work, making women's domestic labor unseen and unpaid. As men went to work, women cared for children, which caused social anxiety among men that boys would become soft and weak due to a lack of male presence in their lives. According to historians of sport and sexuality Eric Anderson, Rory Magrath, and Rachael Bullingham, "The fear of softness was not just about men acting feminine; however, it was directly related to the fear that boys could be socialized to become homosexual."[14] Sigmund Freud's theories influenced societal understandings of the root of male homosexuality; Freud blamed homosexuality on absent fathers and overly influential mothers. As such, the hypermasculinity of sports for boys and men became a project in showcasing male heterosexuality.

The Boy Problem

To understand the development of programming for boys during the era of muscular Christianity, it is important to understand what educators and community leaders of the day referred to as the "boy problem." In nineteenth-century publications for youth educators, two disciplinary methods held prominence: moral suasion and corporal punishment. Moral suasion was an appeal to a child's innate ethical sense and depended on the child understanding that bonds with parents or teachers could be strengthened or withdrawn depending on the child's proper or improper actions. Corporal punishment inflicted pain upon the body, and many saw this as an appropriate recourse should moral suasion fail. Many writers claimed that moral suasion was nearly universally effective with girls but not so with boys. Nineteenth-century educational literature tended to position boys as troublesome, rude, and rambunctious. These characterizations had consequences for theories of discipline. Horace Mann, perhaps the most influential educator of the nineteenth century, promoted the idea that corporal punishment for girls was unnecessary because girls could feel the difference between right and wrong due to their innate sentimentality. On the other hand, he presented corporal punishment for boys, in both threat and practice, as a necessary component for facilitating manliness. For Mann, boys must be trained to disregard bodily pain so that "they will not be unnerved and unmanned" should they be needed for military service in defense of the nation.[15]

Bronson Alcott was another influential educator of the time. For Alcott, boys' lack of ethical sensibility required physical pain as a disciplinary mechanism. He argued that the smack of a flat stick against the hand was a way to speak to boys in their own language: the language of the body. An 1863 essay titled "Against Boys," published in a Boston quarterly collection of essays, describes the dangers of avoiding corporal punishment for boys: "Any idea of appeasing the boy element is, however, quite ridiculous; the animal is implacable, and, like a horse that perceives his rider is afraid of him, becomes unmanageable if petted."[16] In educational settings, therefore, teachers tended to see boys as amoral and physical creatures, only impacted by physical discipline.

Around the same time, Thomas Hughes's Tom Brown adventure stories exploded in popularity. The most popular of the series, *Tom Brown's School Days*, was published in 1857 and chronicles the coming of age of young Tom Brown, a rugby player at a private boarding school.[17] Through physical education, Brown developed a fighting spirit and a moral sensibility that allowed him to defeat bullies and defend his friends. He was the fictional epitome of the muscular Christian ethos—the idea that boys turn into men through regimented discipline and obedience; that Christian moral character is related to athletic training. Within a year of its publication, *Tom Brown's School Days* had sold nearly a quarter-million copies in the United States. American Protestants embraced the athletic Tom Brown as a model for American boys.

Boys' group organizers during the era of muscular Christianity identified two kinds of boys who they saw as in need of intervention. The first were street boys—usually the children of new immigrants and migrants who had factory jobs in

Image 2.2 Illustration from 1896 reprint of *Tom Brown's School Days*. Arriving at a private school named Rugby mid-term, eleven-year-old Tom Brown is mercilessly bullied by Flashman. This illustration depicts Tom Brown along with his friend, Harry "Scud" East, working together to defeat Flashman. *Getty Images/Culture Club.*

cities—affiliated with mischief and petty crimes. The second were middle-class and elite homebound boys, usually born to white Protestant families and perceived as in danger of over-civilization. The rise of corporations increased the demand for educated employees, which expanded the educational time in a boy's life. Reformers blamed schools and churches for being overly bookish and failing to provide outdoor activities.

Child psychologists of the time developed a theory of adolescence called "recapitulation theory." It argued that humans mirror natural evolution in the course of their development to adulthood. Biologically, recapitulation theorists argued, the development of a human in the womb reenacted the evolution of the species by changing through phases from an aquatic microorganism to an advanced human body. Socially, recapitulation theorists argued, children progress through the stages of human evolution from the savage to the civilized. Organizing human cultures on a scale from barbaric to civil granted white Europeans and their descendants a feeling of innate superiority over Indigenous and nonwhite cultures, who they presented as failing to evolve.

Using recapitulation theory, reformers argued that boyhood was movement from savagery to civilization and that female teachers were undermining this process and failing to produce well-developed men. Recapitulation theory presented boys as heathens in need of physical (rather than mental) conditioning to fine-tune their moral sense. Though these theories no longer hold today, they represent at least three serious concerns of the time: most schoolteachers were women, city boys were more housebound than rural boys, and city boys lacked access to manual labor. Although some organizations for boys emerged to try to rehabilitate street boys, over time the focus of boys' work shifted to the sons of middle-class and upper-class men, men who feared that their sons were too soft for leadership roles.

Writers consistently employed the metaphor of "savage" to explain why boys needed physical discipline. The comparison of boys to "little savages" was a way of saying that boys lacked the moral and rational sensibilities of girls. As historian Ken Parille puts it, "as a 'savage' the boy is immoral, immune to reason, primarily concerned with his own bodily needs, and sometimes even brutal."[18] The 1877 *Being a Boy*, by popular writer Charles Dudley Warner, declared, "every boy who is good for anything is a natural savage."[19] An adherent of the recapitulation theory of human development, Warner and others argued that boys must be allowed, even encouraged, to express their savage and primitive instincts so that they could progress through evolutionary phases and eventually become civilized. Historian Julia Grant sums up this point of view: "If boys bypassed this epoch, they could turn into sissies; if they never evolved beyond this stage, they could become hoodlums and hooligans."[20] Part of what constrained reformers' vision of boys' work to white and ethnically European boys was that they tended to see African Americans and

Native Americans as inherently primitive, with savagery as a permanent—rather than developmental—trait.

Reformers assumed that boys growing up on the farm and the frontier naturally progressed though their savage stage to become healthy manly men. However, they argued that boys in the city needed special attention, and three environments emerged to fit this need. Boys' private schools catered mainly to the rich and offered all-male staffs meant to instill discipline and heartiness through a rural setting, sports programming, and male role models. A major advocate for boys' schools was Theodore Roosevelt, who wrote in 1900,

> Nowadays, whatever other faults the son of rich parents may tend to develop, he is at least forced by the opinion of all his associates of his own age to bear himself well in manly exercises and to develop his body—and therefore, to a certain extent, his character—in the rough sports which call for pluck, endurance, and physical address.[21]

Boys' schools were financially out of reach for middle-class families, so they turned to two other emerging environments that promised the same benefits as private boarding schools: summer camps and what historian Clifford Putney has called "paramilitary nature organizations" such as the Boy Scouts.[22]

Summer camps promised that getting boys away from city life and from their mothers would make boys more disciplined and self-reliant. Many of the camps run for middle-class boys were run by the YMCA or churches and held just outside of urban centers. Camp leaders touted the power of nature and of sports in setting boys on the right path toward character, vitality, and manliness. The problem with summer camps was that they were seasonal, leaving boys in their city conditions for most of the year; this is where paramilitary nature organizations stepped in, providing year-round programming for city boys.

Seton's Woodcraft Indians (formed in 1901), the Sons of Daniel Boone (formed in 1905), and the Boy Scouts (formed in England in 1908 and in the United States in 1910) were the dominant organizations of the day, all to be subsumed by Boy Scouts of America (BSA) over the following decades. Boy Scout leaders announced their intention to never hire women (or effeminate men: "No Miss Nancy need apply"), arguing that "REAL, live men—red blooded and right-hearted men—BIG men" were the most effective in dealing with boys.[23] Boys' organizations embraced recapitulation theory; they argued that boys must fully embrace their evolutionary development and needed organized opportunities to access what Ernest Thompson Seton called the "power of the savage." These organizations often relied on dressing as Indians, building teepees, and learning outdoor survival practices.[24]

Image 2.3 Seton's Woodcraft Indians. Ernest Thompson Seton hosted Woodcraft Indian activities on his estate, Wyndygoul. This image is from a 1904 gathering of white boys, ages approximately twelve to sixteen. According to Seton's annual field guide of 1903, "It adds great pleasure to the life of such boys when they knew that they can go right out in the holidays and camp in the woods just as the Indians did, and make all their own weapons in Indian style as well as rule themselves after the manner of a band of Redmen."[25] *Courtesy of the National Scouting Museum, through the generous donation from Julia M. Seton and family.*

Primary Source

Primary sources provide firsthand accounts of the topic under consideration. They emerge from particular times and places and allow us to imagine the context and thought processes that give rise to a perspective.

Excerpts from *The Boy Problem* by William Forbush
Public Domain

Context:

- William Forbush (1868–1927) was a Protestant pastor and the author of numerous texts addressing programming and ministry for boys. In 1893, he founded the Knights of King Arthur, a Christian club for boys based on medieval legends, and this organization became the largest organization for church boys in the early twentieth century, reaching a membership of 130,000 by 1922.

- *The Boy Problem* was published in 1901 and is Forbush's treatise on the temperament and religious needs of boys. Relying on the recapitulation theory of adolescence and white Protestant understandings of Christian civilizational superiority, Forbush presents boys' childhood as a stage of savagery to be built upon and superseded as the boy matures into a civilized man.

Discussion Questions:

- What were Forbush's assumptions about the "race life"? What were his assumptions about Christianity?
- According to Forbush, how should religious educators approach boys? What were his ideas on the right way to reach boys with Christianity?
- *The Boy Problem* argues that boys need special attention during their development, and Forbush does not extend this argument to girls. What do you think the consequences were of focusing exclusively on boys?
- When you reflect on your adolescence, what (if any) remnants of Forbush's philosophy of childhood were present in your life?

Reproducing the Race Life[26]
The psychologist, who believes that each child reproduces the Race Life, regards the years of infancy as rehearsals of prehistoric and feral ages, and the years of early childhood as reproductions of the protracted and relatively stationary periods of the barbarian days. It is because these ages were so long and so deep, because man has been a savage so much longer than he has been a Christian, that this subconscious heritage needs to be recognized, and the work of habit-making, which is the analogue of that past, must, during childhood, be made the central endeavor of all nurture. This work of nurture Dr. Coe finely calls "capturing a boy's presuppositions." It is conscience-building. We do well probably to button our own moral codes, like aprons, around the child for a time, but we do better if we train him always to "speak the truth in his heart."

In summary, we may call this the Old Testament era of the boy's life. The Bible, that marvelous manual of pedagogy, has been thought to reflect in either Testament childhood and adolescence. "The key of the Old Testament," says Sheldon, "is obedience." This we have said is the key to childhood. The law must come before the gospel, the era of nature before the era of grace. Those old heroes were only great big boys, and it is an underlying sympathy with them which explains why boys of this age prefer the Old Testament to the New. There are sound reasons why it should first be taught them.

> **The Way of God with a Child**[27]
> A normal child will say his little incantations which we call prayers, invoke his tooth when it aches or his pocket fetish when he is in a tight place, and look for miracles of deliverance when he is in trouble. We need not question or rudely disturb such imaginative and savage-like faith. It is faith—the only faith that is genuine in a child. In the meantime, we, of course, may habituate him to right conduct and religious observances, rejoice in the dear, uncovenanted graces of his heart, furnish him vacant formularies which he will first grotesquely and then maturely populate, and give him thus the materials and the skill for building life. Probably if children really do in any way "rehearse the race life" they do it more in their religion than in any other way. With them, as with savages, it is probably fear which first teaches them really to pray. Thus they learn to depend, and for a child to depend, or a man to cease to make excuses, is to pray.

Muscular Christianity for African American Men and Boys

Whereas white men embraced traditional gender roles and understandings of masculinity in an attempt to cling to the past, some African American men were determined to use the concept of "true manhood" to propel racial progress and turned to the YMCA to do so. When the American YMCA was founded in 1852, most African Americans in the United States were enslaved. Following the Civil War, the YMCA encouraged separate Black YMCA facilities. Initially lacking the financial resources for this, it was not until the late nineteenth century that African American YMCAs began to thrive. Middle- and upper-class Blacks did not challenge the segregationist policies of the YMCA, arguing that it was better to have separate facilities for Black men, an approach that YMCA historian Nina Mjagkij calls "accommodationist and gradualist"[28] and that other scholars have referred to as a "politics of respectability."[29]

According to Mjagkij, Black YMCA leaders hoped they could train Black men to become "prime examples of the type of men whites aspired to be and thus prove to white men that indeed they were gentlemen who deserved to be treated as such."[30] Black YMCAs sought to develop their members to adhere to a Victorian gentility combined with physical prowess, to make "men who were industrious, thrifty, self-reliant, honest, pious, and culturally refined Christian gentlemen, as well as physically fit and healthy individuals ready to face the demands of a rapidly industrializing society."[31] According to the rationale of Black YMCA leadership, developing Black men to fit these ideals would display true manhood and, therefore, gain the respect of white society.

By 1930, a network of nearly sixty Black-controlled YMCAs had a membership of nearly thirty-four thousand men and boys. This growth was connected to significant demographic change as the percentage of African Americans living in cities grew from 13 percent in 1870 to 44 percent in 1930. For Black elites already living in cities, the newly arriving population of young, rural Black men were at risk of succumbing to the temptations of the city, bringing shame to their families and their race.

The strategy of politics of respectability required attention to Black men's sexuality and, in shunning promiscuity and emphasizing parental and spousal responsibility, Black YMCA leaders hoped to undermine stereotypes of Black men's insatiable sex drive, a rationale that white men employed to justify lynchings. For Black YMCAs, physical education was part of a moral project. Mjagkij writes,

> The associations' physical exercise programs were broadly designed to provide men with strong, healthy bodies, as well as the moral and spiritual fortitude to resist unsavory habits, carnal desires, and urban temptations.... Moreover, physical education programs were often accompanied by personal hygiene and health lectures that emphasized bodily cleanliness as an essential component of masculine fitness, vigor, and virility.[32]

Black YMCAs also offered vocational training to help newly arrived migrants increase their job opportunities. Aside from churches, Black YMCAs were one of the few places where Black men could gather in large numbers without white surveillance or interference. The YMCA announced a policy of desegregation in 1946, two years before the desegregation of the U.S. Army and eight years before the Supreme Court ruling in *Brown v. Board of Education*.

For Black men and boys, the Boy Scouts was another opportunity to pursue a politics of respectability despite the organization's overt racism. In the 1910s and early 1920s, BSA relied on negative African American stereotypes as a foil to scouting values and practices. BSA chapters would perform blackface minstrel shows as fund-raisers. The BSA national magazine encouraged this, running one article with the title "African American Face Makes Green Backs." According to historian Benjamin Jordan,

> Blackface performance and other stereotyped literary and verbal forms enabled BSA leaders to caution boy members about the pitfalls of not developing the values and skills essential for success in America's corporate-industrial, urban mainstream.[33]

This imagery taught white Scouts that being industrious and thrifty were valuable attributes and that Black Americans were too lazy or too unprepared to become good members of industrialized society.

In 1925, BSA applied for and received a Rockefeller grant to form an internal committee that they called the Inter-Racial Service. One BSA leader, Stanley Harris, had conducted research on segregated scouting in the Louisville, Kentucky, area and recommended that other local councils adopt the "Louisville Plan" of starting one or two Black troops with no publicity, having Black troop leaders (supervised by white BSA officials), and allowing local councils to determine Black troop access to Scout resources such as uniforms, swimming pools, camps, and instructors. According to Harris, "The activities of the colored department parallel those of the white but are kept distinctly separate... to avoid any possible clash between white and colored scouts."[34] Ostensibly separated to keep the peace, BSA discussed the benefits of scouting differently for Black and white Scouts. Whereas they touted (white) scouting as a means to develop bravery, reverence, self-reliance, and leadership, they described the benefits for Black Scouts as training to become loyal and efficient laborers, avoiding juvenile delinquency, and developing habits of cleanliness that would mitigate southern sanitation and disease problems.

Local BSA councils often severely limited African American troops' access to swimming pools, which undermined their ability to complete the require swimming test to be promoted to First Class and the advanced ranks of scouting. As late as the 1950s in Richmond, Virginia, discrimination around pool use kept Black Scouts from advancing. BSA local councils often excluded African American members from camps, a serious obstacle to advancement in Scout rank because camps served as a time of intensive instruction and testing for merit badges. Showcasing one's advancement through the acquisition of merit badges formed the basis for scouting, so boys who could not access the means to earn these badges for their uniforms looked less capable than those who could. BSA training instructed Scouts to always salute a fellow Scout in uniform. Another slight to Black Scouts was the withholding of uniforms, therefore withholding both salutes and a means to showcase merit badges. The BSA Inter-Racial Service instructed local

Image 2.4 Boy Scout Troop No. 111 from Orange County, North Carolina, preparing to depart for Camp Shenandoah, June 27, 1969. In the South, segregated Boy Scout troops operated until the 1970s. Organized by Black community leaders in 1967, Troop No. 111 was the only Black Boy Scout troop in Orange County. Its founders hoped that Boy Scouts would provide Black youth with opportunities for character development and positive mentoring in an era of segregation and inequality. *Courtesy of the Orange County Historical Society.*

councils to only allow Black Scout uniforms if local white residents agreed. Like segregation, BSA framed this decision as preserving safety of Black Scouts.

Despite significant limitations that all but decreed that Black Scouts would be limited to second-class Scouts, Black boys and men still sought participation because of the status bestowed on Boy Scouts in the larger white society. According to Jordan,

> Since being a Boy Scout carried significant status in the eyes of the American public, government officials, and employers, even Scouting with restrictions represented a half-way step to demonstrating modern manhood and civic leadership that many African American boys and men eagerly grasped.[35]

By 1944, Boy Scouts had around one hundred thousand Black members. However, with the closing of Black schools after the 1954 desegregation decision of *Brown v. Board of Education*, the African American troops sponsored by these schools disincorporated, and numbers declined.

Urban advocates for boys' and men's physical education spurred a movement of providing public recreational spaces in cities, but racial tensions often made these spaces into zones of tension and discrimination. An example of erupting tensions over recreational spaces is the Riot of 1919. Throughout the 1910s in Chicago, African Americans' use of recreational facilities provoked violence and intimidation. Though the Black population of Chicago grew rapidly in the early twentieth century due to the great migration, the city designated only one stretch of beach, the Twenty-Fifth Street Beach on the South Side, for African Americans. The city of Chicago did not legally segregate the beaches, but white ethnic minorities immigrating in high numbers from Ireland, Italy, and eastern Europe tended to police the beaches and enforce racial segregation through intimidation.

On the day in question, tensions were already running high due to white dissatisfaction with the presence of several African Americans on the Twenty-Ninth Street Beach. Unaware of this, several Black teenage boys had built a raft at the Black designated Twenty-Fifth Street Beach, planning to sail down the coastline into "white waters." A white man on the shore began throwing rocks at the teens, dislodging Eugene Williams from the raft. He drowned. When word of this spread to the Black beach, several African Americans requested that a police officer arrest the white man who had thrown rocks at the boys. The policeman refused, and the resultant violence between African Americans and the white ethnic gangs of the area led to the deaths of twenty-three African Americans and fourteen whites, as well as property damage to homes and businesses. In Julia Grant's analysis, "Although the recreation movement surely enhanced opportunities for some youth, it paradoxically had the potential to exacerbate the ethnic and racial components of the boy problem"[36]—that is, the recreation movement relied on the idea that white boys' barbaric behaviors were a normal and natural part of their development, but uncouth behaviors from Black or native boys indicated their ongoing and essential depravity.

Conclusions

Over the early decades of the twentieth century, Americans accepted the muscular Christian premise that boys and men could achieve strong character through physical education and mastery of the natural world. Theodore Roosevelt summarized this point of view, writing in 1897, "We don't want to see the virtuous young man always have shoulders that slope like those of a champagne bottle, while the young man who is not virtuous is allowed to monopolize the burly strength which must be possessed by every great and masterful nation."[37] Roosevelt's approach to masculinity became normative as organizations such as the YMCA and Boy Scouts grew in number and prominence. Diagnoses of neurasthenia significantly declined in the 1920s as several cultural and geopolitical factors seemed to confirm white men's prominence nationally and abroad: a strict anti-immigration bill passed in 1924 rolled back non-Protestant immigration; participation and victory in World War I seemed to confirm American masculine prowess; and American imperial expansion into its overseas colonies of Hawai'i, Puerto Rico, Guam, and the Philippines allowed some Americans to think of these spaces as new frontiers, replacing westward expansion with global expansion.[38] The muscular Christian claim that sport was a means for building character took root in American culture and remains a significant assumption about the value of sport today.

Resources for Further Study

Media

"Muscular Christianity with Dr. Clifford Putney," *The Anthony Bradley Show*, podcast, May 11, 2021, https://podcasts.apple.com/us/podcast/muscular-christianity-with-dr-clifford-putney/id1560890129?i=1000521276703.

Online Archive

Scouting America (previously Boy Scouts of America) provides a rich archive of historical documents. Philmont Scout Ranch Document Archive, https://www.philmontscoutranch.org/museums/archives/.

Reading

Axel Bundgaard, *Muscle and Manliness: The Rise of Sport in American Boarding Schools* (Syracuse, NY: Syracuse University Press, 2005).

Benjamin René Jordan, *Modern Manhood and the Boy Scouts of America: Citizenship, Race, and the Environment, 1910–1930* (Chapel Hill: University of North Carolina Press, 2016).

Clifford Putney, *Muscular Christianity: Manhood and Sports in Protestant America, 1880–1920* (Cambridge, MA: Harvard University Press, 2001).

Chapter 3

Jewish Immigration and Antisemitism

From 1880 to 1924, eastern European Jews immigrated to the United States in record numbers. Prior to 1880, about 250,000 Jews of German descent lived in the United States. Over the next forty-five years, two million Jews would join them, settling primarily in the American northeast. This influx of Jewish immigration was part of significant demographic change in American northern cities: nearly six million rural Black Southerners moved to the urban north in the "great migration," and four million Catholic immigrants from Ireland and southern Europe arrived during the same period. This demographic change spurred the white Protestant majority toward nativism; white Protestants feared that newly arriving immigrants and migrants would affect American power structures and disempower white Protestants, who had dominated American government and commerce since the founding of the nation. One manifestation of this nativism was antisemitism: discrimination against Jews.

During this time, American Jews used sports for a number of purposes. They formed Young Men's Hebrew Associations (YMHA) that paralleled the muscular Christian institution, the Young Men's Christian Association (YMCA). Like YMCAs, YMHAs developed sports programming for their members. YMHA sports programming intentionally showcased Jewish athleticism to counteract stereotypes that Jews were overly intellectual and to argue that Jews were capable of assimilation into American culture. In addition to sports participation, Jews became sports fans, particularly of baseball, America's national pastime. Attending Major League Baseball games to cheer on Jewish baseball players such as Andy Cohen became a significant part of Jewish communal life for some Jewish immigrants. Baseball also provided an avenue for entrepreneurialism: until the 1950s, sports were racially segregated, and some Jews found the business of Black baseball to be a lucrative endeavor. While some Jews pursued the development and promotion of Black baseball teams, others saw moneymaking opportunities outside the law and organized gambling rings. As American Jews engaged sports through these avenues, the shadow of antisemitism was their constant companion and influenced their actions and larger American responses to Jewish athletes and entrepreneurs. This chapter traces American Jewish involvement in sports from the wave of Jewish immigration in the 1880s to the years following World War II to show that American Jews used sports as both a means to demonstrate assimilation and an avenue for economic profit.

Before jumping into American history, a short introduction to Judaism as a religion may be useful. Judaism is a relatively small religion, comprising about 0.2 percent of the world's population and about 2 percent of the population of North America.[1] Judaism as we know it today developed sometime between the Babylonian destruction of the First Temple in Jerusalem in 586 BCE and the Roman destruction of the Second Temple in 70 CE. Many of the stories of Judaism center on themes of exile and return. Beginning with the story of God's creation of humans in the Hebrew Bible book of Genesis, the first humans, Adam and Eve, lived in the garden of Eden but God exiled them for disobedience. A god of both justice and mercy, God both punishes humans for wrongdoing and offers them new opportunities to form a relationship with God. This theme continues in the exile of Moses, who after leading the Israelites out of slavery in Egypt wandered with his people for forty years before God communicated with Moses on Mount Sinai and offered a new covenant, a promise of return to a relationship with God and to a home.

Whereas belief is a central requirement for Christianity, for Judaism the emphasis falls on telling the stories and following the laws. The holiday most widely practiced by Jews around the world is Passover, a commemoration of the Israelite exodus from Egypt. For eight days, Jews do not eat leavened bread to recognize the hurried flight from Egypt when there was no time to allow bread to rise. The Passover Seder meal is usually a family gathering with special foods that connect with the narrative of Exodus and storytelling meant to connect the people sitting at the table with the lineage of Jewish history. As world religions scholar Stephen Prothero puts it, "To gather for Passover is to stand in a tradition of a people who have gathered for millennia to retell this story in their own languages and on their own terms."[2] With such a long history, and with so much of Jewish history featuring exile and diasporic living, it is no surprise that Judaism developed several branches and a range of approaches to what it means to be Jewish. In the United States today, there are three main branches of Judaism: Reform, Conservative, and Orthodox. Reform Judaism focuses on ethics and social justice and emphasizes integration into American society. In contrast, Orthodox Judaism in the United States emphasizes being set apart and uses clothing, diet, and strict religious observance to separate themselves from larger American society. Whereas both the Reform and Orthodox branches of Judaism began in Europe, Conservative Judaism emerged in the United States as a middle ground between the two, open to advances in modern thought while at the same time preserving some of the religious observances of Orthodox Judaism.

YMHAs and the Goal of Assimilation

America's first wave of Jewish immigrants was comprising around twenty thousand Reform German Jews who arrived between 1820 and 1880 and thrived in the United States. Upon hearing of pogroms, antisemitic sanctions, and poverty in Russia, they successfully lobbied for the United States to serve as a sanctuary for eastern European

Jews. However, the new eastern European immigrants who arrived in the 1880s and 1890s appalled gentiles and Jews alike—they lived impoverished lives primarily in New York City's Lower East Side where they crowded together in dirty, unhealthy conditions. Eastern European Jews were more Orthodox, and German American Jews worried that this new group of Jews would undermine their own precarious identity as Americans. Therefore, they were determined to assimilate this population. They were interested in countering the idea that Jews were "un-Americanizable"—a weak and alien race that rejected the physical in favor of the intellectual and religious.[3] Although American Jews ranged in their commitments to orthodoxy, they were united as a cultural group that experienced discrimination and stereotyping from wider American society.

In the 1880s and 1890s, the stereotype of the weak, unathletic Jew circulated widely in American culture. For example, in an article extolling Anglo-Saxon superiority, the *North American Review* declared,

> The Jews, who alone refuse active exertion, either as a means of livelihood or as a source of amusement, are perhaps the sole instance of a successful people... who explicitly or implicitly reject the duty of exercise; this no doubt is a survival of the oriental feeling that the burden of labor should fall on slaves.[4]

Although this article describes Jews as "successful," it also surmises that Jews reject physical activity because they see it as debasing and in the manner of enslaved laborers. In this and other publications of the day, the narrative was that Jews neglected physical development in favor of intellectual and economic capabilities. Often, authors presented this as Jews failing to grasp the value of athletics for cultivating masculinity and character.

The YMCA's invention of basketball in 1891 soon led to adoption of the sport across the country. Following James Naismith's aspirational description of the game as a vehicle for moral development, the YMHA saw the game as using competitiveness to teach self-control and cooperation. The YMHA embraced the muscular Christian claim that sporting competition could serve as moral education for boys, and in a 1906 Bulletin article titled "Basketball and Morals," the author stated,

> A boy who learns by his athletic life to do everything he can honorably to win, but to submit cheerfully to defeat rather than indulge in trickery and meanness, will carry the same spirit in all his recreation, in all his after life... it is not simply a question of physical exercise and physical development, but that a great moral question is involved... character must be put above victory.[5]

This hearty acceptance of the moral values of sport greatly influenced YMHA policies and practices.

In December 1907, the president of Harvard University, Charles Eliot, gave a speech before the school's Menorah Society. In his speech, Eliot described Jews as physically inferior to all other races. He believed that Jews in the United States had a new opportunity to develop physically and overcome this historical shortfall. He scolded the Jews of Harvard for neglecting outdoor activities and encouraged them to prioritize physical development alongside intellectual development. Eliot's speech elicited public and anxious responses from American Jews. The 92nd Street YMHA, the largest YMHA in the New York City area, responded by agreeing with Eliot and further investing in physical education for American Jews. Historian Ari Sclar writes, "The institutional response to Eliot indicated the strength of the stereotype at a time when the question of Jewish physical regeneration had important implications regarding Jews' place in American Society."[6] One of these implications was the question of whether Jews could fully assimilate to American life or would remain perpetual foreigners.

Sclar describes what he calls the "champion model" of institutional response. The champion model posits that Jewish athletic institutions should focus on specialization and on developing winning athletes and teams to showcase Jewish manliness to wider society and thus help Jewish socialization into American culture. In 1912, YMHAs in New York City embraced the champion model and formed competitive basketball teams focused on elite specialization rather than open participation. The YMHA called for players to directly represent the institution and, by extension, American Jews. They also called on YMHA members to indirectly represent the organization and community by attending games; game attendance became a duty of membership and a financial boost for the YMHA.

Jewish women also engaged with sports through settlement houses, Young Women's Hebrew Associations (YWHA), and Jewish Community Centers (JCC). Settlement houses were common in cities that experienced high rates of immigration and provided resources on learning English, vocational skills, and gender norms. The Jewish Welfare Board, formed in 1921, became the national governing body for the YM-YWHAs and promoted the merger of these into JCCs over the course of the 1920s and 1930s. With these mergers, women faced challenges accessing athletic spaces because the mergers meant that men and women shared the same gym rather than having their own dedicated spaces. As these organizations reformed as JCCs, one priority was making sure that women had access to physical education. This access largely reflected the gender norms and assumptions of the time. For example, Ruth Green of the Washington, D.C., JCC created a flyer to advertise the JCC's sports and exercise offerings for women that read, "Hi Gals! Seen the Gym lately? Now's the time to check your chassis for Salesgirls' slouch, Government Spread, Housewives' Hips. We've got a cure for all so come and get it."[7] In this way, JCCs positioned women's sport as a way to achieve beauty standards of slenderness and downplayed competition. This contributed to the larger goal of assimilation by encouraging Jewish immigrant and second-generation women to adhere to the gender standards of white Protestant America.

While YMHAs and YWHAs continued to promote Jewish men's athleticism and Jewish women's fitness throughout the 1910s and 1920s as evidence of Jewish ability to assimilate, American Jews faced a significant antisemitic backlash when the news story broke that Jewish gangsters were involved in fixing the outcome of the 1919 World Series.

The 1919 Black Sox Scandal

The White Sox entered the 1919 World Series as a team the media promoted as self-reliant, rugged heroes. Some dubbed them "the gods of baseball," and they enjoyed fame beyond Chicago.[8] The Series pitted the White Sox as American League champions against the National League champions, the Cincinnati Reds. The Series of best of nine games occurred in the first weeks of October in both Cincinnati and Chicago. The teams played the final game of the Series in Chicago, where the White Sox lost 10–5, making the Reds the winners of the World Series. In the months following the 1919 World Series, reporters raised the possibility that a conspiracy of players and gamblers had fixed the outcome. The baseball establishment dismissed these claims as muckraking, but on September 28, 1920, a grand jury indicted eight White Sox players for accepting bribes to fix the Series.

Abe Attell, a featherweight boxing champion in the 1910s and occasional bodyguard for Arnold Rothstein, a well-known and powerful New York gangster of Jewish background, was instrumental in fixing the Series. He led players to believe that Rothstein was behind the fix, using this to convince the players that he had the funds to bankroll the operation. Central to Attell's success was Chicago White Sox first baseman Chick Gandil, who convinced a number of other players to go along with the fix and commit to losing the Series.[9]

By spring and summer of 1921, the phrase "Black Sox scandal" had become ubiquitous in the American press. This phrase was appealing as a play on "White Sox" but also resonated with racial tropes of Blackness as corrupted and inferior as well as cleanliness tropes about the value of hygiene. As historian Daniel Nathan puts it, reporters and baseball magnates embraced the convenient fiction that "Gamblers and corruption (as opposed to an exploitative labor arrangement and poor working conditions) were the dreaded diseases plaguing professional baseball and contaminating an otherwise healthy and admirable institution."[10] Everyone was talking about "cleaning up" baseball. In this rhetoric, "dirty" players and gamblers were polluting the otherwise pure sport of baseball.

An undercurrent of antisemitism was present in the media coverage, largely due to the nation's nativist temperament in the early twentieth century and the conspicuous presence of known Jewish professional gamblers at the 1919 World Series. As Nathan puts it,

> Rothstein and Attell (along with several other lesser Jewish gamblers) were portrayed by the media as the Big Fix's driving force in large part because their ethnicity fit the popular cultural stereotype of the deceitful, dishonest, and money-hungry Jew. Rather than unduly castigate the players (who probably initiated the scheme) or the labor conditions and relations that engendered the game fixing, the media focused on the menace that professional gamblers (often code for Jewish gamblers) posed.[11]

In media coverage of the Big Fix, the press consistently referred to the players as "boys," a term that implied their innocence and that (Jewish) gamblers manipulated them for profit.

This was part of a larger trend of defending the innocence and value of baseball itself and vilifying outside sources of corruption (Jews).

The most virulently antisemitic stories about the Series ran in Henry Ford's *Dearborn Independent*. Ford distributed the *Dearborn Independent* through his auto factories and Ford Motor dealerships across the country, so it had a wide readership, boasting numbers of 700,000 to 900,000. If the readership numbers claimed by the *Dearborn Independent* are accurate, this would make the paper second only to the *New York Times* at the time.

Ford had purchased the weekly paper in 1919, and from May 1920 to January 1922, the paper ran a series of stories about a vast Jewish conspiracy to attack and weaken American values through corruption in banking, alcohol, jazz, baseball, and Hollywood. Ford included a translation of *The Protocols of the Learned Elders of Zion* in the *Dearborn Independent*, a fraudulent turn-of-the-century Russian publication that described a Jewish conspiracy to destroy Christian civilization. Ford presented this as a factual piece and based further stories on the idea that a small group of powerful Jews were plotting the downfall of America and Europe.[12] In the worldview of these pieces, Jews were intentionally brainwashing the larger American public for their own gain. Overall, the series of articles ran for ninety-one issues, and Ford had the stories collected and bound in a four-volume set titled *The International Jew: The World's Foremost Problem*. He distributed half a million copies of these volumes across the United States.

Image 3.1 Front Page of *The Boston Post*, September 29, 1920. In their publications, many newspapers used a size of font that they had employed previously only for the outbreak of a war or the assassination of a political leader, showing the significance of this news story. *Public Domain.*

Primary Source

Primary sources provide firsthand accounts of the topic under consideration. They emerge from particular times and places and allow us to imagine the context and thought processes that give rise to a perspective.

Excerpts from "Jewish Gamblers Corrupt American Baseball," *Dearborn Independent*, September 3, 1921.[13]

Context:

- The *Dearborn Independent* dedicated two issues to Jewish influence in baseball; the first ran on September 3, 1921, and is excerpted below. The September 10, 1921, issue claimed that Jews were intent on transforming the "clean" game of baseball into vaudeville style entertainment for profit. According to the article, "American baseball fans who value the game as a sport should wish its utter destruction rather than consent that it become a rendezvous for the gangs that now fill the Jew-controlled burlesque houses."[14] The *Dearborn Independent* presented baseball as pure and American to position Jews as the opposite—dirty and un-American.

Discussion Questions:

- How would you describe the tone of the article? What audience do you imagine that the author intends to reach?
- What criticisms of Jews appear in the *Dearborn Independent* article below? Which of these do you consider to be antisemitic? Why?
- What assumptions about baseball appear in the article? Do you agree with these assumptions? Why or why not?
- What connections do you see between the antisemitic claims, the assumptions about baseball in the article, and the cultural and historical context of the early-twentieth-century United States?

The "Cleanest Sport" Near its Doom from "Too Much Jew." Baseball has passed under the control of "the Sport Spoilers." Can it be Saved?

There are men in the United States who say that baseball has received its death wound and is slowly dying out of the list of respectable sports. There are other men who say that American baseball can be saved if a clean sweep is made of the Jewish influence which has just dragged it through a period of bitter shame and demoralization.

Whether baseball as a first-class sport is killed and will survive only as a cheap-jack entertainment; or whether baseball possesses sufficient intrinsic character to rise in righteous wrath and cast out the danger that menaces it, will remain a matter of various opinion. But there is one certainty, namely, that the last and most dangerous blow dealt baseball was curiously notable for its Jewish character.

There has been time enough for others to tell the truth if they were so disposed. Many sport editors have come as near telling it as their newspapers would permit them. But it becomes daily more evident that if the whole matter is to be laid bare, so that Americans may know where to look for danger, THE DEARBORN INDEPENDENT will have to do it.

And this is not of our own choosing. Baseball is a trivial matter compared to some of the facts that are awaiting publication. Yet it is possible to see the operation of the Jewish Idea in baseball as clearly as in any other field. The process is the same, whether in war or politics, in finance or in sports.

To begin with, Jews are not sportsmen. This is not set down in complaint against them, but merely as analysis. It may be a defect in their character, or it may not; it is nevertheless a fact which discriminating Jews unhesitatingly acknowledge. Whether this is due to their physical lethargy, their dislike of unnecessary physical action, or their serious cast of mind, others may decide; the Jew is not naturally an out-of-door sportsman; if he takes up golf it is because his station in society calls for it, not that he really likes it; and if he goes in for collegiate athletics, as some of the younger Jews are doing, it is because so much attention has been called to their neglect of the sports that the younger generation thinks it necessary to remove that occasion of remark.

If fans wish to know the trouble with American baseball, they have it in three words—too much Jew. Gentiles may rant out their parrot-like pro-Jewish propaganda, the fact is that a sport is clean and helpful until it begins to attract Jewish investors and exploiters and then it goes bad. The two facts have occurred in pairs too frequently and under too many dissimilar circumstances to have their relationship doubted.

When you contrast the grandstands full of Americans supposing they are witnessing "the only clean sport," with the sinister groups playing with the players and the managers to introduce a serpent's trail of unnecessary crookedness, you get a contrast that is rather startling. And the sinister influence is Jewish. So patent was this that even newspapers could not cover the facts this time.

The only fact of value brought out of all the trouble is that American baseball has passed into the hands of the Jews. If it is to be saved, it must be taken out of their hands until they have shown themselves capable of promoting sports for sports' sake. If it is not taken out of their hands, let it be widely announced that baseball is another Jewish monopoly, and that its patrons may know what to expect.

1924 Immigration Law Targets Jews

The nativism that appeared in press coverage of the Black Sox scandal was an indication of a larger trend, and by the 1920s, white Protestant politicians strenuously argued for limits on immigration from eastern Europe (predominantly Jewish) and southern Europe (predominantly Catholic). In 1921, Congress established a 3 percent quota system that set immigration quotas using the 1910 census because the 1920 census was not fully compiled. This system calculated the allowable number of immigration visas for a country based on 3 percent of the 1910 population from that country residing in the United States. The 3 percent system would limit immigration to 350,000 people a year and favor immigration from northern and western Europe.

In response to the 3 percent quota system, nativists argued that immigration should be based on a 2 percent quota system and use the 1890 census. They argued that after 1890, the sources of European immigration had shifted and that the 1890 census would provide a more accurate count of what American demographics should be. John Trevor, a New York lawyer and lobbyist for immigration restrictions, argued that the 1921 3 percent quota system discriminated against native-born Americans by failing to measure the national origins of the entire population. His calculations would result in 16 percent of total allowed immigration allotted to southern and eastern Europe and 84 percent to northern and western Europe.

Historian of American immigration Mae Ngai suggests that eugenics had a significant impact on nativist approaches to immigration. Eugenicists used scientific methods to support their claims that intelligence, morality, and other social characteristics were fixed in race and unchangeable. One such scientist was Harry H. Laughlin, director of the Eugenics Record Office at Cold Spring Harbor, New York, and an expert tasked with providing information to the House Committee on Immigration and Naturalization. Ngai writes, "Laughlin supplied Andrew Johnson [chair of the committee] with copious amounts of data on 'degeneracy' and 'social inadequacy' (crime, insanity, feeblemindedness) showing the alleged racial inferiority and unassimilability of southern and eastern Europeans."[15] Eugenicists such as Laughlin substantiated nativist fears that newer immigrant arrivals were damaging American culture and society.

In May 1924, Congress passed The Immigration Act of 1924, largely based on Trevor's concept of national origin quotas and Laughlin's concept of racial immutability. In determining immigration quotas, the law excluded immigrants from the Western Hemisphere and their descendants (immigrants from central and South America, and to a lesser extent, Canadians), "the descendants of slave immigrants" (African Americans), "the descendants of the American aborigines" (Native Americans), and "aliens ineligible for citizenship or their descendants" (Chinese, Japanese, and all South Asians).[16] In so doing, the law erased all nonwhite people from representation in population analysis. The Quota Board developed quota systems by ignoring intermarriage between white and nonwhite persons and by assuming that country of origin was immutable and passed generationally (ignoring intermarriage among those of European descent).

Practically, this had the effect of allowing larger immigration numbers from northern and western Europe and limiting immigration numbers from non-European countries and from eastern and southern Europe. In the immigration quotas for 1929, for example, Great Britain and Northern Ireland (assessed together as one country of origin) had 65,721 allocated spots, more than twice as much as the second-highest country of origin, Germany, at 25,957, and more than three times as high as the third-highest country of origin, Irish Free State, at 17,853. Compare this to Poland at 6,524; Italy at 5,802; and Russia at 2,784.[17]

In the late 1920s, groups such as YMCAs, church congregations, and the League of Women Voters criticized the quota system for restricting the admission of family members of men who had immigrated prior to 1924, enforcing family separation. Despite these protests, Congress accepted the findings of the Quota Board and signed them into law in 1929. For American Jews, the declining numbers of new arrivals meant a shift from emphasis on assimilation to emphasis on maintaining a sense of Jewish community as second- and third-generation Jews grew up integrating their American and Jewish identities.

Sport as a Middle Ground between Judaism and American Culture

Historian of Jews and sports Peter Levine has argued that while Jewish institutions promoted sports as a method of assimilation, everyday Jews used their sports participation as a way to form a middle ground, a bridge between Jewish and American identities. Jewish involvement in men's professional basketball is a good example of this. The SPHAs, named for the South Philadelphia Hebrew Association, dominated eastern professional basketball from 1931 to 1947. They played in the American Basketball League (ABL), the major league for professional basketball until the formation of the Basketball Association of America (BAA) in 1946 and the National Basketball Association (NBA) in 1949. The ABL collapsed in 1931 due to the Great Depression and relaunched in 1933 with a smaller circuit in the East Coast, centered on New York City—this was dominated by Jews. The 1930s SPHAs player Yock Welsh described it as the "pinnacle of athletic achievement to be able to wear that jersey with those four Hebrew letters on it."[18] Players and fans took pride in the Jewish identity of the SPHAs.

The SPHAs had a loyal Jewish following. As player Harry Litwack put it, "It wasn't just a South Philadelphia team. It was a team for all Jewish people in Philadelphia. We were the best around and we were Jewish. It was an amazing combination."[19] The SPHAs, like other professional teams of the time, followed their games with a dance included with the price of admission. This made game attendance about more than supporting the team and provided a social space for Jews to reinforce community attachments and participate in the activities of the American mainstream. As Levine puts it, "Jewish fans who attended their games relished in the triumph of ethnic heroes who symbolically served

PHILADELPHIA HEBREWS - SPHAS

Eddie Gottlieb manager of the Sphas, is seen looking at his seven players who comprise the team seeking the championship of the American Basketball League. The photo shows, left to right: Manager Gottlieb, Harry Litwack, George Wolfe, Inky Lautman, Lou Forman, Gil Fitch, Shikey Gothoffer and Cy Kaselman.

Image 3.2 South Philadelphia Hebrew Association. This group portrait of manager Eddie Gottlieb and seven players on the SPHAs was taken around 1940. The SPHAs were unabashed about their Jewish identity and played in uniforms embroidered with six-pointed stars and the Hebrew letters samech, pey, hey, and aleph. *Courtesy of the Special Collections Research Center, Temple University Libraries, Philadelphia, Pennsylvania.*

as manifest signs of their own American possibilities."[20] Professional basketball in the 1930s allowed Jewish fans to access the mainstream experience of basketball games and dances as festive events while also experiencing connection to their own Jewishness through the names of players, uniforms, and settings like Hebrew associations. By the late 1940s, Jewish presence in professional basketball declined. This was largely because the newly formed professional leagues did not allow part-time commitments, so players had to choose between sport and other opportunities, and because the immigrant neighborhoods that had given rise to teams like the SPHAs waned as second- and third-generation Jews moved to the suburbs.

The history of basketball at Rabbi Isaac Elchanan Theological Seminary (RIETS), now an affiliate of Yeshiva University, an Orthodox college in New York City, mirrors the story of the SPHAs in that RIETS administrators, faculty, and students also saw sports as a bridge between their Jewish and American identities. Bernard Revel became president of RIETS in 1915; and in 1928, he finalized plans to move the campus to Washington Heights in northern Manhattan and slated a gymnasium as part of the proposed eight-building campus. With the collapse of the stock market in 1929 and the beginning of the Great Depression, RIETS was unable to complete their planned gymnasium, and students had to make do with a basement space with low ceilings and poor ventilation for physical education classes.

Despite the lack of facilities, the renamed Yeshiva College launched varsity sports in 1931 with basketball as its flagship sport. Boston's Jewish newspaper, *The Jewish Advocate*, praised Yeshiva's integration of sports with education of the next generation of rabbis, writing in 1935, "Today our young rabbis-in-training attend smokers [gatherings in smoking lounges], play basketball, study embryology, and are just as collegiate as students of engineering, law or business administration."[21] By the 1940s, Yeshiva had also formed a cheering squad from its all-male student population who performed acrobatics and led cheers for the ball teams. Historian of American Jews and sports Jeffrey Gurock argues, "Yeshiva students were proud of their team because the very existence of their competitive squads evidenced to the world that they—second-generation American Orthodox students—were regular guys."[22] Like the SPHAs, sports participation and fandom at Yeshiva allowed American Jews to integrate Jewish and American culture in a form that created pride in both.

Black Baseball and Jewish Entrepreneurs

Antisemitism made Jews (particularly eastern European immigrant Jews) unwelcome in many white businesses. Therefore, they pursued innovative or undercapitalized enterprises such as Black baseball. Compared to the major leagues, Black baseball was not a stable enterprise, but it was much more financially accessible for Jews than white baseball. Late-nineteenth- and early-twentieth-century white owners of Black teams were Irish or German, but by 1930 Jews became the primary white ethnic group running and promoting Black baseball.[23] The small group of second-generation eastern European Jews who came to occupy a central role in Black baseball from the 1930s to the dissolution of the Negro Leagues were Jews more by culture than by religious practice. Two Jewish entrepreneurs in particular played an outsized role in shaping and promoting Black baseball: Syd Pollock and Abe Saperstein. By examining these two figures, we can see how some American Jews financially benefited from sports by relying on racist stereotypes of African Americans.

Saperstein worked alongside Pollock to promote comedy baseball in the 1930s. Pollock owned a Black novelty team called the "Ethiopian Clowns" who played baseball and performed clowning routines. Clowning routines might include juggling, lighting fireworks, acrobatics, or comedic sketches. The team players were mostly from southern Florida but took on presumed African names such as Kalahari, Selassie, or Tarzan. They would play in grass skirts with their faces painted in stylized war paint. The Clowns used their costumes and face paint to their advantage: when the Clowns played white teams and fell behind, they would rotate their best three or four batters; because they were disguised, the white teams would never notice the ruse.[24] Pollock also booked games for the Black team, the Zulu Cannibal Giants, also known for grass skirts, war paint, and for speaking gibberish that listeners might presume was African. From these examples, we can see that some Jewish entrepreneurial success in baseball relied on exploiting Black stereotypes.

In 1941, the Ethiopian Clowns won the Denver Post Tournament, and Pollock and Saperstein considered creating their own Negro league with the Ethiopian Clowns at the center. Pollock and Saperstein saw Negro baseball as different from the major leagues and saw clowning as an important component. The Black press grew concerned about this attempt to put clowning at the level of serious league play and raised the possibility of boycotting the Ethiopian Clowns. For example, Lem Graves of the *Journal and Guide* argued that the Clowns were only funny to white audiences who "enjoy seeing a Negro act the fool," and that the clowning style of play "should be kept out of organized baseball."[25] Despite criticism, Saperstein and Pollock decided to form the league and promote clowning. The league failed, but the Negro American League (NAL) admitted the Clowns in 1943 with the provision that they drop "Ethiopian" and their antics. Pollock agreed and changed the name but had no intention to stop clowning.

Jackie Robinson signed with the Brooklyn Dodgers in 1945 and was the first African American to play Major League Baseball (MLB). As MLB began to racially integrate, MLB teams passed over Black baseball comedians in favor of young talent that whites could train in their minor leagues. Assuming that Black league baseball was doomed, Saperstein and Pollock formed more comedy teams in the mid-1940s to travel with the Clowns. Over the following years, Saperstein shifted his energies to his novelty basketball team, the Harlem Globetrotters, and Pollock continued to promote the Clowns, who played as a novelty team into the 1980s.[26] Saperstein and Pollock are examples of how some Jews saw the entertainment value of sports as an entrepreneurial option, and in the decades of the Negro Leagues, some Jews were able to succeed as sports entertainment businessmen.

Second-Generation Jewish Immigrants and the 1936 Olympics

The International Olympic Committee (IOC) had decided in 1931 that Germany would host the 1936 Olympics, largely due to the cancellation of the Germany-hosted 1916 Olympics and the IOC's banning of Germany from Olympic competition for the 1920 and 1924 Olympic Games as a punishment for their role in World War I. Offering Germany the host role for the 1936 Olympics was a way of making amends and reintegrating Germany into the Olympic fold. Adolf Hitler, who had come to power in Germany in 1933, was originally disinterested in hosting the games, but his minister of propaganda, Joseph Goebbels, convinced him that the Olympics were an opportunity to showcase "New Germany" on an international stage.[27]

By April of 1933, the National Socialists (Nazis), led by Hitler, had begun legal actions against Jews including barring them from certain professions and from sports teams. This impacted Jewish German athletes who had intended to compete in the upcoming Olympics, and several moved to England to continue their training. Conditions in Germany were growing worse for the Jewish population, and American Jews began to suggest boycotting the 1936 Olympic Games. The IOC took up the issue at their planning meeting in June of 1933 and insisted that Germany allow German Jews to compete. The sports commissioner for Nazi Germany, Hans von Tschammer und Osten, believed that German sports were for Aryans only and barred Jews from sports organizations. By requiring membership in these organizations to qualify for Olympic competition, Germany was able effectively to ban Jewish participation while still following the IOC rules.[28]

In January 1934, Germany issued official invitations for the 1936 Olympics. American Olympic Committee (AOC) President Avery Brundage visited Germany the following September to observe the conditions of Jewish athletes as a precondition for U.S. acceptance of the invitation. German Olympic Committee member Karl Ritter von Halt coordinated Brundage's visit, determined which athletes Brundage would talk to, and served as a translator for their interactions. Brundage returned to the United States convinced that Jewish athletes and sport leaders were satisfied with their treatment and conditions. Based on Brundage's report, the AOC voted unanimously to participate in the Olympics.

At the same time, the American boycott movement was growing in strength. A 1935 Gallup poll showed that 43 percent of Americans favored a boycott. Brundage responded to these concerns by suggesting that because there were not many Jewish athletes, Nazi policies would affect only a few individuals. Brundage insisted that participating in the Olympics was a neutral position, whereas a boycott would implicate the Olympics in "racial, religious, or political" concerns.[29] In September 1935, the Nazis implemented the Nuremburg Laws, depriving Jewish residents of citizenship and rights. American IOC member Charles Sherrill demanded that Germany allow Jews to participate on the German Olympic teams. When the Germans invited three nominally Jewish athletes to return to the country to train and compete (two complied; only one eventually competed), Sherrill dropped the matter, saying, "I would have no more business discussing that in Germany than if the Germans attempted to discuss the Negro situation in the American South..."[30] African Americans were divided on the boycott. Some argued that Black athletes received better treatment in Germany than they did in the United States and that the Olympics were an important showcase for Black talent. Others argued that fighting discrimination in all its forms was the most important goal.[31]

Ultimately, the United States did participate in the 1936 Olympics, though individual athletes decided to boycott. Six American Jewish athletes went to Berlin to compete; however, American coaches removed two of them from their events on the day prior to their competition, replacing them with African American athletes who went on to win gold medals.[32]

Image 3.3 Hitler on his way to the 1936 Olympics in Berlin. On their way to the opening ceremony, Adolf Hitler and his entourage drove under the Brandenburg Gate decorated with flags showing the five rings of the Olympic Games interspersed with flags showing the Nazi symbol, the swastika. *Getty Images/Photo 12.*

Nazi attacks on European Jews continued in the late 1930s. The German annexation of Austria in March 1938 resulted in the mass deportation of Austrian Jews to Poland and to concentration camps. Nazi troops in Germany attacked Jewish homes and synagogues on November 9 and 10, 1938, in what would become known as Kristallnacht, the night of broken glass. Kristallnacht included the burning of more than two hundred synagogues, the destruction of more than seven thousand Jewish-owned businesses, the murder of about one hundred Jews, and the transport of thirty thousand Jews to concentration camps. President Franklin D. Roosevelt verbally condemned Germany's actions while at the same time refusing to adjust America's tight immigration quotas that prevented European Jews from immigrating to the United States.

The American public deeply opposed American involvement in the conflict in Europe. The United States entered World War II after the Japanese attack on Pearl Harbor, Hawaii, on December 7, 1941. By 1942, the U.S. government had multiple confirmed reports of Nazi massacres of Jewish civilians as well as Hitler's intentions to annihilate all of Europe's Jews.[33] Again, President Roosevelt issued a verbal condemnation of these actions; Roosevelt claimed that the only way to impact the atrocities against European Jews was to end the war. Roosevelt's formation of the War Refugee Board in January 1944 did allow for immigration intervention on behalf of Jewish refugees, but the War Department refused to allocate military resources for the purpose of rescuing concentration camp internees, citing the need for these resources in combat.[34] By the time the war ended, the Nazi regime had systematically murdered six million Jews.

Conclusions

The professional baseball player Hank Greenberg was the most famous Jewish athlete in the 1930s. Playing for the Detroit Tigers during the 1934 season, fans anxiously awaited Greenberg's decision on whether to play baseball on the Jewish high holiday of Rosh Hashanah, the Jewish New Year. Though not a religious Jew, Greenberg had casually mentioned that he might attend religious services instead of play in the scheduled late-season game against the Boston Red Sox. The flurry of newspaper articles that followed featured fans, community members, and even rabbis encouraging Greenberg to put his commitment to the Tigers ahead of his religion. He did decide to play and was instrumental in the Tigers' 2–1 victory. Ten days later was Yom Kippur, the Day of Atonement and the holiest day on the Jewish calendar, usually observed with a full day of fasting and prayer. The Tigers played the Yankees that day, and Greenberg did not play, spending the day instead at a synagogue in Detroit. The press generally lauded this choice (perhaps because the Tigers were favored to win the game anyway), and Greenberg emerged as a hero for American Jews across the country symbolizing both Jewish pride and Americanization.[35]

In the 1930s and 1940s, during the Nazi atrocities in Europe, Hank Greenberg was a necessary symbol of Jewish strength for American Jews. Post–World War II, Sandy Koufax became America's most famous Jewish baseball player, but with different symbolic importance. Throughout his career, Koufax always refused to pitch on Rosh Hashanah and Yom Kippur. The press had treated Greenberg's choice as a critical dilemma. Sports historian Peter Levine describes Greenberg's dilemma as "how to balance loyalty to parents, religion, and tradition with commitment to his American profession and his desire to fully participate in his American life."[36] By the time Koufax sat out of the 1965 World Series, this dilemma no longer existed for most American Jews. Americans had accepted that one could be Jewish explicitly and still succeed in America's national game.[37]

For Jewish Americans from the 1880s into the twentieth century, sports provided multiple avenues for Jews to grapple with religious and national identity. Some played sports to demonstrate assimilation. Sporting events featuring Jewish teams or prominent Jewish athletes served as sites for community celebration and affirmation. Sports offered financial opportunities in both illegal and legal spheres as Jews came to dominate sports betting and administration for Black baseball and novelty teams. Although early generations of Jewish immigrants relied on sport as a means for American acceptance, by the 1960s, most Jewish Americans felt demonstrably American; and though many continued to play sports and to promote sports entertainment, these activities were no longer necessary to prove assimilation. America had accepted that a person could be American and Jewish.

Resources for Further Study
Media
Malcolm Gladwell, *Revisionist History*, Series 10: Hitler's Olympics, podcast series, June 27, 2024, https://www.pushkin.fm/podcasts/revisionist-history#episodes.

Online Archive
The United States Holocaust Memorial Museum hosts an online photo story and timeline exhibition titled "Nazi Olympics: Berlin 1936." https://www.ushmm.org/exhibition/olympics/.

Reading
Jeffrey S. Gurock, *Judaism's Encounter with American Sports* (Bloomington: Indiana University Press, 2005).
Peter Levine, *Ellis Island to Ebbets Field: Sport and the American Jewish Experience* (New York: Oxford University Press, 1992).
Steven A. Riess, ed., *Sports and the American Jew* (Syracuse, NY: Syracuse University Press, 1998).

Chapter 4

Sports Ministry

Sports ministry is a Protestant Christian enterprise that developed out of a sense that athletes are special and that Christian athletes need targeted education and tools to help them navigate the world of secular sports. Sports ministry first emerged in an organized way in the United States after World War II. Sports ministry can entail sports training in Christian contexts (such as teams at denominational high schools and colleges), education for athletes and coaches on how to combine sports and Christianity (such as summer camps and retreats), and hosting teams and competitions with the idea of promoting the values of Christianity (such as exhibition events and traveling teams). Today, more than a hundred sports ministry organizations in the United States involve tens of thousands of athletes, coaches, and fans of all ages. A sports ministry organization exists for nearly every imaginable sport, from basketball and soccer to surfing and rodeo. The two largest sports ministry organizations are the multisport ministries of Fellowship of Christian Athletes (FCA) and Athletes in Action (AIA). Each has grown significantly since its founding and continues to expand in terms of staff, members, and revenue. Although these two organizations began by targeting professional athletes in men's sports, they have since developed different focuses for their ministries with FCA focusing on middle- and high-school "huddles" (clubs) and summer camps and AIA focusing on college athletes and forming traveling exhibition teams.

The extent of national organizations is striking but only hints at the growth of sports ministry at a local level. As more and more athletes grew up affiliating their athletic and religious experiences, careers in sports ministry seemed increasingly viable options. Athletes unable or unwilling to pursue careers as professional athletes are able to coach or play for Christian teams at multiple levels—from youth club teams to Christian high schools and colleges to semiprofessional and professional Christian teams. Coaching positions at explicitly Christian colleges and universities are especially appealing career options for Christian athletes. About thirty-five new jobs in Christian coaching and sports ministry are posted each month on ChristianEmployment.com,[1] and the National Christian College Athletic Association notes that its job posting page receives two thousand views per month.[2]

By following the trajectory of sports ministry from its origins in the 1950s and 1960s to today, we can see two significant developments. First, sports ministers' original attempt to

Table 4.1 Growth of FCA from 2005 to 2024[3]

Year	Annual Revenue	Total Staff	Camps Hosted	Camp Attendees
2005	$53.5 million	698	139	27,954
2010	$70.2 million	864	286	45,823
2015	$109 million	1,300	619	94,505
2019	$115.7 million	1,954	805	89,323
2024	$243 million	2,992	1,058	114,548

harness celebrity power led to significant ethical dilemmas as voices inside and outside sports ministry developed critiques of using celebrity power without attending to the repercussions. And second, the growth of athletic opportunities for women following the implementation of Title IX in the 1970s and 1980s brought sports ministry's attention to women's roles and women's bodies at a time when evangelicals were publicly promoting traditional gender roles and taking a hard stand against homosexuality. Sports ministry has long been rife with contradictions between ideology and practice, and this chapter highlights how Christians in sports ministry have navigated and offered solutions to the ethical challenges of combining sport and evangelical Christianity.

Before we dive into the history of sports ministry, it may be helpful to have more information on American evangelicalism, the branch of Protestantism behind most of sports ministry. Evangelicals see themselves as *in* but not *of* the world. This means that they understand the world as temporary and corrupted, and they take it as their mission to reach as many people as possible with the message of salvation through Jesus Christ. In the simplest terms, evangelicals tend to hold these core beliefs: the inherent sinfulness of humans, the power of God to intercede in human affairs, and heartfelt dedication to Jesus Christ as the pathway to heaven. They understand the Bible as the infallible word of God that can exercise power over people's hearts and minds. Most evangelicals adhere to a narrow understanding of salvation: only those who openly declare their belief in Jesus's divine sacrifice are able to enter heaven after death. All others are doomed to hell. Because they see the stakes as eternal, they prioritize outreach to nonbelievers and have developed multiple strategies for outreach that engage popular culture: Christian popular music, Christian television and movies, Christian theme parks and museums, and sports ministry.

Harnessing the Celebrity Power of Sport

Don McClanen, founder of FCA, had the idea for a fellowship of Christian athletes in 1947. While he was a student at Oklahoma A&M, he managed to get a two-minute meeting with Branch Rickey, the manager of the Brooklyn Dodgers who had taken the controversial step of signing the first African American in the league, Jackie Robinson, the year before.

The two-minute meeting stretched to five hours, and the two discussed McClanen's idea. FCA formed officially in 1954 when McClanen wrote letters to a number of athletic celebrities that he knew to be Christian. He told them, "If athletes can endorse shaving cream, razor blades, and cigarettes, surely they can endorse the Lord, too. So my idea is to form an organization that would project you as Christian men before the youth and athletes of this nation."[4] FCA cultivated an ecumenical big-tent idea of Christianity and focused on bringing Christian athletes together for community building. However, McClanen was not the only Christian with the idea that Christian athletes were special and required a special ministry, and over the next two decades, more sports ministry organizations formed that targeted professional and college athletes. These tended to be more theologically conservative and evangelical in nature.

The 1950s was a period of innovation for American evangelicals who developed new strategies to spread their message of Christian salvation. One of the largest, most influential evangelical networks that emerged in the mid-twentieth century was Campus Crusade for Christ (now called Cru).[5] On the campus of UCLA, Bill Bright began the organization in 1951. Campus Crusade was a weekly worship service targeting college students. Bright's ministry defined itself through "aggressive evangelism." This was different from "friendly evangelism," a tool used by other evangelistic groups to gain the trust and respect of a person. Aggressive evangelism prioritized declaring one's identity as Christian as well as encouraging others to follow suit as the first pieces of information that Christians should share.

To assist Crusade members in this task, Bright developed a twenty-minute presentation for staff to memorize called "God's Plan for Your Life." He developed a condensed version of "God's Plan for Your Life" in 1965 called *The Four Spiritual Laws*.[6] Bright boiled down salvation through Jesus Christ to four concise statements, followed by a short example prayer that the reader could use to start a personal relationship with Christ. The four spiritual laws are:

1) God loves you and has a wonderful plan for your life,
2) Humans are sinful and separated from God,
3) Jesus Christ provides the only avenue for humans to have meaningful access to God, and
4) Humans must individually pray to receive Jesus to access God and salvation.

The genius of the booklet was its high degree of portability and simplicity; it treated conversion to Christianity as a step-by-step process that can and should be the same for everyone.

At the same time as evangelicals were developing new communication strategies to expand their reach, televised sport was also changing. In the 1960s, ABC Sports was home to one of the most innovative and influential people in televised sports: Roone Arledge. Creator of sports coverage innovations such as the slow-motion instant replay, sideline commentary, and halftime interviews, Arledge started at ABC on May 1, 1960, as the producer of National

Image 4.1 Athletes in Action's exhibition weightlifting team, mid-1960s. AIA founder Dave Hannah (left) stands on stage with Olympic weightlifter Russ Knipp (center) and sports ministry author Wes Neal. The team traveled to churches and schools, demonstrating weightlifting feats and sharing an evangelical message. *Courtesy of Athletes in Action, a Cru ministry.*

Collegiate Athletic Association (NCAA) football programming. ABC officially started its sport wing, "ABC Sports," in March 1961, and this became the laboratory for Arledge to develop his "up close and personal" aesthetic. Arledge's sports coverage philosophy was to emphasize personal narratives and make sport into human dramas. He told *TV Guide* in a 1964 interview,

> The action on the field is only half of what's going on. The peripheral action is just as important… There's something impersonal about 100,000 people, but if you can see the reaction of just one cheerleader when a touchdown is made or the look on the face of one fan when a player drops the ball, then you really know what's going on.[7]

For Arledge, the drama surrounding sports was useful in attracting spectators who, like his wife, might not care about the game itself but could be interested in the personalities and stories of athletes and coaches. Arledge's approach became the norm for sports coverage over the following decades. His work on *Wide World of Sports*, *Monday Night Football*, and coverage of the Olympics all demonstrated the success of his methods in gaining and retaining viewership.

In the mid-1960s, Dave Hannah, founder of Campus Crusade's sports ministry branch Athletes in Action, described a vision of an athletic ministry that echoes McClanen's sense of the power of celebrity endorsement:

> The idea for the project came to Hannah one day as he watched a Campus Crusade music group share an evangelistic message through its performance. Hannah thought out loud, "Why couldn't an athletic team be used in the same way?... Athletes are used to sell everything from candy bars to cars. Why not have them tell about something far greater—the message of Jesus Christ?"[8]

Hannah's vision was to create the best amateur basketball team in the world and develop a television network that would broadcast the games coast to coast. Hannah explained, "The better we are, the more people will watch us. The more people who watch us, the more we reach for Christ."[9] For Hannah, winning was a means for fame, and fame was a means for evangelism. Despite this grand vision, AIA's basketball team did not garner much attention from its founding in 1967 through its 1975 season. Standing outside both college and professional basketball, Hannah's team was relying on an outdated model of amateur basketball that had not held sway since the 1940s. However, the late 1970s did bring some success as AIA won the 1976 AAU title and defeated several ranked college teams.

Historian Paul Putz summarizes the differences in perspective between FCA and AIA:

> Broadly, the FCA, rooted in college and high school sports within predominantly white Protestant communities in the Bible Belt, continued to possess an establishment mentality with a desire to nurture a big tent community of Christians. AIA, with a more global perspective and with a more demanding set of expectations for its adherents, viewed itself less like a moral guardian and more like a band of elite Christians infiltrating the sports world.[10]

FCA had emerged as an ecumenical organization, but with the emergence of more conservative sports ministry groups such as AIA, FCA followed the trend toward evangelicalism. The theologically diverse FCA lacked the clarity offered by AIA's Four Spiritual Laws, and by the 1970s, theologically conservative evangelicals in sports ministry became the dominant voices of the movement.

Grappling with the Morality of Athletic Celebrity

In the 1970s, *Sports Illustrated* writer Frank Deford leveled a scathing critique against what he called "Sportianity." He wrote, "To put it bluntly, athletes are being used to sell religion. They endorse Jesus, much as they would a new sneaker or a graphite-shafted driver."[11] When Deford's critique appeared, reevaluations of sport from an ethical perspective were increasingly common. Deford and others assumed that Christian engagement with sport would entail a moral obligation to improve sport. This made Christian athletic celebrities and sports ministers easy targets for critique because they engaged sport with little difference from secular athletes and institutions. Deford claimed, "Sportianity does not question the casual brutality [of sports]... It does not censure the intemperate behavior of coaches… The fear of taking a stand on moral issues is acute."[12] According to Deford, Sportianity involved a declaration of Christian beliefs yet did not require ethical improvements. Deford wrote, "In the process of dozens of interviews with people in Sportianity, not one remotely suggested any direct effort was being considered to improve the morality of athletics."[13]

Deford conjectured that this lack of attention to sporting morality stemmed from sports ministry's dependence on athletic celebrity. As Deford saw it, the ministry benefited from sports' promotion of hero-worship of winning athletes. Because sports ministry used the system for evangelism, sports ministers would be unlikely to seek significant changes in the organizing principles of competitive sport. "[N]o one in the movement—much less any organization—speaks out against the cheating in sport, against dirty play; no one attacks the evils of recruiting, racism or any of the many other well-known excesses and abuses… Sportianity seems prepared to accept athletics as is, more devoted to exploiting sport than serving it."[14]

Deford wrote three articles for *Sports Illustrated* on "Sportianity." In the second and third articles, he tempered his critique somewhat and introduced "Sportians" who expressed concerns about moral issues in sport. For example, Deford pointed to a 1972 article titled

Image 4.2 Pages excerpted from "Sports and War," published in *The Christian Athlete* in January 1972. The article featured juxtaposed pictures of injured athletes and fallen soldiers in Vietnam, comparing linebackers to the front line. *Courtesy of Fellowship of Christian Athletes.*

"Sports and War" that appeared in FCA's *The Christian Athlete* while Gary Warner served as editor.

The article decried the growing emphasis on winning and cautioned against treating the world like a sporting competition.

> In the midst of the most complex time in our nation's history, we are witnessing a phenomenal growth of our athletic institutions. Sports has become the national conversation, complete with its own peculiar grammar and vocabulary. It has absorbed our passions in its fantasy world of winners and losers. Sports has proven compatible with our view of the world as a dichotomy of winners and losers. In fact, we seem to retreat into sport in order to deny the complexity and ambiguity that marks the political, social, and religious issues of our time.[15]

The article went so far as to argue that sports ministry needed to take seriously the conflation of sports and war in the United States and rethink Christian involvement in both. Rather than using sport as a platform for outreach, this article called on sports ministry to bring Christian beliefs and practices to bear on actual athletic behavior.

Warner knew that "Sports and War" would be controversial. When he became editor in 1968, Warner's vision for the magazine was to be a forum for reflection on serious issues. In a 1975 interview, Warner discussed the conflict between his vision for the magazine and the vision of the FCA board. Warner emphasized that the problems of sport will not go away simply by converting more and more athletes to Christianity. He said, "You must be gut level honest and deal with the issues. Discuss them. Get both sides. But the board would rather have us not stir the waters. Just print the good story about the good ole boy who does good things."[16] According to Deford's reporting, FCA strongly considered firing Warner after the publication of "Sports and War" and did impose censorship on the magazine following the article's publication.[17]

Evangelicals first perceived sport as an ideal resource because of the power of athletic celebrities to attract cultural attention, but when they began to engage the world of sport, they encountered a problem with their strategy. Sport raised the question: do the ends justify the means? Sporting celebrities could draw attention to Christianity, but if they behaved in morally questionable ways on (or off) the field, was this attention achieving its goal of promoting Christianity? If one's power (both in the sports world and as an evangelist) was contingent on winning, then winning remained a central and unchallenged goal of sport. Taking on these issues, sports ministers started to talk about the project of sports ministry differently. Although celebrity athletes were still the cornerstone of the movement, some significant voices began to promote sports participation as a way to feel connected to the divine and to experience a sensation of Christ-likeness, a very different goal than outreach to nonbelievers.

The career and publications of Wes Neal illustrate one example of this self-reflection. Neal was a weightlifter who traveled with Athletes in Action's weightlifting team in the 1960s. When Neal entered sports ministry, he felt that Christian athletes could and should be different from non-Christian athletes, yet he noticed that their faith did not seem to influence their athletic behavior. In the 1960s, Neal appeared on a television sports show in California. "The host asked me about lifting and I used that question to share the four spiritual laws. Afterwards, I felt that I had done wrong on that. I didn't respect his question. I used his question to talk about something else."[18] Neal experienced a crisis of conscience about using his athletic celebrity as an evangelistic tool. He felt that his identity as a Christian should infuse his sporting experience, not simply be a sound bite at the end of the game. This desire to infuse sport with Christianity led Neal to question and redefine the desired outcome of combining sport and evangelicalism. For Neal, sport could be an opportunity to experience a connection with God using his athletic body.

Because Neal's goal for Christian athletics was no longer limited to evangelism, he came to understand his Christian athletic obligation as "to give every ounce toward something and to do it as unto the Lord."[19] He called this a "Total Release Performance" and understood it as a sensation of Christ-likeness, of being one with Jesus Christ. For Neal, this experience became the ultimate goal of any sporting activity. He believed that sport in itself could provide a sense of intimacy and closeness with God, a feeling that the athlete is fully saturated with the love and power of Christ.

Neal's publications instruct Christian athletes on how to cultivate a mental state conducive to interaction with the Holy Spirit. He taught athletes that a Total Release Performance required mental preparation, writing, "it is your mind that the Holy Spirit engages most of the time."[20] Neal saw the mind as an access point for the Holy Spirit: "The word 'mind' refers to all of our senses which are alert to external objects—the primary organ being the brain. The human mind, acting independently, can produce great works. But it can also produce chaos. It was designed by God to work in a dependent way with His Holy Spirit."[21] Because Neal understood the mind as a "meeting ground with God," much of his instruction involved creating a state of mind intentionally in tune with Jesus Christ. He told me, "I picture myself as Jesus—this is not heresy; there is no way that we *are* Jesus, but I see myself as Jesus living in me. I'm not copying his behavior, but I'm in a union with His spirit." Neal described this union to me as a renewing of the mind with purity. "It's a combination of losing yourself and building yourself—less of me, more of Christ... It's an awesome awareness."[22] For Neal, isolated concentration on the Holy Spirit made mental clarity possible, and this allowed an athlete to experience a Total Release Performance, an experience of renewed purity. By the end of the 1970s, Neal's approach was showing up across sports ministry.

Using evangelical athletes to "sell" salvation required a compartmentalization of sporting and religious lives that some sports ministers such as Neal and Warner found dissatisfying. In an attempt to investigate and remedy their dissatisfaction, Neal and Warner promoted the idea that sport could be an avenue for connection with the divine. This emergent understanding of sport remains quite compelling for Christian athletes and is central to most sports ministry organizations today. However, it is important to note that the impulse toward winning did not go away. The tension remains: should a Christian athlete try to win to influence others or should they play compassionately to experience connection to the divine? The quest to integrate these goals continues to animate sports ministry, and this quest gained new complexity in the late twentieth century when women began to outnumber men as the primary participants in sports ministry organizations.

Sportswomen and New Challenges for Sports Ministry

In the 1970s, organized feminists presented disparities in athletic resources as a political problem. The Commission on Intercollegiate Athletics for Women, formed in 1966, and its successor, the Association for Intercollegiate Athletics for Women, formed in 1971, drew attention to athletic inequalities at the college level. Across the country, colleges allocated paltry resources to women's sports compared to men's. A typical Big Ten Conference school in the Midwest allocated $1,300 to men's athletics for every dollar spent on women's sports; a typical mid-Atlantic university allocated more than $2 million to men's sports and only $1,900 to women's; and on the West Coast, a typical institution with a $2 million sports budget allocated less than 1 percent of it to women's sports.[23]

Advocates for women's sports turned to the newly passed Title IX to argue for equal funding for men's and women's athletics. The 1972 legislation guaranteed equal funds for men and women in all institutions that receive federal funding, reading in part, "No person in the United States shall, on the basis of sex, be excluded from participation in, be denied the benefits of, or be subjected to discrimination under any educational programs or activities receiving federal financial assistance." At first, institutions were unsure whether Title IX applied to athletics; and following a compliance deadline in 1978, there were several legal clarifications on the exact meaning of the legislation. In 1984, the Supreme Court mandated a narrow interpretation of Title IX, making it difficult to challenge sex discrimination in athletics. However, with the passage of the Civil Rights Restoration Act of 1987, legislative challenges to sex discrimination in sport dramatically increased. When Title IX became law, one in every nine women participated in sports. By the early twenty-first century, the statistics were one in 2.5.[24]

The 1990s ushered in a new era in women's sports. Due to Title IX, more women than ever grew up with increased access to athletics and therefore, more women than ever pursued careers in professional sports. The 1996 Olympics, dubbed by NBC "The Year of the Women," boasted a higher percentage of female athletes than ever before. Partly due to the publicity and victory of the Women's U.S. Olympic basketball team, the NBA Board of Governors approved the concept of the WNBA, which began its first competitive season in 1997. In addition, the Women's U.S. national soccer team won the FIFA Women's World Cup in 1999, with perhaps the most memorable moment being Brandi Chastain's victory celebration after scoring the Cup-winning penalty shot against China.

As male soccer players frequently do, she took off her jersey and waved it over her head, causing a scandal by revealing her sports bra and muscular torso. However, the resulting commotion was only possible because so many people were watching; Chastain's sports bra was broadcast to an estimated viewing audience of forty million.[25]

Starting in the 1990s, women began to outnumber men as participants in sports ministry. Sportswomen challenge traditional understandings of gender just by playing sports. While men who play sports tend to confirm understandings of masculinity by showcasing a set of traits culturally regarded as masculine—strength, precedence, agency, and leadership—women in sport have access to these same traits, challenging the idea that these traits belong solely to men. Because sportswomen challenge gender norms, some Americans perceived women's sports as sites of sexual deviance. Sports ministry organizations struggled with how to navigate a stereotype and reality of women's sports: the presence of lesbians. Evangelical Christians in general and sports ministry leaders in particular construe romantic intimacy between persons of the same sex as a sin, an act that displeases God. Policing sexual behavior is normative in evangelical settings. However, most evangelical institutions make a distinction between sexual behavior and sexual desire. Although the majority of sports ministry participants see homosexual *behavior* as sinful, they tend to posit that homosexual *desire* is a human failing that can be changed with God's help.

Since the 1980s, sports ministry and other evangelical Christian institutions have used the phrase "emotional dependency" to describe homosexuality. For example, FCA and AIA distributed the pamphlet *Emotional Dependency and How to Keep Your Friendships Healthy*, published in 1984, at events for female athletes and coaches that they hosted in the late 1980s and 1990s.[26] The pamphlet includes multiple fictional accounts of how "emotionally dependent" relationships develop. These texts and other evangelical materials describe homosexuality in negative terms and present dedication to Christ as a way to avoid falling into what they saw as inherently negative relationships. Homosexuality appears in these texts as a disease in need of healing.

Experiencing God's Power for Female Athletes, a sports ministry resource for women published in 1999, includes a fictional narrative about Jill and Becky, two college athletes who spent increasing amounts of time together, laughed at inside jokes that only the two of them share, and made others uncomfortable by "hugging each other for long periods of time. It wasn't long before rumors started on the team that Jill and Becky were in a lesbian relationship." The authors warn, "What happened in Jill and Becky's relationship is not that uncommon. What started out as a positive friendship turned into an emotionally dependent relationship,... [crossing] physical boundaries and [leading] into a homosexual relationship."[27] For these authors, all homosexual relationships are by their nature emotionally dependent and detrimental.

Primary Source

Primary sources provide firsthand accounts of the topic under consideration. They emerge from particular times and places and allow us to imagine the context and thought processes that give rise to a perspective.

Excerpts from *Experiencing God's Power for Female Athletes: How to Compete, Knowing and Doing the Will of God*, by Deb Hoffman, Julie Caldwell, and Kathy Schultz.
Courtesy of Cross Training Publishing, © 1999, all rights reserved.

Context:

- The authors of this book are Christian sportswomen with ties to sports ministry organizations including FCA and AIA. They wrote this book to provide a resource that addresses issues that they categorize as "identity as a female, stereotypes as a female athlete, and emotional dependency."[28]
- This book includes recommended daily Bible study on themes that affect Christian sportswomen. The excerpt below comes from the chapter titled "Relationships as Female" and addresses homosexuality.

Discussion Questions:

- How do the authors understand homosexuality? What do they see as the appropriate Christian understanding of homosexuality? How do they support their point of view?
- What factors do the authors present as leading a woman to homosexuality? Why do they think Christian women in sports need to consider these factors?
- What do you make of this presentation of homosexuality? What do you see as the consequences of this point of view?

Relationships as a Female, Day 3[29]
Unfortunately, there are many stereotypes that claim female athletes are lesbians, or participating in athletics or certain sports will lead you into homosexuality. Competing in sports does not "make" someone gay. However, it would also be wrong to say that all female athletes are only involved in heterosexual relationships…

Crossing the Line
There is an abundance of gay characters portrayed in television and movies, as well as books and propaganda aimed at convincing the public that people are born gay. There are churches today that "bless" homosexual unions and encourage a homosexual relationship between two people that is loving, monogamous,

and committed. In fact, individuals who do not agree with homosexuality are often labeled as homophobic and told that if they cannot accept this "alternative lifestyle," then *they* are the ones who need help.

The contrasting, anti-homosexual viewpoint among some people who call themselves Christians is just as damaging. They carry signs with slogans such as "God hates fags" and "AIDS is God's solution for homosexuality" at various pro-gay rallies and conferences. These people claim that homosexuals are perverts and condemned to hell. How do we determine what to believe about homosexuality? Where can we turn for honest answers?... The Bible never portrays homosexual relationships in a positive way and it condemns *any* sexual act outside the marriage relationship... Biblical marriage is defined as between one man and one woman....

Factors that Influence

What "causes" someone to be gay?... Most Christians who help people out of the homosexual lifestyle agree on certain common factors that seem to influence the lives of women involved in homosexuality. Even then, many people experience these factors and are never involved in a homosexual relationship. Keep in mind that the following are factors that can *influence* whether someone is susceptible and drawn to same-sex relationships, but do not guarantee that will happen.

- A relationship between a mother and daughter that is not nurturing and protective... Rather than develop her identity as a woman based on the influence of her mother, the girl looks for affirmation and nurturing in other female relationships. This can lead to emotional dependency... or a lesbian relationship.
- A relationship between a father and daughter that does not affirm the daughter's femininity and gender... Without a healthy role model early on, females do not learn how to relate effectively to men. Their response may be turning to other women to get these needs met.
- Peer influence can also be a factor. If a girl enjoys activities that are not considered "feminine," peers can sometimes tease or make hurtful comments that are remembered. She may internalize these comments and feel rejected because of her gender, or feel that she should have been a boy instead of a girl. Traumatic events, such as sexual abuse and emotional and verbal abuse, can lead to a sense of shame and destroy the ability to trust others... Not all women who are abused end up in a homosexual relationship, but there are some estimates that as many as 80% of lesbians have been sexually abused in some way...

Within the area of athletics, there is sometimes a subculture of women who are involved in homosexuality. Again, this is not to say that all female athletes are lesbians, but given some of the factors that may contribute to involvement in homosexual relationships, it makes sense that if a woman is looking for emotional fulfillment and nurturing from a female, she might find such a relationship with a teammate or coach.

In the 1990s, the phrase "gay Christian" seemed like a contradiction in terms; if one word was true, the other could not be. The United States did not recognize gay marriages as legal, and even liberal Protestant denominations were hesitant to ordain openly gay individuals.[30] Around this time, gay Christians began to challenge the idea that being openly gay contradicted Christian commitment. For example, Candace Chellew-Hodge identified as a "recovering Southern Baptist" who "believed the lie that she couldn't be both a lesbian and a Christian."[31] She published *Bulletproof Faith: A Spiritual Survival Guide for Gay and Lesbian Christians* to help gay Christians focus on God's unconditional love and withstand attacks from conservative Christians who condemned homosexuality. She lists a number of "bullets" aimed at gay people: there are "ex-gay" ministries proclaiming that queer Christians can change and then blame them for lack of faith when change does not happen; there are mainstream churches that accept queer Christians as members, but not leaders; and there are messages, sometimes coming from family or close friends, telling queer Christians that they are unworthy or unloved.[32] Chellew-Hodge turned to the Bible to argue against Christians who condemn homosexuality. She points to three main sexual immoralities condemned in the Bible: adultery, prostitution, and rape. When Christians encounter biblical stories of heterosexual immorality, they do not usually use these to condemn heterosexuality as a whole.[33] Chellew-Hodge's point of view gained traction with a younger generation of evangelicals, both gay and straight, who had trouble reconciling messages of a loving God with messages of damnation for gay people.

In sports ministry today, there is a generational divide on the issue of same-sex relationships and intimacy. Institutional leadership tends to be older and attached to traditional ways of doing ministry, such as praying for salvation or declaring commitment publicly, whereas those in the field (college campuses, high schools, summer camps) tend to be younger and more open to thinking of Christian commitment as a journey rather than focusing on a singular moment of salvation. One campus sports minister at a large Division I state university told me,

> When the folks who are now the leaders of sports ministry were doing ministry on the ground [twenty years ago], they saw the issue of sexuality as a black and white issue. There was a lack of sympathy and empathy, an elevation of sexual ethics above all else. This generation doesn't elevate purity culture and doesn't see the issue as cut and dry. We do have conversations about sexual ethics for Christ-followers. But, I don't think a person has to agree with me for God to do something in their life. A different answer doesn't mean that we can't have community or that God can't use you. We keep ministering to a student who may have cheated on his exam with Chat-GPT or something, why would we stop ministering to someone working through sexual ethics?[34]

Sports ministers who are willing to talk about sexual ethics in a broader manner and have open conversations that include queer sexualities can face repercussions such as losing funding or losing their sports ministry position.

In response to more and more college students identifying as LGBTQ, Cru, the parent organization for Athletes in Action, developed a curriculum for campus ministers in 2021 titled "Compassionate and Faithful." The curriculum included videos by Preston Sprinkle, a controversial pastor who heads the Center for Faith, Sexuality and Gender. Sprinkle's approach to gender and sexuality adheres to Christian traditional understandings of sexual intimacy and marriage: sex outside of marriage is sinful, and marriage is between one man and one woman. Where he becomes controversial is in his approach to queer people seeking Christian community. Sprinkle advocates an understanding of same-sex attraction that uses the same sexual ethics as opposite-sex attraction: lust is sinful and sex outside of (straight) marriage is sinful. He differs from some conservative Christians in that he does not present same-sex attraction as sinful in and of itself.

In October 2023, Liberty University, a conservative Christian college in Virginia, hosted Rosaria Butterfield as its convocation speaker. Butterfield identifies as an ex-lesbian, and as part of her convocation address, she named organizations that she saw as un-biblical on issues of sex and gender. In addition to Sprinkle's Center for Faith, Sexuality and Gender and Revoice, an organization that supports gay Christians, Butterfield named Cru, causing a gasp from the audience.[35]

Butterfield's address caused an uproar in evangelical circles and led to Cru pulling Sprinkle's trainings from its curriculum. Sprinkle's encouragement to refer to people by their preferred pronouns as well as his use of the term "gay Christian" as a synonym for

Image 4.3 Rosaria Butterfield addresses ten thousand students at Liberty University's convocation in October 2023. Her address traced her journey from a monogamous lesbian and professor of English at Syracuse University to her present life as a pastor's wife and mother. She told the audience that lies that "discourage repentance and encourage the pride of victimhood" have become normalized in organizations such as Cru. *Courtesy of Liberty Marketing.*

same-sex-attracted Christians generated backlash from Cru donors.[36] Ministry Watch, an organization that alerts Christian donors to practices and ideologies of Christian ministries, described Cru's update to its training materials:

> One document that previously called transgender pronouns "an issue of conscience... a profound way to demonstrate that you recognize them and desire to show respect," now warned that using biologically incorrect pronouns "may unintentionally communicate a position that Cru does not hold (and Scripture does not teach)."[37]

Cru's backpedaling on pronouns and other language choices shows that the organization is beholden to ways of approaching homosexuality held by older generations of evangelicals and less popular with the current generation of sports ministers and Christian athletes.

Over the past decade, new sports ministry resources have emerged that do not shun queer sexuality but unabashedly include LGBTQIA+ persons in their ministry. Formed by two gay Christian athletes who became ministers, Christian Athlete Circles (CAC) is one such organization. Georgia McKee came out as a lesbian in college while heavily involved in FCA and when asked to sign a faith and purity statement that explicitly condemned homosexuality, she left the organization. Kelsey Davis came out as a lesbian in high school and had a strong desire to learn about and belong to a Christian community. She became copresident of her high-school's FCA chapter and was involved with the organization through college and into her professional soccer career. When Davis eventually told FCA that she was gay, the organization was clear that they should part ways. McKee and Davis met in 2020 and formed CAC hoping that the organization could help others who had experienced exile from sports ministry because of their sexuality.

Davis described how her experiences led her to cofound CAC:

> When I was a student athlete in the early 2000s, I had a conversation with a Catholic priest who said to me, 'I can't officially tell you that your sexuality is okay, but I can tell you that God loves you and that you are okay with me.' It was like he really did love the person in front of him, even while his religious institution said that I was wrong. In sports ministry, there are ministers who are supportive of various sexual orientations and identities that work in the wider sports ministry system that doesn't support loving the whole person. It's sad, I feel for those chaplains. I've also been that student athlete who has to do a don't-ask-don't-tell dance to be accepted. If FCA is the only option to connect to my faith, I guess I'm going to swallow it and stay closeted.... It's not good for anyone. Not for athletes, not for chaplains, not for institutions.... At CAC, you don't have to hide parts of yourself in order to belong.[38]

At first, CAC tried to emulate the model of FCA and AIA and form a campus ministry for college athletes. McKee was enrolled in divinity school at a Division I college in the South and proposed forming a campus CAC ministry. However, the school had supported the presence of AIA for more than thirty years and was hesitant to support another sports ministry. McKee understood it as, "They thought they already had a sports ministry, so they didn't need another ministry. The existing sports ministry organizations have a monopoly over college campuses."[39] Davis agreed, saying, "Starting a new athlete ministry is really hard to do on college campuses. Joining something new, especially a progressive Christian ministry, can be viewed as risky. If most of your teammates are going to another sports ministry, and you're going to this start-up, progressive ministry, where does that put you with your team?"

CAC decided to pivot to creating resources for gay Christian athletes and holding online sessions for wider participation across multiple campuses. As CAC's website describes,

> We have too many stories of having ministries "pray away the gay" and other forms of spiritual abuse due to the exclusive theology of these existing para-church organizations. We seek to build an athlete ministry that is rooted in belovedness, original goodness, and dignifies the individual and the collective by honoring diversities and our unity in Christ as mutually inclusive endeavors.[40]

Heather Davis, married to Kelsey Davis, helps run CAC. She told me that athletes reach out to CAC wondering how they could be Christian and gay. She said, "We are trying to reclaim the word 'Christian' as best we can. We're trying to provide resources to fight a toxic theology that is literally killing people."[41] Organizations such as CAC offer a critique of existing sports ministries' approach to sexuality and provide different resources that they hope will reach queer Christian athletes with the message that their sexuality does not mean that they cannot belong in a Christian community.

Conclusions

When sports ministry first emerged in the 1950s and 1960s, evangelical Christians saw prominent athletes as impressive spokespeople who, given the right training, could become ambassadors for Christianity. Over the next few decades, more sports ministry organizations formed with the explicit purpose of cultivating athletes as Christian role models for the American public. As this project succeeded in publicizing the Christian identity of athletes and establishing ministries for athletes from high school to professional, both insiders and outsiders confronted an ethical dilemma. As critic Shirl Hoffman put it, "There are simply no easy, straight-faced, intellectually respectable answers for how evangelicals can model the Christian narrative—with its emphases on servanthood, generosity, and self-subordination—while immersed in a culture that thrives on cut-throat competition, partisanship, and Darwinian struggle."[42] For Hoffman and others, sport is structurally contradictory to Christian values.

In the 1990s, as women began to outnumber men as participants in sports ministry, sports ministers focused on homosexuality as a significant issue confronting sportswomen. This coincided with evangelical Christians taking a public stand against gay marriage and proclaiming the sinfulness of homosexuality. Prominent televangelists such as Jerry Falwell and Pat Robertson blamed the 9/11 terrorist attacks (2001) and the destruction wrought by Hurricane Katrina (2005) on Americans' acceptance of abortion, homosexuality, and feminism.[43] For women in sport, the issue—how to understand homosexuality—was not abstract; their teams were often made up of women with a variety of sexualities. As women in sports ministry grappled with traditional understandings of sexuality as well as their own lived experiences of sports, some came to different conclusions than their older, more traditional counterparts. Organizations such as Christian Athlete Circles offer an alternative to the dominant message of sports ministry that same-sex attraction and same-sex intimacy are contrary to God's will, showcasing potential avenues for sports ministry to transform in the future.

Resources for Further Study

Media
Brian Bolt and Chad Carlson, *Sport.Faith.Life*, podcast series, https://sportfaithlife.com/podcastblog/.

Online Archive
Fellowship of Christian Athletes provides a searchable archive of its magazine, *Sharing the Victory*, https://www.fca.org/resources/fca-magazine-archive.

Reading
Annie Blazer, *Playing for God: Evangelical Women and the Unintended Consequences of Sports Ministry* (New York: NYU Press, 2015).
Gwendolyn Oxenham, "Play Away the Gay," *Under the Lights and in the Dark: Untold Stories of Women's Soccer* (London: Icon Books, 2017), 109–36.
Paul Emory Putz, *The Spirt of the Game: American Christianity and Big-Time Sports* (New York: Oxford University Press, 2024).

Chapter 5

Muhammad Ali

When Cassius Clay returned from the 1960 Olympics in Rome, he was twenty years old and proud of his gold medal in boxing. He met a friend in his hometown of Louisville to go out for a meal, and the restaurant refused to serve Clay and his friend because they were Black. Disillusioned and upset, he would later tell the story of standing on the Jefferson County Bridge looking down at the Ohio River and throwing his gold medal into the water. He described watching the heavy medallion drag the red, white, and blue ribbon under the dark waters.[1] In 1964, Cassius Clay would take the name Muhammad Ali and become the most famous Black Muslim in America. He would refuse to serve in the Vietnam War and lose some of his best boxing years to a legal struggle for exemption from military service. As the Vietnam War declined in popularity over the 1960s, mainstream America went from characterizing Ali as a brat or a villain to praising his strong moral compass.

The story of Muhammad Ali is the story of the Nation of Islam, a religious movement that promoted Black separatism and Black superiority. It is the story of the Vietnam War, a war that sent more than fifty-eight thousand men to their deaths and relied disproportionately on Black people to serve on the front lines. It is the story of a Black athlete's public religious convictions and the fear that those convictions provoked in white America. This chapter explores Ali and his context to showcase the complexity of American race relations in the 1960s and 1970s. In this chapter, I refer to Muhammad Ali as Cassius Clay when addressing events before his name change in 1964 and as Muhammad Ali when addressing events after his public name change. Media outlets and state governing agencies continued to refer to Muhammad Ali as Cassius Clay well after his name change, so in this chapter, you will see two names consistently appearing for our main character.

Nation of Islam

To understand Muhammad Ali and how the public responded to him, we need to examine the Nation of Islam, a religion founded by Elijah Muhammad. Born Elijah Poole in 1897 in Cordele, Georgia, Elijah Muhammad grew up during the period of the highest number of lynchings of Black men in American history. When he was a teenager, a white mob lynched his close friend and neighbor, Albert Hamilton, for supposedly attacking a white girl. Police had imprisoned Hamilton in Crisp County Jail, where one week previously white mobs had overrun the facility and lynched three Black men. In a repeat of this offense, a white crowd dragged Hamilton from the building and into the Black part of Cordele. There, they shot him more than three hundred times and hung his body, taking pictures that they made into postcards and sold in nearby towns. This was the context of Elijah Muhammad's youth in Georgia.[2]

In 1919, Elijah Muhammad married Clara Belle Evans, and the two moved to Macon, Georgia, hoping to escape racially motivated violence by living in a city with a larger Black population. Lynchings, church burnings, and murders of Black men continued across the South; and in April 1923, Muhammad traveled to Detroit, Michigan, seeking a better life for himself and his family, who joined him in Detroit several months later. In 1931, Elijah Muhammad met W. D. Fard, who presented himself as a peddler from Mecca, Saudi Arabia, and Muhammad came to see him as a new prophet of Islam. Fard had moved to Detroit in 1929 and began spreading a message of Black Islam to the African American residents. Fard disappeared in 1934 after being implicated in a murder committed in 1932, and he named Elijah Muhammad his successor. After Fard's disappearance, Muhammad wandered for much of the 1930s and served a jail sentence from 1943 to 1946 for draft evasion during World War II. After his release, Elijah Muhammad developed the major theological tenets and practices of the Nation of Islam.

The Nation of Islam relied heavily on Islam but departed from the tradition in significant ways. Islam is a global religion dating to the seventh century and emerging from the Arabian Peninsula. The central miracle of Islam is the Qur'an, a series of revelations described by the prophet Muhammad as coming directly from God. The central statement of faith for Muslims is: there is no god but God, and Muhammad is the messenger of God. This statement is both a statement of monotheism and a statement that Muhammad's revelations and Muhammad's actions during his life are the basis for correct Muslim living. The word "Islam" means submission, and a "Muslim" is one who submits. Fard claimed to be a new messenger of God and presented himself as divine. When Elijah Muhammad changed his last name from Poole to Muhammad, he was signaling both that he was the messenger of Fard and that he was now a prophet for the Nation of Islam.

The Nation of Islam was similar to Sunni Islam, the largest sect of Islam globally, but it also had enough significant differences that global Muslim leaders did not recognize the Nation of Islam as Islam. According to Muslim theology, only God can be called divine, but the Nation of Islam claimed that Fard was a divine being. Sunni Muslims believe that Muhammad was the last prophet and final messenger of God, making Elijah Muhammad's claims to be a prophet heretical. Fard taught that white people were devils designed to oppress Black people, but most Muslims see all humans as children of God, so Fard's claim that whites were devils was heresy to them.

The idea of white people as devils is central to the theology of the Nation of Islam (NOI) and is important for understanding mainstream backlash against the religion. Elijah Muhammad wrote in his 1965 book, *Message to the Blackman in America*, that sixty-six

Image 5.1 In this photograph taken in 1960, Elijah Muhammad appears wearing his signature black cap, embroidered with stars and crescents. *Getty Images/Hulton Archive.*

hundred years ago the god-scientist Yakub was born. Yakub began to study genetics to create a new order of people to rule over the current population of entirely Black-skinned people. He set about genetically engineering a new population, selecting for recessive light-skinned characteristics. *Message to the Blackman in America* describes the outcome of Yakub's experiments:

> The Yakub made devils were really pale white, with really blue eyes; which we think are the ugliest colors for a human eye… There was no good taught to them while on the Island. By teaching the nurses to kill the black baby and save the brown baby, so as to graft the white out of it; by lying to the black mother of the baby [that her baby was in heaven when it had been murdered], this lie was born into the very nature of the white baby; and, murder for the black people also born in them—or made by nature a liar and murderer.[3]

In Elijah Muhammad's story of Yakub, Yakub bred white people to not only have pale skin and blue eyes, but he made lying and murder essential to their being, creating a race of white devils.

The audience for Elijah Muhammad's teachings remained relatively small over the 1940s and 1950s, and the Nation of Islam did not reach far beyond the boundaries of Detroit. During this time, Malcolm Little was serving a prison sentence for larceny and burglary. His siblings who lived in Michigan and had converted to the Nation of Islam shared Elijah Muhammad's teachings with their imprisoned brother. Changing his name to Malcolm X upon his release in 1952 and dismayed to find that the Nation of Islam was such a small group, Malcolm X embarked on a nationwide recruitment campaign and managed to grow the organization from hundreds of people centered in Detroit to a network of thousands spanning fifty cities across the country.

In the spring of 1955, a Black journalist named Louis Lomax received permission from Elijah Muhammad to make a documentary about the Nation of Islam. Lomax's film crews began filming at NOI mosques in New York City, Chicago, and Washington, D.C., and interviewing Elijah Muhammad, Malcolm X, and other ministers of the Nation. Lomax's documentary, *The Hate That Hate Produced*, aired on television in a five-part series from July 13 through 17, 1959. Television commentators contextualized the program by declaring that the statements of hate coming from NOI's pulpits would cause a federal investigation if they were coming from white Southerners. Calling the group "homegrown Negro American Muslims" who are "the most powerful of the black supremacist groups," a commentator summarized Elijah Muhammad's message as: "the good news for the black man is he is on the verge of recapturing his position as ruler of the universe, and the bad news for the white man is that his long and wicked reign with shortly be over."[4] Malcolm X watched it and surmised that the documentary was written to shock white audiences. And provoke shock it did, as the white press railed against NOI, and prominent Black civil rights spokespeople gave statements meant to reassure the larger population that NOI was a fringe movement and not representative of Black America.

In the media blitz that followed the release of the film, TV and radio programs often invited Malcolm X to appear on panel shows and defend NOI against white and Black detractors. In response to Black civil rights leaders promoting integration as the solution to racial inequality, X would respond,

> No *sane* black man really wants integration! No *sane* white man really wants integration! No sane black man really believes that the white man will ever give the black man anything more than token integration. No! The Honorable Elijah Muhammad teaches that for the black man in America the only solution is complete *separation* from the white man![5]

Malcolm X's stances continued to infuriate the white press, but Elijah Muhammad's message was reaching a larger audience than ever before.

Elijah Muhammad was soon speaking to large, packed gatherings. In his autobiography, X summarized Elijah Muhammad's message during these gatherings: you are not Negros ("There is no such thing as a race of '*Negroes.*' You are members of the Asiatic nation, from the tribe of *Shabazz*! 'Negro' is a false label forced on you by your slavemaster!"); you have long been exploited by white people and have made white people rich ("You have sweated blood to help him build a country so rich that he can today afford to give away millions—even to his *enemies*! And when those enemies have gotten enough from him to then be able to attack him, you have been his brave soldiers, *dying* for him."); and that it is white hypocrisy to declare that racial integration would mongrelize the white race ("Turn around in your seats and look at each other! This slavemaster white man already has '*integrated*' us until you can hardly find among us today any more than a very few who are the black color of our foreparents!").[6] Elijah Muhammad would end with a call to action, to separate from white society and pursue a Black society run by and for Black people. These were the central messages of NOI when a young Cassius Clay first encountered the religious movement in 1959.

Cassius Clay to Muhammad Ali

Cassius Clay joined NOI in 1961, but he originally kept his association a secret, fearing that it would jeopardize his athletic career. He established a relationship with Malcolm X in 1962 when they met at a mosque in Detroit, and their friendship and mentorship grew stronger over time. Against the wishes of Elijah Muhammad, X traveled with Clay to Miami in February 1964 for Clay's fight against Sonny Liston, the World Heavyweight Champion at the time. Elijah Muhammad thought that Clay would lose and feared associating NOI with a loser.[7] X saw the fight as a God-given opportunity to prove Black Muslim superiority. Clay won the fight quickly and thoroughly and announced his commitment to NOI at a press conference the following morning.

X began to challenge Elijah Muhammad's directives and teachings, and Elijah Muhammad replaced him with a figure whose popularity was bodily rather than intellectual: Muhammad Ali. Muhammad Ali became a source of trepidation for many Americans, white and Black, due to his rejection of Christianity and call for isolation of the races. Elijah Muhammad used the public attention to heighten interest in Ali, seeing him as a charismatic replacement for Malcolm X. In March 1964, X announced plans to cooperate with other Black leaders interested in pursuing an activist strategy for Black liberation and a new mosque in New York City. X consistently received death threats after his break with Elijah Muhammad and was assassinated on February 21, 1965. Three members of the Nation of Islam were arrested and convicted of the murder; Elijah Muhammad denied any knowledge of the plot to kill Malcolm X.

Nine months later, the November 22, 1965, fight between Muhammad Ali and Floyd Patterson highlighted an ideological divide in America. Patterson was a member of the National Association for the Advancement of Colored People (NAACP), lived in the suburbs with his white wife, believed in the narrative of the American Dream, and was deeply opposed to Jim Crow policies that segregated whites and Blacks. Ali's stance that separation was good and necessary appalled Patterson. Leading up to their fight,

Image 5.2 Muhammad Ali with Malcolm X. This photograph appeared in the *New York Daily News* on March 2, 1964, documenting Ali and X together a week after Ali's defeat of Sonny Liston. According to the article that accompanied the photo, Ali arrived in Harlem to meet with X and was surrounded by a hundred adoring kids from the neighborhood, who chanted, "You are the greatest," to which Ali responded, "Allah is the greatest."[8] *Getty Images/New York Daily News Archive.*

Patterson told *Sports Illustrated*, "I have nothing but contempt for the Black Muslims and that for which they stand. The image of a Black Muslim as the world heavyweight champion disgraces the sport and the nation. Cassius Clay must be beaten and the Black Muslims' scourge removed from boxing."[9] In response to reporters' insistence that NOI was a hate group, Ali responded, "Elijah isn't teaching hate when he tells us about the evil things the white man has done any more than you're teaching hate when you tell us about what Hitler did to the Jews. That's not hate, that's history."[10]

Ali defeated Patterson over a grueling twelve rounds—Ali backed off knocking Patterson out several times to prolong the fight. After his victory, Ali told the press,

> But it was not you [Patterson] that I was trying to beat and knock out. It was those backing you. I was talking back to them. I was saying, "I am America. Only, I'm the part you won't recognize. But get used to me. Black, confident, cocky. My name, not yours; my religion, not yours; my goals, my own—get used to me! I can make it without your approval! I won't let you beat me and I won't let your Negro beat me!"[11]

Ali's boisterous self-confidence made him controversial in the mainstream but lent him authority among a growing segment of the Black population who were open to learning more about NOI's call for Black separation from an inherently evil white population.

Rejection of the Vietnam War

Cassius Clay registered for the draft on April 18, 1960, as required by law. In March 1962, the Armed Forces classified him as 1-A (draftable); this is the default designation that every man has until the Armed Forces evaluates him for eligibility to serve. On January 24, 1964, Clay took the Armed Forces qualifying exam and scored below the required aptitudes. He retook the exam in March 1964 and failed again. In November 1965, the Pentagon issued a directive that lowered the qualifying aptitude score for military service from the thirtieth percentile to the fifteenth. Ali had scored in the sixteenth percentile and, in February 1966, the Armed Forced reclassified him as 1-A. The Defense Department further dropped qualifying scores as part of an initiative called "Project 100,000" that would allow another 100,000 men per year to serve in the military. The program ran from 1966 to 1971 and resulted in approximately 346,000 men serving in all branches of the military, split evenly between volunteers and draftees. The men who qualified under the new standards were disproportionately Black and died three times more often than soldiers admitted under the previous standard.[12]

Some, like sports reporter Robert Lipsyte, found the military's drop in standards suspicious, insinuating that the Pentagon was directly targeting Ali.[13] In fact, the FBI had been interested in NOI since at least the 1950s and had used Elijah Muhammad's teachings that whites were devils to justify wiretapping and other surveillance measures. According to declassified FBI documents, FBI director J. Edgar Hoover characterized "black nationalist" groups as devious, duplicitous, and in danger of toppling the U.S. government. The term "black nationalist" formed a big umbrella and allowed the FBI to investigate figures and organizations as wide-ranging as the Black Panthers, the NAACP, Dr. Martin Luther King Jr., football star Jim Brown, and musician Jimi Hendrix.[14] After Malcolm X's assassination in 1965, the FBI turned its attention to Muhammad Ali. FBI documents show that the FBI had targeted Ali as early as 1964 for "neutralization," a catch-all term for intervention into a person's life to deprive them of power to sway public opinion.[15]

From at least January 1, 1966, the Louisville branch of the FBI was closely watching Muhammad Ali regarding his draft status. Writing to the FBI director, the Louisville office requested to "follow the draft status of Cassius Clay bearing in mind the possibility he may claim a C.O. [conscientious objector] status and a possible trial may ensue in the event he is found eligible for the draft."[16]

In the history of U.S. wars, Quakers have been the most successful at attaining conscientious objector status. Quakerism is a branch of Protestantism that holds pacifism as a key tenet. During the American Civil War, Quakers succeeded in having an exemption clause added to legislation on military drafting that those who hold a religious conviction of pacifism would serve noncombat roles if drafted. For some, serving in noncombat roles such as hospitals still violated their religious principles because they were still supporting the war effort. The Quakers kept up their cause for religious exemption. When the U.S. government instituted conscription again during World War I, the board overseeing drafting of soldiers granted exemptions to members of well-recognized religious sects with creeds that prohibited participation in war. During World War II, military service exemptions became even broader: one did not have to be a member of a denomination such as Quakerism; one simply needed to show that one's religious convictions did not allow for participation in war. Despite this broad approach, in practice one still needed the status of a long-standing peace church to effectively achieve exemption status. During World War II, Elijah Muhammad had instructed members of NOI to refuse to serve, and they were arrested rather than granted conscientious objector status. To qualify for CO status during the Vietnam War, the petitioner had to demonstrate that he was opposed to war in every case;

Image 5.3 Muhammad Ali (far left) at the Nation of Islam's Annual Muslim Convention in Chicago in February 1966. Ali and others are escorting Elijah Muhammad (far right) out of the building following the day's events. Ali is dressed in a Fruit of Islam captain's uniform. *Getty Images/Bettmann*.

his objections were morally or religiously based, not politically motivated or self-interested; and the objection was sincere. This standard for CO status is still in place.

In February 1966, Ali's lawyer requested deferment for military service on a number of procedural grounds including financial hardship for Ali's family if he could not box. Ali was in Miami and nervously awaited the draft board's decision. Reporters swarmed him, and this was when Ali delivered a line that would become famous—"I ain't got no quarrel with them Vietcong." The media backlash was swift and punishing, calling Ali an "adult brat."[17] The Illinois Athletic Commission called on Ali to apologize for his "un-American remarks," and Ali came before the three-person commission on February 21, 1966. Ali apologized for saying to the press what he should have said to the draft board, but he did not apologize for the content of his remarks.

In general, ministers qualify for CO status, and the FBI began gathering intelligence on Ali's activities within NOI to make the case that Ali was not a minster. For example, on February 26–27, 1966, NOI held its Annual Muslim Convention in Chicago. Ali was in attendance, wearing a Fruit of Islam (FOI) captain's uniform. FOI was a men's organization within NOI that offered military-style training to equip members to defend NOI leadership and property. Elijah Muhammad established a strict code of conduct for FOI including prohibitions on alcohol, pork, drugs, gambling, dancing, and entertainment.[18] As a paramilitary organization, FOI had a hierarchical ranking system, and Muhammad Ali appearing in a captain's uniform seemed to represent his important status in NOI.

An FBI report submitted the day after the Annual Muslim Convention in Chicago included a statement from an informant:

> [Ali] holds no position whatsoever in the FOI and does not even attend FOI meetings… Officials in the NOI want to force him to attend FOI meetings to discipline him, as they are extremely dissatisfied with his attitude and the way he speaks so spontaneously. They feel he needs much more discipline than he presently has to be a satisfactory Muslim.[19]

The Chicago FBI branch offered the Louisville branch further fodder for their cause in a report on March 17, 1966, that included an informant reporting on a conversation between Elijah Muhammad and his son Herbert Muhammad. According to the informant, Herbert Muhammad had asked Elijah Muhammad how he felt about Muhammad Ali's attendance at the Annual Muslim Convention, and Elijah Muhammad had emphasized that Ali was welcome to attend and to sit in a prominent place but Ali would not be speaking at the convention. According to the report, Elijah Muhammad said of Ali, "He's no minister… He won't speak unless I ask him to say something and I will tell him what to say."[20] The Louisville FBI branch used these reports to argue that Ali was not a minister in NOI and therefore should not receive conscientious objector status.

Primary Source

Primary sources provide firsthand accounts of the topic under consideration. They emerge from particular times and places and allow us to imagine the context and thought processes that give rise to a perspective.

Compare news coverage of Muhammad Ali from *Sports Illustrated* and *Muhammad Speaks*

Context:

- Jack Olsen's "Learning Elijah's Advanced Lessons in Hate" ran in *Sports Illustrated* on May 2, 1966. It was the fourth of a five-part series exploring Muhammad Ali. Olsen describes Ali in the opening to part one of the series: "He is the best known athlete in the world. He is also the most hated, and an enigma even to those closest to him."[21]
- On May 12, 1967, NOI's publication *Muhammad Speaks* ran an extended interview between Elijah Muhammad and the nation's leading news medias, American Broadcasting Company (ABC) and National Broadcasting Company (NBC), regarding Muhammad Ali.

Discussion Questions:

- How does Olsen present Muhammad Ali? What do you make of Olsen's tone? What do you make of the choice to refer to Muhammad Ali as Cassius Clay?
- How does Muhammad Ali present the beliefs and practices of his religion? What do you make of Olsen's responses?
- How does Elijah Muhammad explain Muhammad Ali's choice to keep boxing? To refuse induction?
- What do you see as the most important differences between these two excerpts? What similarities do you see? What can we learn from this comparison?

Excerpts from Jack Olsen, "Learning Elijah's Advanced Lessons in Hate," *Sports Illustrated*, May 2, 1966, 37–53.

Like a child who has learned his catechism, Cassius has all the answers. Do the Muslims teach hate? "In a way, we do. But are we wrong to hate the murders and the unjust treatment that we're getting? Sure, we hate that. But we're righteous people. We rely on Allah, and we don't bother nobody." What about Elijah Muhammad's constant refrain that all white men are devils? "Elijah Muhammad teaches us that he didn't know about that hisself till 35, 40 years ago when God, in the person of master Wallace Fard, came to America and taught Elijah Muhammad. And Elijah Muhammad teaches us that this is just the truth that God taught him."

Now, at 24, Clay appears firmer than ever in his beliefs and further away from his parents and relatives. "We Muslims don't want to break down the doors of a white man's restaurant," he said not long ago. "I don't want a milk shake in a white store, because they'll spit in my milk shake and mix it up, and I won't see it because I can't see spit in a milkshake. So I won't feel comfortable. I want to go in my own restaurant where my own beautiful women are there. I can speak the language I speak.... I'm no longer a Negro. I'm no longer a slave. I am with myself and with my own kind. So therefore I get along with you better. Because now I know what you're like, and I know who I am." This speech so excites Clay that he begins to sound like a tent-show evangelist ending his sermon on a peak of emotion and bombast. I was impressed the first time I heard it. Here was bedrock sincerity, the man's soul bared, a searing look at the true Cassius and his pride and his fears. But after I heard him make more or less the same speech three or four times, I began to wonder if it was bedrock Clay or something he was trying to drum into himself, a lesson he had learned at the feet of the master. Then I began to notice that he had a package of these set speeches and he kept coming back to them, like a man whose whole philosophical outlook is poised on three legs, and if one breaks, all break.

Excerpts from "Exclusive Interview with Elijah Muhammad," *Muhammad Speaks***, May 12, 1967, 3–9.**

Question: Do you see any contradiction between the Muslim faith and boxing?
Answer: There is a lot of difference between boxing and the Muslim faith. Boxing is a sport. Islam is a religion.

Question: I mean in the Muslim religion seeking peace and boxing?
Answer: Muhammad [Ali] was boxing when he accepted Islam. The Christian people want him to just walk away from the title, "Champion of the World." They want him to just walk out, because he is a Muslim. If he were a Christian, it would be all right. Christians box and fight and go to war among themselves. For Muhammad to give up the gloves and walk off the platform because he is a Muslim would be denying himself the credit for his performance as a fighter. His championship would be given away and not won from him in the ring as he won it from the former champion.

Question: What is the Muslim viewpoint towards the draft?
Answer: Muslims are righteous people. They do not believe in making war on anybody—and senseless aggression against people violates a Muslim's religious

> belief ... We are said to be free by the government of America. We are not slaves of the white man any longer. However, he is using the same tactics that his father used 300 years ago—that we have to do these things or suffer punishment. We are free today, 100 years up from slavery and we want to return to our own God, religion and people. All who accept Islam have that privilege.
>
> *Question*: Do you think Muhammad Ali has acted properly in refusing to be inducted into the army?
> *Answer*: In the first place we, the Muslims, don't teach violence. I have been here more than 35 years and we have a record spelling out what we teach and our actions prove what we teach. At no time in those years have we ever attacked or been an aggressor. Our religion and the very words, as-Salaam-Alaikum, mean peace. We cannot be classified as aggressors, when we teach peace.
>
> *Question*: Do you think Muhammad Ali should be excused from the draft because he is a minister?
> *Answer*: I was a minister when I went [to jail in 1942]. This government does not excuse you for righteousness, because by its nature, it is against righteousness.
>
> *Question*: There are ministers who are excused.
> *Answer*: Those are Christian ministers.

When Ali's conscientious objector petition failed, he requested a hearing. At the hearing on August 23, 1966, Ali testified before Judge Lawrence Grauman for the Kentucky Appeal Board that he spent most of his time as a minister for Islam and should therefore be exempt from military service of any kind. Judge Grauman pronounced, "I believe that the registrant is of good character, morals, and integrity, and sincere in his objection on religious grounds to participation in war in any form. I recommend that the registrant's claim for conscientious objector status be sustained."[22] Following this judgment, the Justice Department wrote a letter to the Selective Service Board that Ali was not opposed to war in any form, so the judgment should be overturned. As Oscar T. Smith, chief of the conscientious objector section of the Justice Department, put it, "It seems clear that the teachings of the Nation of Islam preclude fighting for the United States not because of objections to participation in war in any form but rather because of political and racial objections to the policies of the United States as interpreted by Elijah Muhammad."[23]

In March 1967, Muhammad Ali returned home to Louisville to rest. He attended a protest for open housing, protesting for the right of Black people to live in any neighborhood in Louisville. While at the protest, Ali spoke to reporters about his decision not to fight in Vietnam, saying,

> Why should they ask me to put on a uniform and go ten thousand miles from home and drop bombs and bullets on brown people in Vietnam while so-called Negro people in Louisville are treated like dogs and denied simple human rights?... I have said it once and I will say it again. The real enemy of my people is right here.... If I thought the war was going to bring freedom and equality to twenty-two million of my people, they wouldn't have to draft me, I'd join tomorrow... I have nothing to lose by standing up for my beliefs. So I'll go to jail. We've been in jail for four hundred years.[24]

Shortly thereafter, Martin Luther King Jr. came out in opposition to the war in Vietnam in a sermon to New York City's Riverside Church on April 4, 1967. King's speech echoed Ali's stance on the Vietnam War: he challenged young men to pursue conscientious objection as an alternative to serving in the war.[25] Martin Luther King Jr. was also under FBI surveillance. FBI director J. Edgar Hoover described King as "an instrument in the hands of subversive forces seeking to undermine our nation"[26] and described surveilling him to discern "the extent of communist influence on King, the Southern Christian Leadership Conference, and the racial situation in general."[27] Black activists were increasingly concerned about Black men dying in Vietnam; Black men accounted for 29 percent of deaths in the war though African Americans made up 11 percent of the U.S. population.[28]

Ali's lawyers arranged for a last-minute hearing the day before his scheduled induction on April 28, 1967. They were seeking a restraining order to prevent the Selective Service Board from declaring Ali delinquent if he refused to take the step forward to indicate his induction into the armed services. The Justice Department lawyer at the hearing laid bare the fear that Ali's actions might set an inconvenient precedent. He said that if Ali's conscientious objector status claim was upheld, "all the Muslims will refuse to take the oath and where will we get the soldiers?"[29] Reporters continued to criticize Ali, and those who defended him found their columns canceled and readers calling with death threats.[30]

When he was scheduled to be in inducted, Ali did not step forward; he refused on the grounds that he was a minister of Islam. He was convicted of refusing induction and given the maximum sentence of five years in prison and a fine of $10,000. Ali was released from prison pending the appeal of the case, but his passport was taken away, so he could not fight in any international fights. After Ali publicly identified as a member of NOI and refused the draft, he had trouble booking fights in the United States, and most of his fights in 1966 were abroad. Ali's refusal to enter the draft for the Vietnam War had the support of NOI and Black leaders such as Martin Luther King Jr., but the boxing community found him "disgusting" and "unpatriotic."[31] The New York State Athletic Commission and the World Boxing Association stripped Ali of his title.

After refusing induction, Ali criticized the media portrayal of his decision, saying, "I strongly object to the fact that so many newspapers have given the American public and the world the impression that I have only two alternatives in taking this stand: either I go to jail or I go to the Army. There is another alternative and that alternative is justice."[32] From 1967 to 1971, Ali was one of the country's most prominent antiwar public speakers. Ali's words became slogans for posters for activist groups including the Student Nonviolent

Coordinating Committee (SNCC). Former SNCC chair John Lewis recalled that the poster reading "NO VIETNAMESE EVER CALLED ME NIGGER" was ubiquitous in the organizing rooms of SNCC chapters across the country.[33]

Ali's appeal for conscientious objector status went all the way to the Supreme Court, and the Court heard the case in 1971. According to reporting by Bob Woodward and Scott Armstrong, Justice William Brennan was the only member of the Supreme Court who wanted to hear the case. Brennan persuaded his colleagues to hear it because of Ali's prominence; none of the Justices thought Ali had a chance at winning.[34] During oral arguments in the case, Solicitor General Erwin Griswold pointed out that NOI held a doctrine of self-defense and argued, "if the Vietcong were attacking his people, the Muslims would become involved in that war." For Griswold, this constituted evidence that Ali was not opposed to war in every case and therefore did not qualify for conscientious objector status. With Justice Thurgood Marshall recused because he had been solicitor general when the case began, the court voted 5–3 to deny Ali's CO status, agreeing with Griswold that he did not qualify.

The chief justice assigned Justice John Harlan to draft the majority opinion. As Harlan's clerk was preparing the document, another clerk convinced him to read *The Autobiography of Malcolm X* and Elijah Muhammad's *Message to the Blackman in America*. Through this reading, the clerk became convinced that Ali's willingness to fight in a holy war was irrelevant: for all practical purposes, Ali was opposed to all wars. Harlan was doubtful but agreed to read the materials. The following morning, he surprised his fellow Justices by reversing his opinion and demanding that the Court include the materials his clerk had prepared in their opinion. According to Woodward and Armstrong, "Harlan was persuaded that the government had mistakenly painted Ali as a racist, misinterpreting the doctrine of Black Muslims despite the Justice Department's own hearing examiner's findings that Ali was sincerely opposed to all wars."[35] With Harlan's switch, the vote became 4–4, and this tie meant that Ali would still go to jail with his original conviction upheld. Chief Justice Warren Burger, Justice Hugo Black, Justice Byron White, and Justice Harry Blackmun did not want to switch their votes and worried that Harlan's view would set a precedent that all members of the Nation of Islam were eligible for conscientious objector status.

With the Court's year coming to a close, the justices had a dilemma: because written opinions did not accompany tie-vote decisions, Ali's conviction would stand but he would not know why he had lost. Justice Potter Stewart found this option untenable and suggested that the Court simply set Ali free citing a technical error by the Justice Department. The form denying Ali conscientious objector status did not include a specific reason for doing so, allowing the court to throw out the denial. Stewart's solution appealed to the other Justices because it would not set a precedent for future NOI conscientious objection claims.[36] The Supreme Court's decision came out on June 28, 1971, overturning Ali's conviction and freeing him from both military service and jail time.

Muhammad Ali and the Nation of Islam after Vietnam

By the time his case came before the Supreme Court in 1971, public distain directed toward Ali had turned to praise as Americans increasingly questioned the war, admired Ali's struggle for religious freedom, and accepted civil rights' legislation. Ali's refusal to serve in Vietnam made him a figure of scathing critique at the time, but in the long run it redeemed him as a public figure. Historian Michael Ezra has claimed that Ali's image rehabilitation was only possible because NOI abandoned him.[37] In April 1969, Ali made an appearance on *Wide World of Sports* to talk to Howard Cosell about his future. When asked if he would return to the ring, Ali said he would if the money was right. Elijah Muhammad disapproved of this stance and immediately distanced NOI from Ali. Elijah Muhammad announced that NOI would exclude Ali for one year, would refer to him as Cassius Clay, and would not respect him as a Muslim until he had endured his exile and proved his commitment to NOI. In *Muhammad Speaks*, Elijah Muhammad ran an article clarifying his punishment of Ali, saying, "Allah (God) says in His Holy Quran that you cannot serve two gods and be honest with both for you do not have two hearts... Muhammad Ali (Cassius Clay) made a complete fool of himself for accepting the sport that Allah (God) condemns."[38] Elijah Muhammad condemned Ali's choice to return to boxing as worshipping a false God: the money and fame of sport. Ali accepted this dismissal with humility and stated that his comments were foolish and that he hoped NOI would take him back. Ali continued to praise Elijah Muhammad and NOI, and by 1974, Ali was again recognized and lauded in *Muhammad Speaks*.

In 1975, the same year as the end of the Vietnam War, Elijah Muhammad died, and his son W. D. Muhammad assumed leadership of NOI. Upon taking over, he changed the name of the organization to "World Community of al-Islam in the West." The group no longer sought racial separatism and embraced Sunni Islam. Ali expressed support for these changes and remained devoted to the organization. However, NOI member Louis Farrakhan was unhappy with the evolution of the religion, so he split with the group, kept the name "Nation of Islam," and continued Elijah Muhammad's teachings on white evil and Black separatism. In 1985, W. D. Muhammad disbanded the World Community of al-Islam in the West and declared that members were simply Sunni Muslims. The overwhelming majority of Black Muslims in the United States today identify as Sunni Muslims, not as members of the Nation of Islam.

Conclusions

In 1977, as his first official action as president, Jimmy Carter issued a presidential pardon to those who had evaded the draft during the Vietnam War. Affecting more than one hundred thousand men, Carter's decision indicated a significant cultural turn away from militaristic pride and toward the acceptance of those who protested the war. By the 1990s,

Muhammad Ali had the status of an American hero. Ali's story of throwing his gold medal into the Ohio River came full circle in 1996 when he lit the Olympic torch for the games in Atlanta. The International Olympic Committee heralded Ali as a hero and gave him a replacement gold medal at a halftime ceremony during the men's basketball final between the United States and Yugoslavia. President Bill Clinton, himself a protester of the Vietnam War, invited Ali to the White House for the Millenium Dinner on December 31, 1999. The next president, George W. Bush, presented Ali with the Presidential Medal of Freedom in 2005. Bush had supported the Vietnam War and had trained with the Air National Guard in Texas during his eligible years. When Bush tied the medal around Ali's neck, he lauded him as "a fierce fighter and a man of peace."[39]

As a young man in his twenties, Muhammad Ali declared his allegiance to the Nation of Islam and rejected his government's demand that he serve in a war abroad while racism continued at home. As the most famous athlete in the world at the time, Ali brought attention to the Nation of Islam and to the exploitation of Black men in the Vietnam War. Fear and hatred of Ali's stances turned to admiration as Ali stuck by his claims and the American public grew tired of the ongoing combat in Vietnam. In 1984, three years after he retired from boxing, Muhammad Ali was diagnosed with Parkinson's disease—a degenerative disease that diminished his ability to speak and move around. The death of Elijah Muhammad and the subsequent turn to Sunni Islam deradicalized Black Muslims at the same time as Ali's battle with Parkinson's disease made him a sympathetic public figure. He became an advocate for raising awareness and research funds for treatment of the disease. In 2016, Ali died at age seventy-four after living with Parkinson's for more than thirty years. President Barack Obama released a video memorializing Ali, saying,

> We are seeing this incredible outpouring of love and testimony about the impact that he had as an athlete in the ring, as somebody who was willing to speak out on behalf of issues of social justice even at a time when they were not popular, somebody who ended up becoming an ambassador, not just on behalf of one of the world's great religions, but also somebody who sought to bridge a relationship of peace and understanding between religions, a person who for African Americans, I think, liberated their minds and recognized that they could be proud of who they were, and also that they could be pretty and tough at the same time.[40]

By the time of his death, Ali's years as a Black separatist had faded from public memory, replaced by admiration for his moral rejection of war and his contributions to Black pride.

Resources for Further Study

Media

Ken Burns, Sarah Burns, and Dave McMahon, dirs. *Muhammad Ali, Round Two: What's My Name? (1964–1970)*. PBS, 2021.

Online Archives

Issues of *Muhammad Speaks* are available through JSTOR at https://www.jstor.org/site/reveal-digital/independent-voices/muhammadspeaks-28144384/.
Declassified FBI files are available at https://vault.fbi.gov/.
Suggested search terms: Muhammad Ali, Elijah Muhammad, Nation of Islam

Reading

Howard Bingham and Max Wallace, *Muhammad Ali's Greatest Fight: Cassius Clay vs. the United States of America* (New York: M. Evans and Company, 2000).
Maureen Smith, "*Muhammad Speaks* and Muhammad Ali: Intersections of the Nation of Islam and Sport in the 1960s," in *With God on Their Side: Sport in the Service of Religion*, ed. Tara Magdalinski and Timothy J. L. Chandler (New York: Routledge, 2002), 177–96.
David Wiggins, "Victory for Allah: Muhammad Ali, the Nation of Islam, and American Society," in *Muhammad Ali, The People's Champ*, ed. Elliot J. Gorn (Champaign: University of Illinois Press, 1998), 88–116.

Chapter 6

Asian Martial Arts

In the opening to their history of the Black Karate Federation (BKF), karate grandmasters Steve Muhammad (previously Steve Sanders), a member of the Nation of Islam, and Donnie Williams, a Christian bishop, write, "Foremost and above all, we thank the Divine Creator for allowing us to be of service to humanity through the study and teaching of the martial arts."[1] How did unarmed combat techniques developed half a world away become the basis for a Black empowerment karate organization in the United States? The story of how Asian martial arts came to be commonplace and adopted by non-Asians in the United States starts with judo, a Japanese form of self-defense developed in the late nineteenth century with the explicit aim of using physical practice to cultivate moral and spiritual maturity.

To follow this story to the BKF, we need to investigate early American adoptees of Asian martial arts such as President Theodore Roosevelt and other proponents of the strenuous life, consider how the internment of Japanese Americans during World War II impacted the practice and spread of Japanese martial arts, factor in the American occupation of Japan postwar and the U.S. military's use of martial arts training for their troops, and finally turn to the kung fu movie craze of the 1970s invigorated by martial arts superstar Bruce Lee. In following this winding trajectory, we can arrive at a historical moment when Black Americans adopted karate as their own and taught each other the physical, mental, and spiritual benefits of martial arts.

I have chosen to use Western naming conventions in this chapter, and all names are presented with given name first and family name second. In this chapter, you will encounter multiple names and spellings of martial arts. Spellings of martial arts differed in early American writings on the topic because the names are transliterated from Asian character alphabets. *Jujutsu* is a generic umbrella term for numerous systems of combat. *Judo* is a particular form of jujutsu developed by Jigoro Kano and taught at his school, the Kodokan, in Japan beginning in 1882. *Karate* is a martial art developed in Okinawa that moved to Japan in the early twentieth century. *Taekwondo* is a Korean martial art predominantly developed by Koreans who studied judo and karate in Japan. *Gongfu*, or *kung fu*, is a blanket term for Chinese martial arts. What all of these have in common is an emphasis on unarmed defense techniques, a hierarchical training structure, and incorporation of Confucian and Buddhist teachings.

Confucianism is the name that European scholars gave to the Chinese *Rujia* or "School of the Scholars." Confucianism is an ethical system developed by Confucius (from Kung-fu-tzu or "Master Kung": 551–479 BCE). Confucius was born into a chaotic time in Chinese history and developed educational materials that he hoped would instill order, mutual flourishing, and self-development. Some key values of Confucianism that had a lasting impact on Chinese, Korean, Japanese, and Vietnamese cultures are reverence for antiquity, respect for education, and filial piety (deference to elders and ancestors). Central to Confucian understandings of the world are correctly inhabiting one's relationships through care and loyalty. Scholar of world religions Stephen Prothero calls Confucianism the "Way of Propriety," meaning that the core of Confucian understanding of human flourishing is correct relationships, etiquette, and ethics.[2]

If Confucianism is the way of propriety, Prothero describes Buddhism as the "Way of Awakening."[3] Like Confucianism, the central figure of Buddhism is a human being: Siddhartha Gautama (563–483 BCE), a Himalayan prince who grew up protected from every suffering and then abandoned his wealthy, comfortable life to wander and seek a solution to human suffering. The story goes that after six years of wandering, Siddhartha Gautama sat under a tree for forty-nine days contemplating human existence. A sense of awakening came upon him as he began to see that all things are impermanent and that human suffering stems from our desire for unchangingness in a constantly changing world. From this moment onward, he was known as the Buddha or "Awakened One."

Like Confucianism, Buddhism offered humans a means of solving human problems without divine intervention. Whereas Confucianism focused on proper behavior and relationships, Buddhism focused on self-cultivation to tune into the world as it is: constantly changing and therefore empty of any graspable or stable meaning. The story of the Buddha's rejection of his family and his journey of awakening spread from its origins in India to China, Japan, Sri Lanka, Myanmar, the southeast Asian islands, and Tibet (and eventually the world over). Over time, different regions developed variations of Buddhism, but all hold the core teaching that humans suffer because we mistake things that are changing as unchanging, because we want things to be other than they are. The solution to this suffering is to embrace the emptiness of all things. As opposed to clinging to unreality, the experience of emptiness is freedom and an opportunity for bliss in the here and now. Understanding the spiritual philosophies of Confucianism and Buddhism can help us understand the ethical background of martial arts development and training principles. Turning now to the development of martial arts in Japan, we gain historical context for the creation of judo, the martial arts system that became most popular outside Asia.

The Development of Martial Arts in Japan

During the Edo era (1603–1868), when the shoguns of the Tokugawa family ruled Japan, the philosophy of martial arts training shifted from purely combat skills to pursuit of personal development. According to martial arts historian Udo Meonig, the idea of a purely weaponless martial art could only develop in a relatively peaceful society that emphasized personal self-defense over armed combat.[4] During this time, the samurai practiced various traditions of Japanese martial arts sometimes called *bujutsu* (martial technique) or *bugei* (martial art).

Under the Meiji government (1868–1912), Japan initiated a shift toward rapid modernization and Westernization. Japanese aristocratic samurai lost privileges that they had held in the Edo period and began to earn a living by opening their *ryu* ("school" or "style") to the public. The samurai found themselves politically powerless, but at the same time, Japanese culture romanticized and idolized samurai values, traditions, and history. For example, Nitobe Inazō's publication, *Bushido: The Soul of Japan* (1900), was one of the first works to idolize the warrior code. He writes in praise of the samurai,

> A truly brave man is ever serene; he is never taken by surprise; nothing ruffles the equanimity of his spirit. In the heat of battle he remains cool; in the midst of catastrophes he keeps level his mind. Earthquakes do not shake him, he laughs at storms. We admire him as truly great, who, in the menacing presence of danger or death, retains his self-possession.[5]

Inazō credits the religions of Buddhism and Confucianism with instilling the values of serenity, loyalty, and bravery in the samurai. Admiration of the samurai led to an increase in martial arts training across the population. Meonig argues that elements of Japanese martial arts training such as repetition of specific arranged forms (*kata*) and respect for hierarchical authority structures reflect Confucian traditions and rituals.[6]

Amid Japan's cultural shifts, twenty-two-year-old Jigoro Kano opened a training hall in downtown Tokyo in 1882 that he called the Kodokan. Kano emphasized scientific principles, efficiency, and modernism. From the start, Kano hoped to combine physical mastery with ethical cultivation. Kano had noticed that the Japanese aristocracy had come to see jujutsu and bujutsu as barbaric, so he rebranded his style of physical training *judo*, "way of gentleness" or "giving way."[7] He decided to use the suffix *-do*, which means way or principle, rather than *-jutsu*, which means practical application and refers mainly to the physical actions of combat. Kano wrote in 1917: "If the intention is to practice Judo solely as an athletic exercise without comprehending its spirit, such training will accordingly be left wanting in the important aspects of self-improvement. All Judo practitioners must give heed to training both the body and the mind."[8] Kano's philosophy of judo was that it was, first and foremost, a tool for self-improvement with the ultimate goal of benefiting society and humankind. For him, the spiritual *do* included intellectual and moral education for daily life.

The 1922 Kodokan Cultural Association charter listed three statements of purpose. The first statement was "Maximum efficiency in energy usage is key." This statement reflects a central claim of judo—a smaller person can defeat a larger person in combat—and reflects Kano's concern with modernism and efficiency. The second and third statements of purpose were, "Self-perfection is achieved through helping others achieve perfection" and "Mutual self-perfection is the basis for the co-prosperity of humanity."[9] The Kodokan's statements treat judo as more than a sport or a mode of combat: judo is a vehicle for ethical cultivation and human flourishing. The Confucian value of right relationships and the Buddhist value of flourishing through acceptance form the backdrop for Kano's statements of purpose.

Karate arrived in Japan from Okinawa in the early twentieth century. Okinawan karate was a practical art for self-defense consisting of physical conditioning and kata training. Karate's philosophy of "one blow equals certain death" meant that sparring was too dangerous, so kata emerged as a necessary substitute.[10] To gain acceptance in Japan, Okinawan karate masters added philosophical concepts to the martial art and developed a formal, hierarchical structure of authority. Confucian values such as respect for one's elders and teachers became central to karate. One of the Okinawan karate masters to rise to prominence in Japan was Gichin Funakoshi. For Funakoshi, karate was "spiritual training… fostering the traits of courage, courtesy, integrity, humility, and self-control."[11] Funakoshi befriended Kano, and the two shared the conviction that martial arts could train students for the betterment of humankind.

Judo was a major influence on taekwondo, the national martial arts practice of Korea. Japan was the colonial ruler of Korea from 1910 to 1945. By 1940, about one million Korean immigrants lived in Japan, and this number grew to 2.4 million over World War II. Many of taekwondo's founders had studied karate and/or judo in Japan in the 1930s. One of those founders, Choi Hong Hi, articulated the ethical value of taekwondo as "to cultivate the noble character of the person."[12] The name "taekwondo" emerged from a compromise between those preferring *taekyon-do* (referring to a traditional Korean kicking game) and those who preferred *tangsoodo* or *kongsoodo*, names of schools affiliated with individual martial arts masters. The government of the Republic of Korea liked that the name taekwondo was similar to the kicking game *taekyon*, but there is little evidence that *taekyon* influenced the martial art of taekwondo. The new name took off; the Korean Taesoodo Association changed its name to the Korean Taekwondo Association in 1965, and in 1971, Korean President Park Chung-hi declared taekwondo to be Korea's national sport. That same year, the government issued a requirement that all taekwondo schools fall under the purview of the Korean Ministry of Education. This forced taekwondo schools to give up Japanese names and traditions to receive a government permit.[13]

Judo, karate, and taekwondo spread in popularity across Japan, China, and Korea during the late nineteenth and early twentieth centuries, meshing the modern value of efficiency with the Confucian value of hierarchy and the Buddhist value of self-cultivation. At the same time in the United States, the Protestant movement of muscular Christianity was also attempting to combine physical, mental, and spiritual development, and this parallel ideology led to U.S. interest in the martial arts of Asia.

Jigoro Kano traveled to Europe in 1889 and, through garnering fame by defeating a Russian officer in a wrestling match on his steamship voyage, Kano envisioned that judo

Image 6.1 Yamashita Yoshitsugu (left) trains American businessman Samuel Hill on judo techniques at a training session in 1904. Westerners began to visit Jigori Kano's judo school in Tokyo in the late 1880s and 1890s, and Kano sent his prized students abroad as emissaries to promote his new martial art. *Courtesy of Yoshiaki Yamashita Photograph Album, Special Collections and University Archives, University of Massachusetts Amherst Libraries.*

may have international appeal. Kano had several prize students at the Kodokan who he imagined would make good emissaries for judo. Top of these was Yamashita Yoshitsugu. In 1903, when American businessman Samuel Hill requested that Kano send him a judo teacher to toughen up his son, Yoshitsugu traveled to the United States to take the job.

Yoshitsugu was an excellent instructor and spent 1903–1904 teaching judo to Washington, D.C., elites and their sons, including President Theodore Roosevelt, who Yoshitsugu taught in a special training room in the White House. Roosevelt and other early-twentieth-century high-status Americans were interested in Asian martial arts as mixtures of elegance, efficiency, scientific knowledge, and physical skill. Roosevelt wrote in a letter to his son Kermit on February 24, 1905,

> With a little practice in the art I am sure that one of our big wrestlers or boxers, simply because of his greatly superior strength, would be able to kill any of those Japanese,

who though very good men for their inches and pounds are altogether too small to hold their own against big, powerful, quick men who are well trained.[14]

Roosevelt's believed in the superiority of brawn and that Americans could employ the skills of judo to demonstrate their own might.

In 1932, as part of the Summer Olympic Games held in California and western Canada, Kano toured the West Coast delivering lectures on judo. He consistently described judo as training in "maximum efficiency and mutual welfare and benefit."[15] Whereas jujutsu focused on training for combat, Kano presented judo as an ethically principled endeavor. Despite Kano's insistence on the ethical foundation of judo and its primary aims of self-cultivation and community benefit, most non-Asians in the United States who learned judo and jujutsu thought of the practices as a means for physical health, winning wrestling matches, and self-defense. World War II contributed to suspicion toward Japanese Americans from the larger population, and the U.S. government's decision to imprison the Japanese American population of the West Coast concentrated judo instructors in camps for several years. Even as Asian martial arts declined in popularity across the United States, in the camps judo flourished.

Japanese Internment during World War II

In Japan, the Meiji restoration was successful in making the small nation economically and socially on par with Europe and America. In the 1930s, Japan sought to become an empire, not just a nation, and began to militarily impose on China, an ally of the United States at the time. On July 7, 1937, a conflict between the Japanese and Chinese over the Marco Polo Bridge near Beijing launched the countries into full-scale war. As Americans attempted to flee Nanjing, the Japanese bombed an American Navy gunboat and three Standard Oil tankers, leading to the deaths of three Americans. Japan officially apologized for the incident, claiming that they did not see the American flags on the boats, and the United States and Japan reached an uneasy peace. However, Americans began to see Japanese people and practices as suspicious. Shortly thereafter, Japan declared its ambition to rule over all Asian people and to drive Western powers out of Asia. On September 27, 1940, Japan signed the Tripartite Pact with Germany and Italy, intertwining the military conflicts of World War II.

On December 7, 1941, the Japanese attack on Pearl Harbor brought the United States into the war. And on February 19, 1942, President Franklin Roosevelt signed Executive Order 9066, establishing the mass incarceration of Japanese Americans in internment camps. Since the late 1930s, the FBI had been creating a list of potentially dangerous Japanese Americans that included judo teachers because of their strong ties to Japan. The vast majority of Japanese Americans were Buddhist and, according to historian Duncan Ryūken Williams, "Religious difference acted as a multiplier of suspiciousness, making it even more difficult for Japanese Americans to be perceived as anything other than perpetually foreign and potentially dangerous."[16] As the United States entered World War II, the government deprived many Japanese Americans of their rights, property, and freedoms.

The War Relocation Authority (WRA) forcibly removed approximately 120,000 Japanese Americans from their homes and interned them in ten camps located across Utah, Arizona, Colorado, Wyoming, Arkansas, California, and Idaho. The Justice Department ran a second parallel internment, holding 5,264 Japanese American community leaders. The interned population included *Issei*, first-generation Japanese immigrants who had arrived between 1890 and 1924 that U.S. law prevented from becoming citizens; *Nisei*, second-generation Japanese Americans who were citizens by birth; and *Sansei*, third-generation Japanese Americans, most of whom were small children at the time. In the camps, many Buddhist religious leaders saw incarceration as an opportunity to put Buddhist teachings into practice, emulating the Buddha by giving up a comfortable life and journeying through hardships.[17]

One such prison camp was the Manzanar War Relocation Center, in operation from March 25, 1942, to November 21, 1945. At its peak, Manzanar housed 10,121 Japanese Americans, divided nearly equally between male and female and about 25 percent school-age children. Most of the interned were from the city of Los Angeles, a major center of social life and commerce for Japanese Americans before the war. In the camp, incarcerated families lived in twenty- by twenty-five-foot apartments and had access to communal mess halls, laundry facilities, and latrines. Manzanar also included a hospital, schools, worship sites, recreation facilities, and stores. Barbed wire surrounded the camp, along with eight sentry towers manned by armed military. In the camps, sports competitions of baseball, basketball, and volleyball served to combat boredom and establish a sense of normalcy. Judo, kendo, and sumo training also became commonplace in many camps as practitioners found each other and made space for training and competitions. Judo in the camps provided cultural connection and affirmation. Structurally, the camps brought together judo practitioners from different geographical origins, forming a network of U.S. judo instructors and practitioners.

Early in 1943, the WRA launched an "all-out" relocation strategy, pressing camp internees to move to the country's interior and requiring all Issei and Nisei to fill out an "application for leave clearance" that included questions to determine whether the internee was sufficiently loyal to the United States to be trusted outside the camps. This became known as "registration." Registration coincided with the U.S. military considering allowing Nisei to serve in the military. General John L. DeWitt, the leader of Western Defense Command (WDC), did not like the idea of reopening the Armed Forces to Japanese American recruits. According to World War II historian Eric Muller,

> [DeWitt] had ordered the mass exclusion of Japanese Americans from the coast in the spring of 1942 on the basis that it was impossible to determine the loyalty of Japanese Americans. On the strength of this conviction of General DeWitt's, the War Department

had uprooted everyone, and the government had spent many millions of dollars building and running assembly and relocation centers.[18]

For DeWitt, the entire premise of the camps was that Japanese Americans were inscrutable; therefore, Japanese loyalty was inherently uncertain, requiring their internment for the safety of the country. If a survey could determine loyalty, this undermined his entire operation.

DeWitt railed against the questionnaire approach, telling the army's provost martial general, Allen Gullion, "I don't see how they can determine the loyalty of a Jap by interrogation… or investigation. There isn't such a thing as a loyal Japanese and it is just impossible to determine their loyalty by investigation—it just can't be done."[19] Despite DeWitt's reservations, the Army announced on January 20, 1943, that it would open opportunities for military service to Nisei volunteers from the camps. In their plan, Japanese Americans who volunteered for service would serve in a segregated Nisei battalion rather than positions throughout the armed services. By any measure, the project was a disaster. The military had been hoping for 3,500 Nisei volunteers for military service; it got 805.

Image 6.2 Judo class at the WRA Rohwer Relocation Center in McGehee, Arkansas, on November 12, 1942. Judo instructors held training sessions as often as twice a day in the internment camps. At Manzanar, about four hundred students practiced judo daily. *Courtesy of the National Archives and Records Administration.*

Following "registration," requests for repatriation and expatriation to Japan shot up. The month before registration, these requests numbered fifty-two; over the next three months, nearly one thousand persons, 3 percent of the entire population of the camps, requested to be removed to Japan.[20]

Living in the camps, Japanese Americans were shocked to learn of the atomic bombing of Hiroshima City, Japan, on August 6, 1945, that decimated four square miles, killed eighty thousand people instantly, and resulted in radiation poisoning of about eighty thousand more. Many were also shocked to hear of Japan's unconditional surrender a week later, fearing that the U.S. government would see the war victory as a reason to deport Japanese-born internees. Japan's formal surrender came on September 2, 1945, and many internees predicted that the camps would close within two weeks. However, the largest camps remained occupied for the next several months to accommodate relocation of Japanese Americans. Although Japanese Americans experienced harassment and discrimination in their post-camp lives, legal discrimination declined, and in 1952 the Supreme Court overturned the Alien Land Law, allowing Japanese-born Americans to seek citizenship through naturalization.[21]

When the U.S. government forced Japanese Americans to leave their homes for incarceration, many stored their belongings at their Buddhist temples. During internment, ransacking and looting of these temples destroyed what little Japanese Americans had to restart their lives. For example, the largest Zen temple in the United States at the time, the Zenshūji Sōtō Mission in Los Angeles, was repeatedly broken into by gangs of boys despite attempts to protect the space by a real estate broker paid by the temple. During the three years that the temple was vacant, repeated theft and destruction destroyed at least 65 percent of the property within.

In addition to theft and wanton destruction, some Japanese Americans returned to their temples to find them occupied. At the same that Japanese American neighborhoods emptied out due to incarceration, the "great migration" was bringing many Black Americans to cities that had racial housing restrictions. Areas such as Los Angeles's Little Tokyo became enclaves for arriving African Americans. With tens of thousands of Black migrants arriving and moving into a neighborhood that previously had only housed seven thousand Japanese Americans, new arrivals set up makeshift living quarters in churches and vacant Buddhist temples. When Japanese Americans returned to Los Angeles, they sometimes had trouble regaining the rights to their temples, and some experienced drawn-out lawsuits before eventually regaining their sacred spaces.[22]

Despite these difficulties, Buddhist temples resumed activities in 1946 as religious leaders returned from the camps. Religious sites became home to a revival of Japanese cultural activities such as Japanese language education and New Year celebrations. After the war, judo's popularity also expanded with Japanese Americans settling in a range of cities. The four original yudanshakai (black belt associations) of Seattle, Hawaii, Northern California, and Southern California resumed operations, and a fifth yudanshakai opened in Chicago, showing the geographical expansion of judo after the war.

Martial Arts in the U.S. Military

The U.S. occupation of Japan at the end of World War II prioritized full demilitarization of Japan, including a total ban on martial arts. In late 1950 and early 1951, U.S. authorities began to allow judo and jujutsu as sports but not as martial combat training. At the same time, the United States was interested in learning the skills of Japanese martial arts for its own military. In 1950, the Air Force Strategic Air Command (SAC), under the leadership of Curtis Emerson LeMay, launched a major incorporation of judo into its military training. According to LeMay, judo was "a valuable tool for the command's air police and security forces" because it provided "a means of self-defense for combat flyers who might someday be forced to bail out over enemy territory."[23] Over the next few years, SAC airmen studied Kodokan judo, aikido, and karate under Japanese masters. The SAC and Kodokan established an ongoing relationship. By 1962, SAC boasted 160 black-belt judo instructors who had trained more than twenty thousand combat crew in judo.

Several SAC servicemen developed a passion for Japanese martial arts and became instrumental in rejuvenating American interest in martial arts. One of these was Ernie Cates, founder of Neko-Ryu Goshin-Jutsu and a judo champion in both Okinawan and U.S. Military competitions of the 1950s and 1960s. While on a military tour of Okinawa,

Image 6.3 Strategic Air Command soldiers train in judo at a base in California in 1962. The U.S. Armed Forces began holding judo tournaments in the 1950s, playing a major role in the development of competitive judo. *Getty Images/ullstein bild Dtl.*

Cates studied judo at Takashi Matsumoto's dojo in Kodokan style. He described the philosophy:

> Matsumoto would not allow us to, for example, do makikomi style techniques where you dropped down your opponent. He said that you had to be able to protect your opponent when he went down. He said you couldn't do that with these full body drop takedowns like makikomi. Safety was very important and respect for your opponent was very important to him. He was also the only sensei in Okinawa that would teach gaijin [foreigners].[24]

Upon returning to the United States in 1956, Cates and his friend Jim Giles opened a storefront dojo in Jacksonville, North Carolina, near where Cates was stationed at Camp Lejeune. They charged $10 a month for judo and jujutsu training.

In the Jim Crow South, Black and white marines could not mix—they had separate training centers on the base. Both Cates and Giles were white. One day, a Black marine named Ron Duncan asked for instruction at Cates's dojo. Cates tells the story: "I asked him, 'What do you want to learn?' He pulled out a switch blade knife and made a pass at me! I put him on his ass! He told me after that, 'That is what I want to learn!'"[25] Taking on a Black student had to be kept secret, so Cates's wife sewed curtains for the dojo to hide the studio from the street.

Duncan would later go on to develop "Way of the Wind" ninjutsu. The August 1969 Second International Conference of Martial Arts sponsored by *Black Belt Magazine* included a demonstration by Duncan. Hawaiian-born Japanese American CEO of *Black Belt Magazine*, Mitoshi Uyehara, confronted Duncan following his demonstration, demanding to know who had trained him in the secret art of ninjutsu. Duncan refused to answer Uyehara, preserving the secrecy of ninjutsu, even rejecting Uyehara's offer of a cover feature in *Black Belt* if he would divulge his trainer. According to historian of Black martial arts Zachary Price, "Through his performance and his refusal to give up his secrets to the most powerful martial arts authority in popular media, Duncan adhered to the 'code of secrecy' that gave ninjutsu its foundation as well as its mysticism and, to an extent, criticism and skepticism."[26] Duncan understood the figure of the ninja in Japanese mythology to be a trickster figure. He described the figure of the ninja to Price, saying, "He was a conman. He utilized illusions and he played upon the superstitions of the times to get across effectively."[27] The mythology of ninjutsu perpetuated by Duncan (stealthy infiltration of a hostile environment, attacks on enemies, and successful escape) was showcased in Hollywood films of the time, and these films would become significant in growing the popularity of martial arts among the general public in the second half of the twentieth century.

Post–World War II, a number of rapid changes affected Asian martial arts in the United States. Released from internment with little to return to, Japanese martial arts instructors moved to cities across the United States; consequently, martial arts instruction, which had been centered in the West Coast and Hawaii, diffused across the country. At the same time, U.S. servicemen opened their own judo schools and further spread the practices.

Although mainstream suspicion of Japanese Americans had lessened the popularity of Asian martial arts in the lead-up and during World War II, the popularity of martial arts rebounded in the following decades, assisted in large part by the kung fu movie industry.

Everyone Was Kung Fu Fighting

In early 1960s Seattle, a young man training others in martial arts in a local parking lot was about to make global history. Taky Kimura owned a supermarket near this parking lot in Seattle and told martial arts historian James Halpin,

> I thought I was white, until they sent me to the camps. They wouldn't even delay shipping me off one day so I could graduate from high school. They took away my identity because if I wasn't white and I wasn't free and I wasn't American, then who was I? When I got out of the camps I was a derelict, except that I don't drink. I was walking around half ashamed even to be alive. Then I hear about this Chinese kid giving *gongfu* [kung fu] lessons in a parking lot near my supermarket. And there he is, bubbling over with pride, knocking these big white guys all over the place easy as you please. And I got excited about something for the first time in fifteen years. So I started training and bit by bit I began to get back the things I thought I'd lost forever.[28]

That kid was Bruce Lee. In Hollywood in the 1960s, Lee was only able to get stunt man jobs or bit parts. Hollywood executives claimed that white audiences would not identify with an Asian hero, so they denied him star roles. In response, Lee returned to Hong Kong and made kung fu movies that were so popular globally that Hollywood begged him to return. He died in 1973 at the age of thirty-two from a swelling of the brain brought on by hypersensitivity to Equagesic, a powerful aspirin.

Lee's most famous film, *Enter the Dragon*, premiered in theaters a month after his death. The film is the most popular martial arts film to date and grossed an estimated $400 million at the box office worldwide. The opening scenes from *Enter the Dragon* show Bruce Lee winning a martial arts challenge at the Shaolin monastery, the birthplace of Chinese kung fu. Following his success, he discusses philosophy of martial arts with the monastery master. Their conversation went as follows:

> Teacher: I see your talents have gone beyond the mere physical level. Your skills are now at the point of spiritual insight. I have several questions. What is the highest technique you hope to achieve?
> Lee: To have no technique.
> Teacher: Very good. What are your thoughts when facing an opponent?
> Lee: There is no opponent.
> Teacher: And why is that?
> Lee: Because the word 'I' does not exist... A good fight should be like a small play, but played seriously. A good martial artist does not become tense, but ready. Not thinking,

yet not dreaming. Ready for whatever may come. When the opponent expands, I contract. When it contracts, I expand. And when there is an opportunity, I do not hit. [holding up fist] It hits all by itself.[29]

This dialogue references several widely held understandings of martial arts as both physical practice and spiritual avenue. We see the Buddhist idea of the emptiness of all things in Lee's responses and the Confucian priority of honoring hierarchy in Lee's deference to his teacher.

The film also brings together several strains of martial arts through its characters: Lee, from Shaolin; Roper, a white American Vietnam veteran; and Williams, a Black American Vietnam veteran who trained with the Black Karate Federation. The plot of *Enter the Dragon* follows Lee, Roper, and Williams as they travel to a private martial arts tournament, led by a former Shaolin member named Han. Han has broken bad and runs a drug trade from a private island where he also drugs and kills girls. Over the course of the film, Lee uncovers this operation and fights Han to the death, but not before Han brutally kills Williams, stringing up his bloodied body in Han's underground lair. Roper and Lee survive, and the film ends with a thumbs-up between the two as helicopters fly in to liberate the island.

In the film, Williams, with his afro and red velvet bell-bottomed suit, stands out in Hong Kong. A flashback scene shows a training session led by BKF cofounder Steve Muhammad. We see a room of mostly Black men in karate gis practicing punches. Under the BKF icon of the cobra and fist, Williams shakes hands with Steve Muhammad before departing on his journey to Hong Kong. Turning now to the BKF, we can see a number of themes at work: admiration for the ethics and philosophies of Asian martial arts, the impact of American military service on access and promotion of Asian martial arts, the cultural force of Hollywood's kung fu movie industry, and the lived reality of fighting for survival for some Black Americans.

The Black Karate Federation

In the late 1960s, dozens of Black martial artists in Los Angeles began meeting at Van Ness Park to train together. From this, a core group of leaders emerged and began calling themselves the Black Karate Federation.[30] The major karate competitions in 1960s and 1970s Southern California would frequently pit Black contestants against each other to ensure that few Black fighters made it to the final rounds of the competition. However, one tournament rule was that members of the same school could not compete against each other in the early rounds. So, one of the founders of BKF, Jerry Smith, designed a patch for BKF members to wear to establish that they were part of the same school. The patch featured a clenched yellow fist wrapped in a belt of red, black, and green forming the background for a cobra, upright and fangs bared. Smith wanted to incorporate pan-African colors and powerful symbols such as the fist and cobra. According to other founders of BKF Steve Muhammad and Donnie Williams, the decision to use a cobra stemmed from BKF's understanding of martial arts' origins in Africa and development in Asia. They write, "The royal Pharaohs of Egypt, the yoga masters of India and Black Karate Federation practitioners in America have all used the cobra as a symbol of physical, mental and spiritual excellence. This symbol, on three continents, links BKF Kenpo to the oldest martial arts traditions on Earth."[31]

Some 150 BKF students entered the Lima Lama tournament in 1971, walking in single file carrying briefcases containing their folded gis with signature patches sewn on. As Muhammad and Williams put it, "They wanted people to know they were there to take care of business."[32] In wearing this patch, Black fighters showcased connection to each other and were able to fight for fair treatment in tournaments. KC Jones, an early member of BKF told me, "BKF was a like a union, the voice of Black karate participants. You had a mass of people to defend you if you needed it in competition."[33] And like a union, BKF was able to leverage collective action, threatening to boycott tournaments with anti-Black policies such as refusing to hire Black referees.[34] Jones told me that BKF angrily protested two competitions where judges were obviously unfair to Black competitors. "After that, it wasn't a problem anymore." Once BKF came up with its signature crest and fighters began wearing it, tournament officials could no longer pit them against each other. This shifted the outcomes of the competitions from no Black fighters in the top spots to almost all Black fighters in the top spots. As Jones put it, "Sometimes we would bow out against each other, just to take turns getting first, second, and third."[35]

Image 6.4 Black Karate Federation cofounder Jerry Smith (far right) trains students at his school in Los Angeles in the early 1970s. Cecil Peoples takes a swing as (from left to right) Gino Barbary, Sam Pace, BKF cofounder Cliff Stewart, Ernest "Madman" Russell, and Gary "The Rabbit" Goodman look on. *Courtesy of Black Karate Federation.*

Primary Source

Primary sources provide firsthand accounts of the topic under consideration. They emerge from particular times and places and allow us to imagine the context and thought processes that give rise to a perspective.

Excerpts from *BKF Kenpo: History and Advanced Strategic Principles* by Steve Muhammad and Donnie Williams

Context:

- Two of the original five cofounders of BKF, Steve Muhammad and Donnie Williams, first published on martial arts in their 1983 book *Championship Kenpo*. This excerpt is from their 2002 publication and details their understanding of the roots of martial arts and their philosophy for martial arts engagement.
- Steve Muhammad converted to the Nation of Islam, and Donnie Williams became a bishop in a nondenominational Protestant church. Both attribute a spiritual dimension to their martial arts training.

Discussion Questions:

- What connections do you see between Steve Muhammad and Donnie Williams's approach to martial arts and the Confucian values of reverence for antiquity, respect for education, and deference to elders and ancestors?
- What connections do you see to the Buddhist teachings of cultivating the self to accept constant change and embrace the emptiness of all things?
- Both Steve Muhammad and Donnie Williams were Vietnam War veterans. How might U.S. military context play a role in the development of their philosophies?

Need for Survival[36]

The need for survival is a driving force for all living beings. From the earliest humans who used sticks and stones, to modern man and his strategic use of nuclear and bio-genetic warfare, there may never be an end to conflict or a quest for survival. Throughout the ages, from Africa to America, expressions of human activity that create such entities as the Black Karate Federation are products of centuries of struggle and evolution that will no doubt continue to provide a foundation for future generations to build upon.

The strategy used by grandmasters Steve Muhammad and Donnie Williams since the early days of the BKF in Los Angeles has been to focus on cultivating mental and physical discipline and to be able to use that discipline and apply it to all walks of life, particularly in the area of spiritual growth. They have realized that without a healthy spirit, one's body, one's house, one's community and one's nation cannot endure.

BKF Creeds[37]

There are three creeds or statements of belief within the BKF. Ed Parker wrote the first. It is as follows:

"I come to you with only karate, empty hands. I have no weapons, but should I be forced to defend myself, my principles, or my honor, should it be a matter of life or death, of right or wrong; then here are my weapons, karate, my empty hands."

Bruce Lee wrote the second creed. It is as follows:

"Be composed, but don't stand still.
Be mobile, but don't move.
Don't attack, strike.
Hit your opponent on his first move.
Move only to counter or attack.
Don't stand still, and yet don't move."

Donnie Williams wrote the third creed:

"Karate is my skill.
I will defend my friends and loved ones to the end.
When I present myself day or night,
They will always know I will walk, run, then fight."

In the early 1970s, BKF would jog in formation through their neighborhood in Los Angeles chanting in cadence. They would end their jog at Sportsman Park (later renamed Jesse Owens Community Regional Park) at the corner of Central and Western Avenues. According to Muhammad and Williams, "On one particular occasion, while more than 100 students and their families trained at the park, police helicopters circled overhead and squad cars converged on the park. In another for instance, there were reports of strange, unidentified people who would drive up to the school and take pictures through the windows."[38] In 1973, before Steve Sanders changed his name to Steve Muhammad, he told *Karate Illustrated* (now *Black Belt Magazine*) that announcers at karate competitions would often mistakenly affiliate him with the Black Panthers. He said, "We are not militants and we are not street fighters… I have nothing against the Panthers. They do their thing and I do mine. But I am not a Panther! I am Steve Sanders, a black karateka."[39] KC Jones told me that the BKF Crenshaw school was under FBI surveillance and had been infiltrated a number of times since it opened in 1971. I asked how they would know if someone was a spy. "You get pretty good at knowing 5–0 when you see them. We let them stay. Hey, we'll beat you up just like everybody else."[40] Williams and Muhammad believed that the FBI wiretapped their phones and surveilled BFK students with frequent police stops and questioning.[41]

Today, BKF is incorporated as a nonprofit and focuses on community outreach rather than training for competitions. The brick-and-mortar BKF schools closed during the COVID-19 pandemic and had not reopened as of 2025. According to Jones, BKF teachers are teaching out of parks, YMCAs, and converted garages, "like the early days."[42] Cultural historian Zachary Price analyzed African American martial arts teachers and communities, coming to this conclusion: "By crossbordering and grounding in the cultural template of an Asian cultural property, Black people attempted to refine the kinetics of what were non-Western and non-Eurocentric based artforms for their own purposes to address the dismemberment of their bodies and the political and economic conditions under which they lived in the US."[43] Price's analysis emphasizes that the martial arts traditions that caught on in the United States developed in Asia, not in Europe or the United States. These martial arts traditions provided an alternative to sports invented by white people, which may have increased their appeal for Black populations.

Conclusions

Most international multisport competitions are dominated by sports invented in Europe and the Americas. Perhaps this is why, from its founding in the 1880s, leaders of judo sought to present the sport as globally viable, paving the way for karate, taekwondo, and kung fu to achieve some international presence in sporting competitions. The Paris 2024 Summer Olympics included 329 medal events. Of these, fifteen were judo events and eight were taekwondo, comprising 7 percent of all medal competitions. Although previously included in the summer Olympics, karate and wushu (kung fu) did not have medal events in the Paris Games. These four are the only sports included in the Olympics that originated in Asia.

The success of judo as an international sport is deeply tied to the context of its invention in Japan, early adoption of judo by late-nineteenth-century American elites, the diffusion of Japanese Americans across the country following Japanese internment during World War II, American military fascination with judo during and after American occupation of Japan, Hollywood investment in martial arts movies, and the subsequent adoption of a range of Asian martial arts styles in the United States beyond Asian American communities. Judo and other Asian martial arts successfully took hold in the United States because they appeared as paths for moral development, not purely combat or self-defense. The Confucian emphasis on hierarchical relationships and correct behavior combined with the Buddhist emphasis on self-cultivation through presence and acceptance undergird martial arts philosophies around the globe. These ethical components remain integral to many martial arts practices and are one example of the integration of Asian religious perspectives in American physical culture.

Resources for Further Study

Media

Terry Bullman, creator. *Human Weapon.* Season 1, episode 5, "Judo: Samurai Legacy." Aired August 17, 2007, on the History Channel.

Jimmy Smith and Doug Anderson, hosts. *Fight Quest.* Season 1, episode 10, "USA: Kajukenbo." Aired February 29, 2008, on the Discovery Channel.

Online Archive

The National Park Service provides an archive of oral histories, photographs, and documents from the Manzanar War Relocation Center. "Manzanar Virtual Museum Exhibit," https://www.nps.gov/museum/exhibits/manz/index.html.

The Densho Archives contain primary sources that document the Japanese American experience from immigration in the early 1900s through World War II incarceration and redress in the 1980s. "Denshō," https://densho.org.

Reading

Paul Bowman, *The Invention of Martial Arts: Popular Culture between Asia and America* (New York: Oxford University Press, 2021).

Zachary F. Price, *Black Dragon: Afro Asian Performance and the Martial Arts Imagination* (Columbus: Ohio State University Press, 2022).

Duncan Ryūken Williams, *American Sutra: A Story of Faith and Freedom in the Second World War* (Cambridge, MA: Belknap Press of Harvard University, 2019).

Chapter 7

Muslim Athletes

At 6 a.m. on September 11, 2001, Hamza Abdullah received a phone call from his roommate telling him to turn on the television. He was eighteen years old and playing college football at Washington State University. He left his room and joined his other roommates, all members of the football team, watching the live news coverage of the twin towers of the World Trade Center in New York City billowing smoke. He remembers sitting on the couch, unable to do anything except watch the television coverage for the next two hours. "I was thinking, what does this mean? Are we going to war? My older brother was in the Navy. Was he going to go to war? Would there be a draft?"[1] With these questions on his mind, Hamza and his roommates left the house for their 9 a.m. class. The classroom mood was somber, and the professor sent the students home, telling them to call their families. Hamza headed to a friend's dorm to continue watching the television coverage with friends.

That afternoon, Hamza had football practice at 2 p.m. When he arrived, his coach was at a loss. The coach predicted that the weekend's game against University of Colorado would be canceled. He asked the team, do you want to practice today? Hamza did not want to practice, but as a younger player, he followed the inclinations of the senior players, who did want to practice. "I remember going through the motions, but I was anxious to get back to the TV and to hear from my brother." Hamza's brother was twenty years old, and Hamza did hear from him later that day, learning that the Navy was sending him to a secure location. Most of his attention that day was consumed with thinking about what might happen to his brother.

In the days and weeks that followed, as it became clear that the perpetrators were Muslim, Hamza's teammates started asking him questions, wondering what he believed and wondering about general practices in Islam such as daily prayer and fasting. "I was the only Muslim on the team, the only Muslim they knew. As a young kid, I was taught to spread peace. Now, I was being asked to speak for Muslims around the world. I was not up to that task." This gave Hamza a desire to learn more about Islam. The future NFL player began a journey of self-education that would last through his professional football career and beyond. (A note on names: There are two athletes with the last name Abdullah in this chapter. They are not related. For clarity, I refer to them by their full name when introduced, and by their first names thereafter.)

Image 7.1 Hijacked United Airlines Flight 175 from Boston crashes into the south tower of the World Trade Center in New York City and explodes at 9:03 a.m. on September 11, 2001. In a meticulously planned attack, terrorists loyal to al Qaeda leader Osama bin Laden hijacked four airliners. They flew three of the planes into buildings: the twin towers of the World Trade Center and the Pentagon in Arlington, Virginia. A fourth plane crashed in rural Pennsylvania. The attacks killed 2,976 people and injured thousands more. *Getty Images/Spencer Platt.*

Many American Muslims who lived through the 9/11 attacks found themselves involuntary ambassadors for Islam. According to religious studies scholar Steven Fink, "Wanting to disabuse neighbors and co-workers of misunderstandings about Islam, these Muslims who had previously placed Islam on the margins of their lives recognized a need to educate themselves about their own religion before they could educate others."[2] Although many Muslims in the United States thought of their religion as cultural heritage, the challenges of explaining Islam after 9/11 led many American Muslims to conclude that they needed to demonstrate to those around them that the Muslims who attacked the United States were not accurate representatives of their religion, and therefore they chose to demonstrate their religious identity more publicly. This took a number of forms: for some, it meant attending prayer services at mosques, fasting for Ramadan, and engaging in conversations with others about religion; for women in particular, it often meant donning the hijab, a traditional headscarf worn in many Muslim communities.

This chapter addresses challenges that Muslim American athletes face. In the decades following 9/11, American Muslims have faced Islamophobia, racism, and general ignorance about their religion. As visible members of a minority tradition, Muslim athletes in the United States have encountered systemic barriers to their full participation in sports, including clothing restrictions and fasting during Ramadan. As the number of Muslim athletes in the United States has increased, some sports' policies have changed to better include and assist Muslim athletes.

Before we turn to the experiences of Muslim athletes, it may be helpful to briefly address the history and practices of Islam as well as the demographics of Muslims in the United States. Islam is a monotheistic religion that emerged in the Arabian Peninsula twelve hundred years ago. In the early seventh century, the Arabian Peninsula was a desert land inhabited by competing clans and tribes. The man who would become the prophet of Islam, Muhammad, was born around 570 CE and began to receive revelations when he was approximately thirty years old. A misconception that Westerners sometimes have about Islam is that Muhammad is like Jesus—the holy founder of a religion. Although Muhammad is central to Islam, Muslims do not see Muhammad as divine the same way Christians see Jesus. The central miracle of Christianity is the resurrection of Jesus after death; the central miracle of Islam is the Qur'an, words that Muhammad received from God.

By the seventh century, Arabs had developed finely honed skills in linguistic scrutiny, and they considered poetry to be the highest form of art. People believed that Muhammad's revelations were from God because of their extraordinary linguistic beauty.[3] This is one reason why the Arabic language is important to Muslims regardless of their native tongue: Muhammad received God's messages in the language of Arabic, and speaking these words aloud is a religious practice called recitation. Like Christians honor the central miracle of their tradition by practicing communion, ingesting bread and wine to commemorate Jesus's last supper before his death, Muslims honor the central miracle of their tradition by reciting the words that Muhammad received from God, preserved in the Qur'an. In Christianity, the Bible is the record of a miracle; in Islam, the Qur'an is the miracle itself.

Islam means "submission," and to be a Muslim is to be "one who submits" to God. "Allah" is the Arabic word for God and refers to the God of the Hebrew Bible and Christian New Testament. Most Muslims today observe five central tenets of Islam, often called the "five pillars of Islam." The first and central pillar is adherence to the Shahadah, a statement of faith that affirms monotheism and the importance of Muhammad's revelations: "There is no God but God, and Muhammad is the messenger of God." The remaining four pillars are *salat* (daily prayer), *zakat* (charitable giving), *sawn* (fasting during the month of Ramadan), and *hajj* (pilgrimage to the holy city of Mecca in Saudi Arabia). In addition to the Qur'an as a source of religious knowledge, Muslims also turn to *hadith*, the record of Muhammad's life, for lessons on how to be a good Muslim.

Islam has two major branches: Sunni and Shia. These groups are inheritors of a schism regarding religious authority that emerged soon after Muhammad's death. Muslims disagreed on whether religious authority was limited to Muhammad's bloodline (Shia) or could be held by Muslims not descended from Muhammad (Sunni). The global population of Muslims in the 2020s is more than two billion, and more than 85 percent of the world's Muslims are Sunni.

In the United States, Muslims make up about 1 percent of the total population, around three million people. With the passage of the Immigration and Naturalization Act of 1965, Congress overturned the previous quota system, opening doors for increasing Muslim immigration by allowing greater immigration from majority Muslim countries. The new legislation stressed two criteria: family reunification and occupational preference. The first criteria preserved the ethno-racial makeup of the United States; the second was meant to strengthen the U.S. labor force. Over the first two decades following the change in immigration law, most Muslims arrived under the occupational preference category and tended to be highly educated. From the mid-1980s to the present, most immigrant Muslims have immigrated via family reunification, though occupational preference is still an avenue for some. From 1965 to 1995, one million Muslims immigrated to the United States. Immigrant Muslims and their descendants comprise about 80 percent of the American Muslim population.

Approximately 20 percent of American Muslims are African American. About half of these grew up in the Nation of Islam, which became Sunni Islam, and about half converted to Islam during their lifetime. A Pew Research Center survey from 2019 noted that only 2 percent of African American Muslims still identified as Nation of Islam. The majority identified as Sunni Muslim or as no particular Islamic denomination.[4] Black Muslims, immigrant Muslims, and their descendants are more likely to live in cities than in rural areas. Many mosques in the United States cater to either Black Muslims or immigrant Muslim communities, though a small number do integrate these populations. Both these populations experienced challenges for sporting participation. By turning to sports' rules that restrict women's clothing and head covering choices, we will see ways that Muslim women who choose to cover their hair and bodies have encountered resistance to their participation in sports.

Veiling and Modest Clothing

For many women who practice Islam, covering one's hair and body is a method of following the Qur'anic exhortation that women (and men) maintain barriers of sexual purity and demonstrate piety through demure comportment and shielding of the body. Veiling is not compulsory in Islam, and many Muslim women do not wear head coverings. The practice of head covering is also not unique to Islam and predates the religion by hundreds of years. Within multiple religious traditions, women have covered their heads to hide their hair as a way of desexualizing themselves—consider Catholic nuns' habits, Orthodox

Jewish women's *tichel*, Hindu *pallu* in religious spaces, and Buddhist head shaving. In the first decades of Islam, the term *hijab* denoted partition or screen as in a physical barrier between the prophet Muhammad's wives and visitors. At the time in the Arabian Peninsula, veiling was a fashion trend that signaled high status. Historian Leila Ahmed has shown that Muhammad's wives wore head coverings not to adhere to the Qur'anic call for partition but as a social symbol of high fashion and status.[5]

Since the 1970s, Muslim women's head covering has increased in popularity around the globe. Ahmed has argued that this trend is due to a postcolonial rejection of European claims of superiority; majority Muslim countries demonstrated a conspicuous difference from European cultural norms by showcasing women's modest dress.[6] Some governments and societies began to require women to dress this way, but in other places, covering was optional. In both settings, the practice of veiling increased dramatically. The hijab, a headscarf that covers the head and neck and leaves the face visible, is the most common form of veiling. Other forms of Islamic women's covering range from the *shayla*, a loose-fitting headscarf that covers the hair and leaves the neck visible, to the *niqab*, a full-body garment that covers the face and leaves the eyes visible, to the *burqa*, a full-body garment that covers the face with a screen over the eyes that allows visibility for the wearer. Most women who wear hijab also wear modest clothing, loose-fitting garments that cover their bodies from wrists to ankles, though modesty standards and preferences vary.

Although many first-generation Muslim immigrants who arrived in the decades after the 1965 change in immigration law did not veil, the practice gained popularity among second- and third-generation immigrants. The Nation of Islam encouraged female adherents to wear modest clothing and head coverings for religious gatherings and in their daily life. With the transition to Sunni Islam in the 1970s and 1980s, former Nation of Islam women adopted the hijab around the same time as second- and third-generation immigrant women. A 2018 sociological investigation of Muslims in the United States found that American Muslim women almost universally presented head covering as "an autonomous, individual, and informed choice," not as an externally imposed requirement.[7]

In the days and weeks directly following September 11, 2001, hate crimes and verbal abuse toward women in hijabs skyrocketed. In response, some non-Muslim women began organizing "headscarf days," donning headscarves in solidarity.[8] As news reports of physical and verbal attacks against women in hijabs circulated, some women discontinued the practice, fearing for their safety and the safety of their families. At the same time, a groundswell of Muslim women adopted wearing the hijab as a means of increasing the visibility of American Muslims. For these women, the hijab showcased their pride in being Muslim and provided a counterpoint to the circulating stereotypes of Islam as violent, oppressive, and un-American.[9]

Women and girls who wear the hijab and modest clothing have encountered challenges when it comes to sports participation. FIFA's disqualification of the Iranian women's soccer team from an Olympic prequalification match in 2011 for their headscarves brought international attention to the issue of headscarves and safety. According to FIFA, headscarves that covered the neck, like the Iranian team wore, were too dangerous to allow on the field due to potential for choking from tugging.[10] Over the next decade, Muslim sportswomen and clothing producers took on the dual challenge of changing institutional rules and designing modest athletic clothing and sports hijabs that would meet safety requirements.

Primary Source

Primary sources provide firsthand accounts of the topic under consideration. They emerge from particular times and places and allow us to imagine the context and thought processes that give rise to a perspective.

Excerpts from "Muslim Women's Swimwear at the University of California, Santa Cruz"[11]
Courtesy of Swimming World Magazine.

Context:

- Swim instructor at University of California, Santa Cruz Julie Kimball wrote the following article in collaboration with her swim student, Tahrier Walid Sub Laban, about the challenges the two faced in accommodating Muslim standards of modest dress for swimming lessons in 2006.

Discussion Questions:

- What, if any, accommodations should sports instructors, coaches, and institutions offer for athletes who prefer modest clothing?
- Have you had any experiences with athletic clothing that challenged your standards of modesty? If so, what did you do in that situation?
- Given the story below, how would you respond to the questions that the authors raise at the end: Is swimming with clothing a liability in the USA? Are public pools welcoming and accessible to all swimmers regardless of appearances? Are public swim classes open to all students?

Muslim Women's Swimwear at the University of California, Santa Cruz
Tahrier was dressed from head to toe in hijab, the standard Muslim dress that includes long shirt, pants and a scarf. It was the first class of spring quarter, 2006, at the Olympic-sized swim pool at the University of California, Santa Cruz. Tahrier approached me and asked to join my beginning swim class. I responded, "Of

course." She then asked if she would be permitted to wear her traditional clothing, which covers all but her face and hands and conceals her curves, in accordance with her faith while learning to swim. I was momentarily taken aback. In my training I had learned that wearing clothing in water is synonymous with danger. I offered to lend her a wetsuit that would cover her body. She responded "No." How about a rash guard with her pants? "NO." She said that these options would be inappropriate because they would show her body figure. Tahrier insisted on wearing her self-chosen outfit, comprised of a long sleeve shirt and boot-legged pants of synthetic material, a cotton T-shirt that hung to mid-thigh, and a head scarf that covered all her hair. "Ok, let's try it."

Throughout the spring quarter, I taught Tahrier along with sixteen other swim students the basic skills to accomplish the crawl and the backstroke. Tahrier diligently practiced these skills while wearing ten pounds of wet clothing and struggling to keep her hair tucked beneath her scarf. She never gave up and she never missed a class.

It was well into the quarter when Tahrier mentioned that she was still swallowing water while swimming the crawl. Her concern was that it would be a problem later in the fall quarter if she were to swim during the celebration of Ramadan when Muslims are required not to eat or drink from first prayer at sunrise to fourth prayer at sunset. Until then, I had not realized how much she was struggling. I quickly concluded that the crawl was not yet appropriate for Tahrier and we redirected toward swimming more elementary backstroke and the breaststroke. Within a few classes, Tahrier was breathing without swallowing water, keeping her clothing and hair in place, and moving steadily through the water. By the end of spring quarter, Tahrier was jumping off the three-meter high dive and swimming to the ladder with self-confidence, using a competent breaststroke technique while fully dressed.

At the beginning of fall quarter, 2006 Tahrier returned to swim class. After a couple of weeks of classes, Tahrier mentioned that she found a web site where one could purchase Muslim women's swimwear. The site, www.ahiida.co, is based in Australia. I e-mailed the company and asked if we could product test the Muslim women's swimsuit since we had never before seen such a product and couldn't be sure that it would meet Tahrier's needs. Aheda, the owner of the company, called me at home, and she agreed for Tahrier to product test the suit. It eventually arrived in the mail. Tahrier was thrilled. The suit met all the criteria for an active Muslim woman to swim and to fulfill her code of modesty. It is a beautiful, light-weight suit that offers UV protection. Also, the suit covers her with a modest fit that doesn't show body form, nor can her hair fall out from under the headscarf, which is sewn to the tunic. Tahrier feels many pounds lighter in the water, doesn't have to worry that her modest appearance is compromised, and can now swim the crawl and backstroke without struggle.

> It had taken a full year for Tahrier to muster up the courage to ask me if she could join the Physical Education swim classes at UCSC. While traveling in the USA, some hotels would not allow Tahrier and her sisters to swim while wearing their clothing in the pools. This brought up several questions: Is swimming with clothing a liability in the USA? Are public pools welcoming and accessible to all swimmers regardless of appearances? Are public swim classes open to all students?

In the early 2000s, Kulsoom Abdullah was enrolled in graduate school at the Georgia Institute of Technology in Atlanta. When she took up weight training for physical fitness, she had no idea that she would end up successfully challenging the clothing rules for Olympic weightlifting. She was originally drawn to weight training as a way to improve at taekwondo but found that she enjoyed the training. After Kulsoom had been training for a few years at a local CrossFit gym, her coaches encouraged her to sign up for a local competition. She attended a small competition held in a high-school gym. She wore the clothes that she wore to train: a cotton hijab, long-sleeved shirt, and oversized sweatpants. At smaller, local competitions, lots of competitors wore their training clothes, and Kulsoom's clothing did not raise any challenges.

When Kulsoom qualified for a national competition, she knew that everyone would be wearing a standard singlet, a tight-fitting garment that revealed knees and elbows. She told me, "No one had ever asked for religious accommodations before. I knew that my request might be denied, but I thought I would still be able to lift and just be disqualified, but they denied my request and wouldn't even allow me on the platform [to lift]." The Council on American-Islamic Relations learned about her denial to compete and asked Kulsoom if they could issue a press release. "I thought I had nothing to lose; they had already said no, that I couldn't compete." The press release came out in the summer of 2011. "After that, media outlets contacted me immediately. I was surprised. I didn't think anyone would care. I think people were fascinated by the idea of a woman in a headscarf lifting weights. I wasn't excited to be in the news, I'm not a front-of-camera person, but I pushed myself to do it because not everyone gets this platform."[12]

USA Weightlifting felt pressure from the media coverage. The board in charge of the rules had been opposed to changing the requirement for bare arms because they were afraid that compression shirts that were common in power lifting and provided an advantage would become the norm. They issued a statement that they would bring up Kulsoom's request for rule changes to the International Weightlifting Federation (IWF) at their next board meeting and they would follow the IWF rules. The next international competition and board meeting was in Malaysia, and Kulsoom did not plan to attend. She did not think that USA Weightlifting's petition would be successful on its own, so she prepared a presentation for them to give at the IWF meeting.[13] "I wanted to show them that

Image 7.2 Kulsoom Abdullah trains for an Olympic weightlifting competition in an Atlanta gym in 2011. After experiencing a denial to compete due to her long sleeves and long pants, Abdullah gave a presentation to the International Weightlifting Federation's (IWF) board on how modest clothing could be incorporated fairly; this was instrumental in IWF's policy change allowing a full-body unitard under compulsory attire. *Bob Andres/Atlanta Journal-Constitution via AP Images.*

it could be fair; they could check for compression shirts. And that it would be good for them as a business to be more inclusive, that it would increase participation and spectatorship."[14] After the meeting, IWF issued a press release that they would allow religious accommodations. Kulsoom became the first woman to wear the hijab at an international weightlifting tournament.

Although Kulsoom was able to petition and achieve a rule change in one meeting of a governing board, other athletes in other sports were not able to achieve changes so quickly. After Kelly "Khadijah" Diggs, a triathlete and Ironman competitor, won her first race in 2014 and the second-place competitor refused to share the podium with Diggs in protest, thinking that Diggs's clothing ("kit") had given her an advantage, Diggs requested rule clarifications that would enable her to compete fully covered and in a headscarf without having to request special exemptions for every race. Diggs told me that, at the time, she was swimming the water portion of the event in "a grandma swimsuit I found on Amazon and a green Dri-Fit over it," not an outfit that would give her a competitive advantage. "I wasn't even wearing a sport hijab when I started out. I was wearing a chiffon hijab, just blowing in the wind. No one cared what I was wearing until I won. That's when it became a problem." Over the next six years, Diggs repeatedly requested that USA Triathlon and Ironman provide rule clarifications on clothing. USA Triathlon eventually provided them, but as of 2025, Ironman still has not offered rule clarifications.

One particularly challenging interaction was at the 2018 national triathlon race in Miami, hosted by Miami Man. Because USA Triathlon had no clear standards for a competitor's kit, Diggs had find the race director before every race and personally have her kit approved for the events. She had done this for this race, but a referee declared that she was disqualified. Diggs politely let the referee know that her kit had been approved by the race director and that she would like to protest the referee's decision. He was rude and belligerent. Diggs remembers him saying, "I don't give a damn if you want to protest. You can wait all you want but this won't be overturned."[15] The referee was surprised when the race director walked up, said, "Hi, Khadijah," and overturned the referee's decision, reinstating Diggs in the race.

Although USA Triathlon eventually clarified its rules, Ironman does not have official rules regarding clothing on the books. For world championships, Ironman follows the World Triathlon rules, but if it is a non-world championship event, Ironman follows the rules of the host country. When I asked if Diggs if she had requested clarifications, she said,

> Oh yeah, they know me. I don't know what this resistance is to recognizing that this sport is not just for middle-aged white men. They respond to me with, we need to make sure that you don't get an advantage. And to that I say, put on this kit. Do you think racing fully covered in ninety-degree heat is an advantage?![16]

A frustration for Diggs is that Ironman seems ready to modify its rules if male athletes request it. For example, the cycling rules previously stated that a biker had to have their shoulders exposed, but after male racers complained about sunburns, Ironman changed the rules on clothing to allow sleeves to the elbow and shorts to the knee. A Canadian racer who legally changed his name to Jesse the Elf and surgically altered his ears to be pointy like a Christmas elf was able to achieve rule changes after one meeting when he requested the ability to race an Ironman wearing a Santa hat.

In multiple sports over the past decade, hijabi athletes have encountered similar challenges—resistance to rule changes that would allow for modest clothing, referees who stand in the way of individual's competing, and even having to choose between their sport and practicing their religion. Bilqis Abdul-Qaadir grew up in Massachusetts, and as a student at the University of Memphis and later Indiana State, she became the first National Collegiate Athletic Association (NCAA) Division I basketball player to compete in a hijab. Upon graduation, she hoped to play professional basketball overseas, but an International Basketball Federation (FIBA) rule prohibiting headgear, including the hijab, posed a barrier to this plan. She learned of this rule during her senior year at Indiana State in 2013. The league told Abdul-Qaadir that hijabs were prohibited to keep basketball "religiously neutral." When she countered that religious tattoos were prominent in the league, they responded that hijabs were a safety hazard for players. She told *CNN*, "I considered taking the hijab off to play. It was a dream since I was a kid, and it was my faith keeping me from reaching my dream. I was so torn."[17] Abdul-Qaadir petitioned for a rule change, hoping for a swift response. But it was not until 2017 that FIBA announced that it would allow league-approved headgear, too late for Abdul-Qaadir's professional basketball career.

In November 2016, a boxing official disqualified fifteen-year-old Amaiya Zafar from Oakdale, Minnesota, from competing in the Sugar Bert Boxing National Championships in Kissimmee, Florida, for a uniform code violation. Her long sleeves and leggings violated the uniform regulations set by the International Boxing Association (IBA) for reasons USA Boxing executive director Michael Martino called "clearly a safety issue," stating, "If someone got hurt during the event, the referee wouldn't be able to see it. We have 30,000 amateur boxers in the United States. So if you make allowances for one religious group, what if another comes in and says we have a different type of uniform we have to wear? You have to draw a line some place."[18]

Zafar was scheduled to fight Aliyah Charbonier, a fifteen-year-old from Claremont, Florida, who went on to win the match. Following her win, Charbonier found Zafar and gave her the championship belt that she had won. "It's just not right," Charbonier told the *Washington Post*. "It's not really a distraction for me what she's wearing... They didn't give her a chance to fight. We tried to tell them that it was all right, but for safety purposes they say they need to have a visual of your arms. It wasn't right."[19] In 2019, the IBA clarified its rules to allow long sleeves and tights under competition clothing as well as sport hijabs.

For most high-school and college athletic programs today, athletes who want to compete in a hijab must file paperwork for a religious exemption. Officials at individual events can refuse to let athletes compete if they do not have the proper paperwork. After a referee disqualified high-school volleyball player Najah Aqeel in Nashville, Tennessee, in 2020 for not having paperwork for her hijab, the concern over disqualification reached Karissa Niehoff, executive director for the National Federation of State High School Associations (NFSH), which sets competition rules for most U.S. high-school sports. She told *CNN* that she did not agree with the official's decision to disqualify Aqeel.[20] Five months after Aqeel's disqualification, NFHS announced new rules stating that volleyball players will no longer need prior approval to wear religious headwear during competition. The organization proposed the rule change for all high-school sports, but a different committee oversees each sport and votes separately on rule changes. In 2021, basketball, soccer, field hockey, spirit, swimming, and diving all lifted the requirement for prior approval for hijabs and modest clothing.[21]

As rule changes regarding headscarves and full-coverage clothing roll out sport by sport due to the activism of individual athletes advocating for hijabi participation, Muslim athletes also negotiate another challenge to their sporting participation: fasting for Ramadan.

Fasting for Ramadan

According to a 2017 survey, about 80 percent of American Muslims fast for Ramadan. Only about 40 percent of American Muslims pray five times a day or attend mosques weekly, making Ramadan a significant and common practice for this population.[22] During the month of Ramadan, fasting Muslims abstain from food and drink from dawn until sunset. Ramadan falls during the ninth month of the Islamic calendar, and because the Islamic calendar is lunar, the dates of Ramadan shift from year to year over the Gregorian calendar. On the Gregorian calendar, Ramadan starts about ten days earlier from year to year, and over the course of about three decades, the dates of Ramadan will migrate across the entire calendar. Most Muslims acknowledge several exemptions from the religious requirement to fast: menstruation, pregnancy, breast-feeding, illness, travel, the very young and the very old, and potential for personal harm. If one breaks the fast for travel or another temporary condition, Islamic institutions tend to recommend that the person make up the day(s) of fasting before the next Ramadan.

Because Ramadan migrates across the calendar from year to year, different sports are affected during different years. When Ramadan falls in the heat of summer, this can be a significant challenge for athletes who compete in outdoor sports. The 2012 London Summer Olympics were held during Ramadan, bringing international attention to the issue of Muslim athletes and fasting. Approximately three thousand Muslim athletes competed in London: all seventeen days of competition fell during Ramadan, and daylight lasted from 4 a.m. to 9 p.m. Although most of these competitors chose to delay their fast until after the competition, some fasted during the Olympic Games, and the Olympic Village made special arrangements to provide predawn and post-sunset meals.[23] Individual choice on whether to fast during Ramadan or delay fasting led to some teams significantly modifying their training schedules. For example, the Moroccan men's soccer team had nine players fasting and thirteen delaying their fasts. This led the coach to arrange two sets of meals and two different practice times while in London: one practice at noon for those delaying their fast and one practice at 6:30 p.m. for all players, allowing those fasting to break their fast directly afterward. The coach told the *New York Times*, "Our full team hasn't eaten a full meal together since July 20."[24]

Hamza Abdullah, whose experiences on September 11, 2001, opened this chapter, has fasted for Ramadan since he was seven years old. He played in the NFL from 2005 to 2011. In 2010, Ramadan fell during August training camp, one of the most arduous times of the year for NFL players. Hamza did not ask for special accommodations for fasting, but his teammate Michael Adams intervened on his behalf. Playing for the Arizona Cardinals at the time, the coach had a rule that no one could eat at the end-of-day team meetings. Hamza's teammate stood up and said, "Hamza gets to eat," and the coach allowed it. Hamza told me,

> I'm not sure if it would have gone the same way with self-advocacy. They might think, this guy's trying to be an individual, trying to get special treatment. I'd like to say yes, that I would have advocated for myself, but with Mike standing up for me, it went well. And he

wasn't a team captain or one of the guys making the most money, he was just standing up for the little guy.[25]

The following year, Hamza experienced a concussion during the first day of Ramadan; that was his only year in the NFL that he did not fast. He wrote in an online guide for Muslim athletes,

> I felt a bit guilty I wouldn't be able to Fast but that night I had a calming dream that put me at ease. I thanked Allah for allowing me to Fast all those years and be able to represent Muslims and educate others about Islam. I also realized, I now would be able to let others know that I wasn't a superhero. I am human and had to break my Fast just like others.[26]

Ramadan occurs earlier each year and most recently has fallen during summer and spring months, moving from August in 2010 to March in 2025. Over the past fifteen years, American media outlets have paid attention to fasting athletes, often running stories of athletes' successes while fasting and rarely covering stories such as Hamza's concussion that undermined his fast for that Ramadan. NBA legends Hakeem Olajuwon and Kareem Abdul-Jabbar observed Ramadan while playing NBA games. Both logged some of their best performances while fasting. News coverage of these fasting athletes inspired the next generation of Muslim athletes including Kyrie Irving, who told the *Denver Post* during Ramadan in April 2022, "It [Ramadan] really simplifies life. And puts it in a greater perspective." Kevin Durant expressed admiration for his teammate, saying, "Everybody who does Ramadan and is playing through it, you've gotta commend them while they're going through it. That's tough to do, especially when you have a job like this."[27]

Athletes at the college level look up to fasting professional athletes. Two Muslim athletes on the Georgetown football team, Alpha Barry (sophomore cornerback) and Mouhammed Sow (freshman defensive tackle), were fasting for Ramadan in April 2024 during their off-season training. Sow told the *Georgetown Voice*, "Tuning into the NBA, watching Kyrie Irving have his best games during Ramadan, I go to workouts [in the morning and] I just know I gotta push the best I can, for real."[28] That same Ramadan, the University Athletic Association interviewed fasting athletes, including Case Western track and field athlete Yusuf Shabaan, who told them that he had watched Kyrie Irving hit the game-winning shot against the Denver Nuggets earlier that month, "I felt that. I know what can happen when you keep the focus." Shabaan also noted the inspiration he took from Men's World Cup Soccer athletes fasting when the World Cup overlapped with Ramadan in 2018. "I would see them on the world's biggest stage, still competing and winning. Even though I was only playing club sports, it demonstrated to me the power and mental strength an athlete can possess when they focus on their goal rather than on what they are, or are not, eating or drinking."[29] Press coverage of athletes who deliver stellar performances during Ramadan has increased national awareness of Ramadan, leading to some changes in institutional policies to accommodate fasting athletes.

Image 7.3 Kyrie Irving celebrates with his team after scoring the game-winning basket on March 17, 2024, while Irving was fasting for Ramadan. Irving hit the game-winning shot at the buzzer to give the Dallas Mavericks a 107–105 win over the defending NBA champion Denver Nuggets. *Getty Images/Glenn James.*

Over the past decade, as more and more college athletic departments hired sport dietitians similar to those who work with professional teams, fasting for Ramadan has fallen under the management of these professionals. They recommend what and when to eat as well as how to adapt training schedules while fasting. For example, the University of Texas athletic department supported its track athlete, Yusuf Bizimana, by coordinating with his coach and sports dietitian to move his workouts to early morning and develop a dietary plan to allow him to fast from sunup to sundown during Ramadan in April 2022. On working with Texas assistant sports dietitian Samantha Fuhrmann, Bizimana said, "Everything she's done for me is great. She's taking care of my diet. She tells me what time to eat, what to drink, what to put in my body."[30] Similar dietary and scheduling assistance has been in place at the University of Connecticut for fasting men's basketball players and at Northwestern University for fasting tennis and soccer players.[31]

Some sports institutions have modified their policies to help fasting athletes. During the 2023 Major League Soccer (MLS) and MLS Next Pro seasons, the league initiated designated drink breaks at sunset for fasting players to break their fast. In years past, fasting players had to use halftime or wait for the game to end to break their fast. Abdirizak Mohamed, a Muslim athlete who plays on the MLS Next Pro team Columbus Crew 2, told the *Religion News Service* that he has struggled in the past to find ways to break his fast midgame, once taking a penalty in another league when a referee accused him of wasting time when he used a game pause to break his fast. "For me, obviously, faith comes first," Mohamed said. "Whenever it's time for us to fast, we always put that before the athlete title." In 2022, Mohamed and other Muslim players in MLS Next Pro began informally negotiating Ramadan stoppages with referees and other teams before games. Jeff Agoos, MLS's senior vice president of competition, said that their new policy for sixty-second breaks stemmed from numerous requests from players and staff about how best to manage player safety while fasting during Ramadan.[32]

In 2024, when Ramadan overlapped with the NCAA men's college basketball tournament, Dan Monson, coach for Long Beach State's men's basketball team, argued that the NCAA should grant accommodations for teams with players fasting for Ramadan and schedule their games at night. During the first round of the tournament, Long Beach was scheduled to play against Arizona at noon. Monson noted that the NCAA could have easily switched the game with another that was scheduled for 5:25 p.m. that would have allowed fasting players on his team to break their fast before playing. He pointed out that the NCAA provides religious accommodations to Brigham Young University (BYU), a Mormon institution, to not play games on Sundays. BYU head coach Mark Pope disagreed with Monson's request for schedule adjustments, despite BYU's player Aly Khalifa fasting for Ramadan. Despite receiving religious exemptions for play dates, Pope told the *Salt Lake Tribune*, "We're a team full of believers, and so we're not necessarily looking for unique accommodations."[33] Perhaps as advocacy for Muslim athletes' fasting increases, more sporting institutions will consider rule modifications and exemptions.

Conclusions

Ibtihaj Muhammad became the first Muslim American athlete to win an Olympic medal while wearing a hijab at the 2016 Olympics in Rio de Janeiro. Growing up in Maplewood, New Jersey, Ibtihaj Muhammad started fencing at the age of twelve at the behest of her mother, who liked the fact that fencing uniforms made it easy to practice modesty. The New Jersey State Interscholastic Athletic Association required student-athletes who wanted to modify uniforms for religious reasons to file a letter with the school's athletic director, and Muhammad brought this letter with her to every fencing competition. She told *CNN Sports* in a 2023 interview, "Everyone knew that I wore hijab, but it was really just kind of like this discriminatory thing that happened to me as a kid. And it was just kind of normal. I didn't know if I was going to be able to play."[34] Although Ibtihaj Muhammad's experience of not knowing whether she would be allowed to compete has been the norm for hijabi athletes for decades, this has started to shift as more and more sport oversight institutions change their rules to allow for hijabs and modest clothing without requiring religious exemption paperwork.

In 2017, Deering High School in Portland, Maine, provided sport hijabs to students with the goal of boosting Muslim girls' participation in sports. Tennis cocaptains Liva Pierce and Anaise Manikunda raised more than $800 online to buy sport hijabs. They solicited private donations to avoid criticism for using taxpayer funds on religious apparel. Pierce told a local reporter, "If a Muslim student didn't want to play tennis because she couldn't be true to her religion and play the sport, that's awful. I don't want that to happen—I don't think anyone wants that to happen." The tennis cocaptains were not Muslim, but Pierce brought up the idea of providing hijabs to Melanie Craig, the school's athletic director, who responded, "If I'm going to buy a football helmet, I'm going to buy a hijab." The cocaptains raised enough money to outfit all teams (lacrosse, soccer, volleyball, softball, field hockey, and track), buying sport hijabs from Asiya, a company headquartered in Minnesota cofounded by Fatimah Hussein, a Somalian native who coaches basketball, and Jamie Glover. Glover noted that Deering High School was the first school to purchase sport hijabs from Asiya for their student-athletes. She said, "For us, [Deering High School's order] is super exciting because we do see this as just another part of the uniform—another piece of equipment that we feel athletes need to be able to play."[35] With Nike's release of their "pro-hijab" in 2018, access to sport hijabs has dramatically increased.

Hard-fought rule changes in women's sports have accompanied a growing awareness of Muslim athletes fasting during Ramadan, and sports programs and institutions have developed ways of coaching and accommodating these athletes. In 2005, when Hamza Abdullah was fasting in the NFL, few Muslims were playing professional football. "I knew Muslim athletes were fasting, I knew I wasn't alone, but sometimes I felt alone. I would love to see a Muslim athletes' association that could advocate for Muslim athletes—just to let Muslim athletes today know that there are people on your side. I would love to find a way to come together and support each other."[36] Khadijah Diggs runs a program in Atlanta called DISK (Diversity Infusion Syndicate), training Muslim and non-Muslim women for triathlons. In 2023, her team of four were all Muslim, and the competition they were preparing for was scheduled to begin on Eid, the last day of Ramadan. This meant that the training for the race had to happen during Ramadan. She told her trainees to trust her with their training; she would be going through it with them.

> At that event, we had seven world championship qualifications and three podiums. We were the only Muslims there. Seeing [one of my trainees] win super-sprint on Eid, I'll never forget it. A lot of times at world championship qualifiers, I'm the only Muslim woman. To have these women trust me to coach them and mentor them during Ramadan, it meant a lot. I was so grateful that these women trusted me.[37]

The Pew Research Center has estimated that the population of Muslims in the United States is growing at around 100,000 per year; by 2040, Muslims may outnumber Jews to become the second-largest American religious group behind Christianity.[38] Resources for Muslim athletes such as sport hijabs and training regimens for fasting during Ramadan have helped increase Muslim participation in sport over the past decades, and this trend is likely to continue, aided by increased representation of Muslims across multiple sports.

Resources for Further Study

Media

Rashid Ghazi, dir. *Fordson: Faith, Fasting, Football*. Glenview, IL: North Shore Films, LLC and Quraishi Productions, 2011.

Online Archive

The Council on Islamic-American Relations provide a series of guides and tool kits for American Muslims navigating a variety of settings in the United States. "Guides and Toolkits," https://www.cair.com/resources/guides-and-toolkits/.

Reading

Rebecca Alpert, "Mahmoud Abdul-Rauf and the National Anthem Ritual in the NBA," in *Religion and Sports: An Introduction and Case Studies* (New York: Columbia University Press, 2015), 127–33.

Steven Fink, *Dribbling for Dawah: Sport Among American Muslims* (Macon, GA: Mercer University Press, 2016).

Terry Shoemaker, "Religions in Sports," in *Religions and Sports: The Basics* (New York: Routledge, 2024), 25–48.

Part 2

American Christianity and Social Issues in Sport

The five chapters in this part of the book critically investigate the ways that American Christian perspectives have informed social issues and controversies in contemporary sports. Muscular Christian claims that sport builds character, has moral value, and is a vehicle for instilling traits traditionally affiliated with masculinity such as individualism, leadership, and self-sacrifice have taken root in American sports, and these understandings are the backdrop for contemporary controversies in sport.

Because most sports are segregated by sex, often from a young age, sport is a space where people learn about and express gender. Taking on the categories of sex and gender can help us explore the consequences of segregating sports by sex. Different understandings of what sex is has ramifications for who can participate in sports, and exploring how American Christianity undergirds gender perspectives can help us understand legislative pushes to ban trans athletes' participation as well as policies shaping sports for women and girls. Bringing this investigation of gender to bear on youth sports, we can consider the troubling gendered messages that some children receive from sports participation.

Paying attention to American Christianity can also help us understand the controversies surrounding Native American mascots, doping, and paying college athletes. Calls to change Native American mascots have brought attention to North America's colonial history, including the ways that westward expansion relied on portraying Native Americans as dangerous heathens resisting Christian civilization. Doping scandals in professional sports also draw to the surface an uncomfortable contradiction: how can sports be morally valuable when the inherent goal of sports is to defeat another? Investigating Americans' moral repulsion regarding performance-enhancing drugs showcases a cultural fixation on shame and confession that runs counter to the realities of big-time sports. Recent years have upended the long-standing requirement that college athletes be unpaid. This, too, has challenged the idea of sport as inherently morally valuable. Focusing on how denominational colleges and sports ministries have reacted to recent changes in the economics of college sports raises questions about who should benefit financially from sports and why.

Taken as a whole, the chapters in Part II raise the question: what is the point of sports? These critical and thematic chapters are an opportunity to think through why sport matters, who benefits from sports, and if our current state of sports is an accurate reflection of our values.

Chapter 8

Sex and Gender

In 2021, Shira Mandelzis was going into her junior year at Riverdale Country School in the Bronx, New York City, and decided to sign up for football. She had enjoyed touch football in middle school, and she was an avid snowboarder and an athletic teen. She knew that the team was all boys, but the team was no-cut, no-tryout, so she figured that she would give it a try. Soon after she registered to play, the school's athletic director let her know about a 1985 New York State Education Department regulation intended to protect girls playing boys' sports. To join the team, Mandelzis needed to submit a record of her performance in physical education classes; an evaluation by a doctor of her medical history, body type, and sexual maturity level (measured using the Tanner scale, which for girls assesses pubic hair and breasts as measures of sexual maturity on a scale of one to five); and complete a physical fitness test of sprints, pull-ups, push-ups, and a one-mile run to assess her strength and endurance. Although she did pass and play on the team, she decided that one season was enough. She told *Atlantic* reporter Maggie Mertens,

> Going through the regulations was so infuriating for me, because there were these freshman [boys] who are 100 pounds and half my size, and all they had to do was sign up. And the fact that my ability to get on the field had to be tested simply because of my gender, when I had more experience than these other people, was just very upsetting for me.[1]

None of the boys had to submit to evaluations of their strength, endurance, or sexual maturity to play football.

Sport experiences can be just as challenging for a boy who wants to play on a girls' team. Colin Ives grew up playing field hockey as the son of a field hockey coach. Although globally men are the majority of field hockey players, in the United States, field hockey is a women's sport. When Ives wanted to try out for the team at his high school in Tarrytown, New York, he had to go through the same process as Mandelzis. He played on his school's team for his freshman and sophomore years. The COVID-19 pandemic meant that there was no season his junior year. When he sought approval to play for his senior year, the other schools in his school's league voted to exclude him from play, citing his physical strength as a danger to the girls. Ives found this to be both inaccurate and belittling to his teammates. He told the *Atlantic*, "There are players on teams that we play that are faster than me, that are stronger than me, that can hit the ball harder than me. So I knew that [the league's] arguments didn't really have any basis in that regard."[2] Ives maintained his love of field hockey and served as a student assistant coach while in college at Wesleyan University in Connecticut.

Mandelzis made a formal request to the New York State Education Department to revoke their guidelines on mixed-gender sports qualifications, and the Board of Regents took up the issue in 2024. It considered a proposed amendment to the guidelines that would require the same criteria for participation regardless of sex. If no selection process was required, as for Mandelzis's no-cut, no-tryout football team, then all students would be allowed to participate equally. The revised guidelines would also discontinue the use of the Tanner scale because it is intrusive and can feel demeaning. When the Board of Regents opened a sixty-day public comment period, it was overwhelmed with comments against the amendment and tabled it indefinitely.[3] As of 2024, the regulations remain in place.

Since 2020, the United States has seen a wave of legislation, lawsuits, and court decisions addressing who is allowed to play on which sports teams. Republicans introduced a Senate bill on September 22, 2020, that would withdraw federal funding from schools that allowed trans women to participate on their sports teams, claiming this was necessary to "protect women's sports." In the U.S. House of Representatives, Democratic Party presidential candidate Tulsi Gabbard introduced the "Protect Women's Sports Act of 2020" intending to restrict Title IX protections exclusively to people assigned female at birth. This act did not pass but was part of a larger legislative push to ban transgender people from sports participation. This coincided with conservative Christian emphasis on an unchangeable gender binary. For example, Alabama governor Kay Ivey signed a ban on gender-affirming care, tweeting in April 2022, "We're going to go by how God made us: if the Good Lord made you a boy, you're a boy, and if he made you a girl, you're a girl. It's simple."[4]

One central narrative in this legislative and court case push was that women have fought hard to be included in athletic institutions, and allowing the participation of trans women, high testosterone women, and women with intersex variations would undermine these gains.[5] For these proponents, protection of the category of "woman" is necessary to preserve women's sports. Scholars and proponents of inclusivity in sports have argued that current attention to trans women and women with high testosterone continues the sexism (discrimination against women) and homophobia (abhorrence of homosexuality) that have long restricted women's athletic options.

What Is "Sex"? What Is "Gender"?

"Sex" is a person's biological designation as male or female. In the U.S., medical authorities identify an infant as male or female at birth and record this information on their birth certificate. This document establishes the sex of the individual, and authorities use birth certificates to determine legal rights, medical benefits, incarceration locations, and military service. In this way, sex is both a biological and a legal designation. Changing one's sex designation is a legal process often requiring evidence of medical alteration of one's sex organs and secondary sex characteristics such as breasts or facial hair.

One's biological designation as either male or female carries with it social expectations. "Gender" is the way that we express and perform these expectations. Rather than thinking of gender as something stemming from biology, it is helpful to think of gender as an outcome of social relationships. Our culture teaches us that being male and acting masculine go together and that being female and acting feminine go together. The performance of gender, the way that a person acts masculine or feminine, relies on existing cultural ideas about masculinity and femininity. These cultural ideas, in turn, allow people to evaluate each other's masculinity and femininity, to assess how closely aligned the person's behaviors and self-presentation are with cultural expectations.[6] Sex, gender, and sexuality go together because society tends to affiliate the expected gender expression of one's biological/legal designation (women acting feminine and men acting masculine) with heterosexuality. Boys who are "sissies" or girls who are "tomboys" contradict gender expectations and might experience suspicions of sexual deviance.

"Intersexed" is a biological term for those who do not fit cleanly into a sex binary.[7] This category may include atypical genitalia, chromosomal abnormalities, or hormonal production outside of the average range. Bodies born with atypical genitalia have always existed, but beginning in the nineteenth century, physicians developed surgical treatments to resolve genital ambiguity, usually by clitoral and/or vaginal construction and consequent designation as female. At the time, the medical establishment believed that atypical genitalia would lead to homosexuality, so they performed these surgeries not for the health or comfort of the patient but to intervene in what they saw as a trajectory toward deviant sexuality.[8] "Trans" refers to a person who does not identify as the biological/legal designation they received at birth but as a different sex. "Nonbinary" refers to individuals who identify as neither male nor female.

Legal redesignation of one's preferred sex can be a complicated process and, like surgeries on ambiguous genitalia, is connected to homophobia. For example, in 2005, New York City adopted a policy common to most jurisdictions: only those who proved they had undergone genital surgery could reissue their birth certificates with sex reclassification. The city changed this policy in 2014 to allow people born in the city to change their sex classification on birth certificates with no requirement for surgery but still required a signed affidavit from a medical professional attesting to the change. The 2014 decision to remove the surgery requirement was likely linked to the 2011 legalization of same-sex marriage in the state of New York. A major concern prior to the legalization of same-sex marriage was that same-sex couples would use reclassification of sex on birth certificates to marry fraudulently. When the surgery requirement was in place, about twenty people a year changed their birth certificate sex designation; from January 2015, when the new policy took effect, to March 2017, more than seven hundred people changed their birth certificates. In 2018, New York City added a nonbinary category of "X" as allowable on birth certificates in addition to M or F.

Given these key terms, it is useful to map out competing perspectives on what sex "really is." Political scientist Paisley Currah helpfully provides four perspectives, showing that different understandings of sex correlate with different positions on sex classification and reclassification.[9] To show how these perspectives matter when it comes to sport, let's briefly consider the case of Lia Thomas. Thomas was a collegiate swimmer who competed on the men's swimming team at Penn for 2017–2019. Thomas came out as transgender and began hormone replacement therapy in May 2019, continuing to compete on the men's team while completing the required year of hormone treatments before the National Collegiate Athletic Association (NCAA) would allow a switch to the women's team. When the COVID-19 pandemic shut down college sports, Thomas took a leave of absence to preserve her final year of eligibility and returned for the 2021–2022 season to compete on the women's swim team. She finished that season with a NCAA championship win for the 500 freestyle, sparking controversy over the NCAA's decision to allow her to compete.

Table 8.1 Theories of Sex and their Consequences for Reclassification and Sports Participation

What sex is	Held by	Position on sex reclassification	Position on sports participation
Sex is determined at birth, sex is determined at conception, and/or sex is defined by reproductive capacity.	Social conservatives; "traditional common sense"	Initial sex assignment of M/F cannot be changed; a person's sex cannot be reclassified.	Participation in sex-segregated sports is based on initial classification as male or female.
Sex is constituted by or verified by genitals.	Mid-twentieth-century medical experts	Evidence of genital surgery allows for reclassification as M/F.	Participation in sex-segregated sports is based on medical designation as male or female.
Sex is gender identity: male, female, or nonbinary.	Mainstream transgender rights advocates; twenty-first century medical experts	Declaration of gender identity F/M/X is grounds for reclassification.	Participation in sex-segregated sports is based on individual declaration of gender identity.
Sex is an effect of gender norms.	Gender radical trans advocates; constructionists	F/M/X classification should be ended for all.	Sports should not be sex-segregated.

Source: Adapted from Paisley Currah, "Table 1.1. Theories of Sex and Their Corresponding Positions on Sex (Re)Classification" in *Sex Is as Sex Does*. Courtesy of NYU Press.

For those who hold that sex is determined at birth or conception (social conservatives and those holding to "traditional common sense"), there is no way to reclassify gender regardless of surgery, hormonal treatments, or gender preference. From this perspective, Lia Thomas should have competed on the men's team regardless of desire to compete as a woman. Conservative Christians were among those who vehemently opposed the NCAA decision to allow Thomas to compete on the women's team. For example, Jon Benzinger, a pastor at Redeemer Bible Church in Arizona, stated on his YouTube channel that Thomas was an abomination hated by God for masquerading as a woman.[10]

For those that hold that sex is defined by one's genitals (dominant stance of the mid- to late-twentieth century), surgery would be grounds for reclassification. Though Lia Thomas was undergoing hormone replacement therapy, from this perspective, Thomas should have competed on the men's team because Thomas had not undergone genital surgery. The NCAA and USA Swimming, the authorities overseeing college sports and American participation in international swimming competitions, hold a modified stance that fits this category: they decree that athletes who demonstrate a level of testosterone consistent with average female levels can compete on women's teams. We will explore the focus on testosterone at length later in this chapter. For understanding this perspective on what sex really is, we can note that sporting authorities tend to develop medical/biological requirements that allow for athletes to compete as women if they were assigned male at birth.

For those who hold that sex is gender identity and can take the form of male, female, or nonbinary (mainstream transgender activists, twenty-first century medical experts), individuals declare their gender identity. This position became dominant among transgender advocates by the mid-1990s. From this perspective, one does not need to pursue medical treatment to reclassify their sex. Some primary and secondary schools have adopted this perspective when considering the inclusion of nonbinary and trans youth in sports teams. Some teammates of Lia Thomas stated in a letter to the NCAA that they support this perspective on sex and gender identity except for when it comes to sport. Their letter stated, "We fully support Lia Thomas in her decision to affirm her gender identity and to transition from a man to a woman. Lia has every right to live her life authentically. However, we also recognize that when it comes to sports competition, that the biology of sex is a separate issue from someone's gender identity."[11] The question from this perspective is: Should sports be treated as a special case or should declaring one's sex/gender identity allow a person to compete in the category they choose?

For those that hold that sex is an effect of gender norms (gender radical trans advocates; those holding the position that sex is social construction), gender classification of M/F/X should be ended for all persons. This is the most radical position and argues that because sex is an effect of gender, it should not carry legal consequences at all. Using this perspective, we might imagine creatively reconstituting sport where competitors are categorized based on size, age, talent, qualifying rounds, or another metric separate from sex. These four perspectives represent competing ideas on how to legally designate sex;

and, as we can see in competing understandings of Lia Thomas's swimming participation, they have differing consequences for understanding sports participation.

The Specter of Gender Fraud

Current concerns about trans women competing in sport harken back to concerns of "gender fraud" in the Olympic Games. Since the 1940s, the International Olympic Committee (IOC) has attempted to verify the gender of sportswomen in a number of ways, despite the fact that in only one instance has a man competed as a woman. The story goes that Heinrich Ratjen was so loyal to Hitler Youth that he bound his genitals and competed as a woman under the name of Dora in the 1936 Olympics. Historians have since revised this account to note that Ratjen's gender ambiguity was not discovered because of sporting participation but was due to a German police officer's ID card challenge at a train station years after the competition. Historian of science and medicine Vanessa Heggie points out, "Although the story of a deliberate Nazi fraud makes better

Image 8.1 American Helen Stephens (left) and Polish runner Stella Walsh after finishing first and second, respectively, in the 100m sprint at the 1936 Olympics in Berlin. Unfounded accusations that these sprinters were men masquerading as women led to demands that the Olympics initiate sex verification testing for sportswomen. *Getty Images/ullstein bild Dtl.*

headlines, Ratjen's story is probably a more homely and familiar one of medical error, gender uncertainty, and embarrassed silences."[12]

Also at the 1936 Olympics, in the one-hundred-meter race, American Helen Stephens and Polish runner Stella Walsh finished first and second, respectively. The Polish press accused Stephens of being a man, and the American press responded that Walsh was a man. Avery Brundage, who would later chair the IOC, was Helen Stephens's team coach, and shortly after she experienced accusations that she was a man, he began to call for systematic sex testing. This led officials to "check" in an unspecified manner and declare that both were, in fact, women. In 1980, Walsh died by gunshot in a violent department store robbery, and her autopsy made public Walsh's "ambiguous" sexual features. In response to demands that the IOC revoke Walsh's medals, the IOC released a statement that Walsh had competed in good faith and had not broken the rules of the day. Despite this, Walsh and Ratjen have become centerpieces of the canon of gender frauds. They fit the conventional narrative that the IOC implemented sex testing to prevent communist countries from disguising their male athletes as women to win more medals.

In the 1960s, Cold War fears of communist cheating led to the implementation of at-event, standardized sex verification for sportswomen. Sex testing at these sporting events was invasive, often requiring that sportswomen submit to a visual examination of genitals and breasts carried out by female doctors.[13] Those who failed the visual test usually underwent further tests. The first athlete to be disqualified via these tests was Ewa Klobukowska of Poland. Upon failing a visual test of her genitals at the 1967 European Cup Track and Field Event in Kiev, she underwent a chromosomal test, which she also failed, having "one chromosome too many" according to the International Association of Athletics Federations (IAAF, now World Athletics), the international governing organization for track and field. Although accounts of Klobukowska's chromosomal test vary, the dominant narrative is that she had a triple-X chromosome variation, a chromosomal arrangement that would not have affected her development as female.[14] Despite criticisms from Polish endocrinologists that testing the arrangement of chromosomes is not an accurate method to determine sex, the IAAF nullified all of Klobukowska's records and victories and barred her from competition.[15]

The case of Spanish Olympic hurdler Maria José Martínez-Patiño, was instrumental in shifting the focus to testosterone as the determining factor in sex designation for international sports. The IOC disqualified Martínez-Patiño in the mid-1980s because she had XY chromosomes. Martínez-Patiño was able to overturn this disqualification by showing that she had complete androgen insensitivity syndrome; her tissues were unable to respond to testosterone or other androgens. She argued that her insensitivity to testosterone should be the deciding factor in allowing her to compete, and both the IAAF (in 1992) and the IOC (in 2000) cited her case as a key determinant in their decisions to discontinue chromosomal sex testing. Sex testing in all its forms presumes that a singular marker of sex (genitalia, chromosomes, testosterone level) can categorize people into a two-sex system. In reality, bodies are much more complicated. IOC's and IAAF's difficulty in determining who belongs in the category of female reveals the complexities present in regulating women's sports. These same complexities are likely present in men's sports but remain hidden because institutions do not require male athletes to verify their sex.

Sporting regulators in the 2010s and 2020s consistently referred to testosterone as "the male sex hormone," which has led to inaccurate assumptions. For example, identifying testosterone as male elides the fact that women also produce testosterone and need it for healthy functioning. Calling testosterone a sex hormone presents it as only impacting sex organs and sexual function, but testosterone plays a role in a wide range of bodily functions unrelated to sex, such as liver function. Cultural anthropologist Katrina Karkazis and science studies scholar Rebecca M. Jordan-Young call the focus on testosterone "T talk" and argue that T talk reinforces the myth that testosterone makes men athletically superior to women: despite the fact that millions of men have vastly more testosterone than elite sportswomen, they are not as fast or as strong as those women. IAAF rebranded as "World Athletics" in 2019 and adopted new eligibility regulations for "athletes with differences in sexual development" in 2023.[16] According to the data included in World Athletics' eligibility regulations, the majority of women have testosterone levels ranging from 0.6 to 2.44 nanomoles per liter (nmol/L), whereas most men have testosterone levels that range from 7.9 to 29.4 nmol/L in blood serum testing. World Athletics provides no data to explain why most men are not as strong or as fast as elite sportswomen despite their higher testosterone levels, and they provide no indication that testing and regulating male athletes' testosterone levels would ensure fairness in men's competition.

Caster Semenya has become the face of World Athletics' and IOC's focus on testosterone levels. Semenya naturally produces high levels of testosterone, which has led sports administrators, media outlets, and other athletes to accuse her of having an unfair advantage. Ugandan scholar and human rights activist Sylvia Tamale offers an illuminating comparison between Olympic champions Caster Semenya and Michael Phelps to show different treatments of men and women with genetic conditions that contribute to their athletic success. Media portrayals of Phelps and Semenya describe them as "freaks of nature." For example, Tamale points to an article from *Men's Journal* that describes Phelps:

> Michael Phelps, on the other hand, is a genetic freak. He is 6'4", but more to the point he has the wingspan of a prehistoric bird. His unusually lengthy torso (it's the right size for a man 6'8") affords him more flat surface area to which to surf the top of the water. And he's got hyperflexible knees and ankles that give his kick more snap, and big hands and feet that push a lot of water. But according to sports scientists, his physique tells only part of the story. Whereas most elite swimmers measure blood lactate levels of 10 to 15 millimoles per liter after a race, Phelps measures as low as five. In other words, he's able to go faster calling on far less lactic acid-producing anaerobic energy reserves than his opponents.[17]

Images 8.2 and 8.3 Caster Semenya (left) competing in the women's 3000m final during the Athletics South Africa Grand Prix in Cape Town, South Africa, on March 23, 2022; Michael Phelps (right) competing in the 2016 Olympic Games on August 8, 2016, in Rio de Janeiro, Brazil. Media coverage of these two athletes tends to refer to them as "freaks of nature" because of their genetic athletic advantages, yet of the two, only Semenya's advantages are called "unfair." *Getty Images/Rodger Bosch; Getty Images/Nolwenn Le Gouic.*

Media portrayals of Semenya also use the language of "freak" but present her as an abnormal version of person, rather than exalting her genetics as is the case with portrayals of Phelps. As Tamale points out, "there are no suggestions from the public that [Phelps] should undergo corrective surgery or administer medication to 'normalize' his lactic acid levels."[18] Meanwhile, Semenya described her experience of medically suppressing her testosterone levels as "hell" with symptoms such as depression, panic attacks, insatiable appetite, constant sweating, and insomnia. She told *CNN*, "It's like digging a hole that you can never fill up. You know, it's like you measure a casket and you get in and then you bury yourself. It was not easy. It was a hard time."[19] In response to Semenya's continued advocacy and quests for legal action to end discrimination against high-testosterone women, World Athletics has stood by its 2023 regulations.[20]

One assumption undergirding sex testing and the policing of women's sport is that sport constitutes a level playing field and that institutions have an obligation to protect the fairness of sport. The wave of proposed legislation across the United States from 2020 to 2023 tended to use the language of "fairness" to justify the exclusion of trans women and girls from participating in sports. However, sport sociologists have long noted that sport is not and cannot constitute a level playing field given genetic variation among athletes and social and cultural factors that influence athletes' access to success such as racism, socioeconomic class, homophobia, and transphobia. As the above analysis comparing Semenya and Phelps shows, sporting institutions are not interested in limiting genetic variations that create an "unfair advantage" for male athletes, revealing a deep hypocrisy in the system. Only sportswomen are subject to demands that they medically intervene in their biology to compete.

Christian Homophobia and the Targeting of Trans Youth

The wave of proposed legislation in the 2020s that would exclude trans athletes across all age groups from participating in sports that do not match their sex assigned at birth has remarkably similarities to conservative Christian activism against gay marriage in the late twentieth century. The American culture shift toward the acceptance of gay and lesbian relationships has taken the teeth out of conservative Christian and Republican efforts to rally support via homophobia, but the issue of trans participation in sports has emerged as an effective political issue for this same population.[21] In comparing conservative Christian antigay and anti-trans viewpoints, we can trace a pattern of how the right lost the culture war on homophobia and consider whether the same trajectory may hold for anti-trans claims.

Conversion therapy, a conservative Christian practice that emerged in the 1970s, promised that Christian commitment can alter one's sexual desires and erase same-sex attraction so that a gay person who desires to be straight can become so.[22] A prominent conversion therapy provider was Exodus International. Exodus relied on culturally established ideas of masculinity and femininity to teach gendered behaviors and "cure" Christians of homosexuality. For example, they recommended a friendly football game to connect men to masculinity or a makeover party to connect women to femininity. Because "sports are just a natural way for guys to connect" and because women struggling with lesbianism "will stay away from skirts, makeup, and jewelry," these tactics taught the participants that they were not different from average men and women and should embrace their gender roles. According to their website, "It's not really about the points at the end of the game or the style of a person's hair; the goal is to change our distorted perceptions of ourselves and heal inner wounds."[23] For Exodus, homosexuality was an affliction that could be healed through Christianity, and that healing could be put into effect by conforming to gender expectations. Those who claimed that God changed them through their participation in organizations such as Exodus identify as "ex-gay" and often showcase their straight marriage and biological children as evidence of God's power over sexuality.

The 2021 Netflix documentary *Pray Away* investigated Christian ex-gay ministries, including Exodus, by following those who founded and led the ex-gay movement as, one by one, they came to realize that what they were preaching (that a person could stop experiencing same-sex sexual desires through commitment to Christianity) was not true for themselves and caused significant harm to those who tried to follow the path they proposed.[24] A central character in the documentary was Julie Rodgers. Rodgers, born in the mid-1980s, grew up in a conservative Christian household, and when she came out to her parents as a lesbian at age sixteen, they enrolled her in programming through Living Hope Ministries, an affiliate of Exodus. Ricky Chelette, the leader of Living Hope, taught the young people who came to him that same-sex attraction was a result of a poor relationship with parents or trauma. When Rodgers told Chelette that she had a great relationship with her parents and that she had never experienced abuse, Chelette suggested that Rodgers had suppressed experiences of abuse and could no longer remember them.

Over the course of high school and college, Rodgers participated in programming at Living Hope several days a week. In consultation with Chelette, her parents withdrew Rodgers from her softball team and decided that she would attend a Christian college so that she would not be gay. Rodgers's parents' decision to remove her from sports participation reflects fears that sports for women can lead to same-sex attraction. As coach and LGBTQ advocate Pat Griffin put it,

> Women in sport have a tradition of assuring ourselves and others that sport participation is consistent with traditional notions of femininity and that women are not masculinized by sport experiences… Femininity, however, is a code word for heterosexuality… This intense blend of homophobic and sexist standards of feminine attractiveness remind women in sport that to be acceptable, we must monitor our behavior and appearance at all times.[25]

For women playing sports, engaging in the traditionally masculine activity of intense sporting competition can raise suspicions regarding sexuality; and in Rodgers's case, her parents saw softball as a factor contributing to her same-sex attractions.

At the national Exodus conference in June 2013, founder Alan Chambers apologized to those who had experienced hurt or shame at the hands of the organization. Chambers and the board announced the dissolution of Exodus International after thirty-seven years. Chambers apologized for stigmatizing parents, causing heartbreak, and heaping shame and guilt on persons who continued to experience same-sex attraction, including himself. "[My ongoing same-sex attractions] brought me tremendous shame and I hid them in the hopes they would go away. Looking back, it seems so odd that I thought I could do something to make them stop. Today, however, I accept these feelings as parts of my life that will likely always be there."[26] Chambers's acceptance of the feelings of same-sex attraction did not mean that he supported acting on those feelings. On the contrary, his solution remained to try to be straight or to be celibate.

From 2004 to 2017, American public opinion on the legalization of gay marriage shifted significantly. In 2004, nearly two-thirds of Americans opposed gay marriage; in 2017, nearly two-thirds supported it.[27] Most major religious traditions in the United States saw an increase in acceptance of gay marriage over this period—including white evangelicals whose acceptance of gay marriage increased from 13 percent in favor in 2001 to 35 percent in favor in 2017.[28] Younger Americans demonstrate the highest levels of acceptance of gay marriage. Gen Z (those born from 1996 to 2010) and millennials (those born from 1981 to 1996) are almost twice as likely as baby boomers (those born from 1946 to 1964) to say that gay marriage is good for American society.[29]

Sociologists Robert Putnam and David Campbell have argued that conservative Christianity's political focus on excluding gay people from marriage throughout the 1980s and 1990s led to more and more young people identifying as "not religious" as a shorthand for "not homophobic." The Pew Research Center reports that the number of Americans who say that they are "not religious" has grown from 8 percent in 1987 to 29 percent in 2021, constituting the largest shift in religious affiliation in modern U.S. history.[30] Putnam and Campbell point to a number of cultural events and changes that may have contributed to increased acceptance of homosexuality over this period. First, public attention to the AIDS crisis in the 1990s increased sympathy for gay men from the American public. Second, as more people openly identified as gay and lesbian, more straight people interacted with openly gay people and came to see them as normal. Third, television shows and movies normalized homosexuality, with popular shows such as *Will and Grace* (1998–2006, 2017–2020) showcasing gay characters.[31]

Primary Source

Primary sources provide firsthand accounts of the topic under consideration. They emerge from particular times and places and allow us to imagine the context and thought processes that give rise to a perspective.

Compare the "Defense of Marriage Act" (1996) to the executive order "Defending Women from Gender Ideology Extremism and Restoring Biological Truth to the Federal Government" (2025)

Public Domain

Context:

- President Clinton signed the "Defense of Marriage Act" into law in 1996. Following passage of the federal law, forty states passed legislation banning same-sex marriages. These bans had consequences for same-sex couples including denial of access to a partner's employment benefits, inheritance, right to cohabitation, custody of nonbiological children, and medical leave to care for a partner or for nonbiological children.
- President Trump signed the executive order "Defending Women from Gender Ideology Extremism and Restoring Biological Truth to the Federal Government" on his first day in office on January 20, 2025. It was one of twenty-six executive orders that President Trump signed that day.

Discussion Questions:

- What similarities do you see between these two documents? What differences do you see?
- What are the intended and unintended consequences of these legal documents?
- What understandings of sex, gender, and sexuality do you see in each?
- How do you personally feel about these legal actions? What is the heart of the matter for you? Where do you feel pulled or see complexity?

Excerpts from The Defense of Marriage Act[32]

Section 2. Powers Reserved to the States.

No State, territory, or possession of the United States, or Indian tribe, shall be required to give effect to any public act, record, or judicial proceeding of any other State, territory, possession, or tribe respecting a relationship between persons of the same sex that is treated as a marriage under the laws of such other State, territory, possession, or tribe, or a right or claim arising from such relationship.

Section 3. Definition of "Marriage" and "Spouse"

In determining the meaning of any Act of Congress, or of any ruling, regulation, or interpretation of the various administrative bureaus and agencies of the United States, the word "marriage" means only a legal union between one man and one woman as husband and wife, and the word "spouse" refers only to a person of the opposite sex who is a husband or a wife.

Excerpts from Executive Order, "Defending Women from Gender Ideology Extremism and Restoring Biological Truth to the Federal Government"[33]

Section 1. Purpose.

Across the country, ideologues who deny the biological reality of sex have increasingly used legal and other socially coercive means to permit men to self-identify as women and gain access to intimate single-sex spaces and activities designed for women, from women's domestic abuse shelters to women's workplace showers. This is wrong. Efforts to eradicate the biological reality of sex fundamentally attack women by depriving them of their dignity, safety, and well-being. The erasure of sex in language and policy has a corrosive impact not just on women but on the validity of the entire American system. Basing Federal policy on truth is critical to scientific inquiry, public safety, morale, and trust in government itself.

This unhealthy road is paved by an ongoing and purposeful attack against the ordinary and longstanding use and understanding of biological and scientific terms, replacing the immutable biological reality of sex with an internal, fluid, and subjective sense of self unmoored from biological facts. Invalidating the true and biological category of "woman" improperly transforms laws and policies designed to protect sex-based opportunities into laws and policies that undermine them, replacing longstanding, cherished legal rights and values with an identity-based, inchoate social concept.

Accordingly, my Administration will defend women's rights and protect freedom of conscience by using clear and accurate language and policies that recognize women are biologically female, and men are biologically male.

Section 2. Policy and Definitions.
It is the policy of the United States to recognize two sexes, male and female. These sexes are not changeable and are grounded in fundamental and incontrovertible reality. Under my direction, the Executive Branch will enforce all sex-protective laws to promote this reality, and the following definitions shall govern all Executive interpretation of and application of Federal law and administration policy:

(a) "Sex" shall refer to an individual's immutable biological classification as either male or female. "Sex" is not a synonym for and does not include the concept of "gender identity."

(b) "Women" or "woman" and "girls" or "girl" shall mean adult and juvenile human females, respectively.

(c) "Men" or "man" and "boys" or "boy" shall mean adult and juvenile human males, respectively.

(d) "Female" means a person belonging, at conception, to the sex that produces the large reproductive cell.

(e) "Male" means a person belonging, at conception, to the sex that produces the small reproductive cell.

(f) "Gender ideology" replaces the biological category of sex with an ever-shifting concept of self-assessed gender identity, permitting the false claim that males can identify as and thus become women and vice versa, and requiring all institutions of society to regard this false claim as true. Gender ideology includes the idea that there is a vast spectrum of genders that are disconnected from one's sex. Gender ideology is internally inconsistent, in that it diminishes sex as an identifiable or useful category but nevertheless maintains that it is possible for a person to be born in the wrong sexed body.

(g) "Gender identity" reflects a fully internal and subjective sense of self, disconnected from biological reality and sex and existing on an infinite continuum, that does not provide a meaningful basis for identification and cannot be recognized as a replacement for sex.

A significant crisis regarding LGBTQ+ youth is high rates of depression and suicide. The Trevor Project, a nonprofit organization formed in 1998 focused on suicide prevention efforts for LGBTQ+ youth, conducted nationwide surveys of LGBTQ+ youth ages thirteen to twenty-four. The 2024 survey found that trans and nonbinary youths considered suicide and attempted suicide in rates higher than gay and lesbian youths. Those who experienced physical harm, discrimination, and those threatened or subjected to conversion therapy were more likely to consider or attempt suicide than LGBTQ+ youth who do not experience these things. Some 12 percent of LGBTQ+ youth attempted suicide in 2024.[34]

Although state legislatures continue to consider bills that impact opportunities for trans youth, some lawmakers and governors are aware of the impact of these policies on mental health. For example, when the governor of Louisiana, John Bel Edwards, vetoed the "Fairness in Women's Sports Act" in 2021 (a law stating that K–12 schools must require students to play on sports teams that match their sex assigned at birth), he released this statement:

> This bill will not be signed into law because it is targeted, unfairly, at children. This legislation will make life more difficult for children who are going through unique challenges gaining acceptance into their schools, communities, and sometimes even their own families. It should be our role, as leaders in this state, to reach out to and lift up these children, rather than to ostracize them. Moreover, the effect of this bill is not so much about how it would affect athletic events,… the real harm of this bill is that it would set as the policy of the State of Louisiana that there is something wrong with these children and that they should be treated differently from whom they really are.[35]

Political targeting of trans youth and increasing awareness of the suicide crisis in this population may carry a similar impact as the AIDS crisis in bringing public attention to the impacts of discrimination.

As more trans and nonbinary people come out, more Americans than ever before know a trans or nonbinary person. Those who identify as trans or nonbinary are more likely to be younger with about 5 percent of ages 18–29 identifying with these categories, compared to 1.6 percent of 30- to 49-year-olds and 0.3 percent of those over 50. A Pew Research Center survey from 2022 showed that 44 percent of adults in the United States know someone who is transgender (up from 37 percent in 2017) and 20 percent know someone who is nonbinary. These percentages are higher for younger people: for ages 18–29, 52 percent know a trans person and 37 percent know a nonbinary person.[36]

Personal stories of trans athletes have emerged in recent years. For example, Hulu released *Changing the Game* in 2019, a documentary profiling the challenges of three transgender teenagers as they navigated playing sports in their home states of Texas, Connecticut, and New Hampshire. The athletes' experiences were constrained by the laws of their states. Mack Beggs, a transgender boy and competitive wrestler in Texas, competed against girls because state laws prevented him from wrestling in the boy's

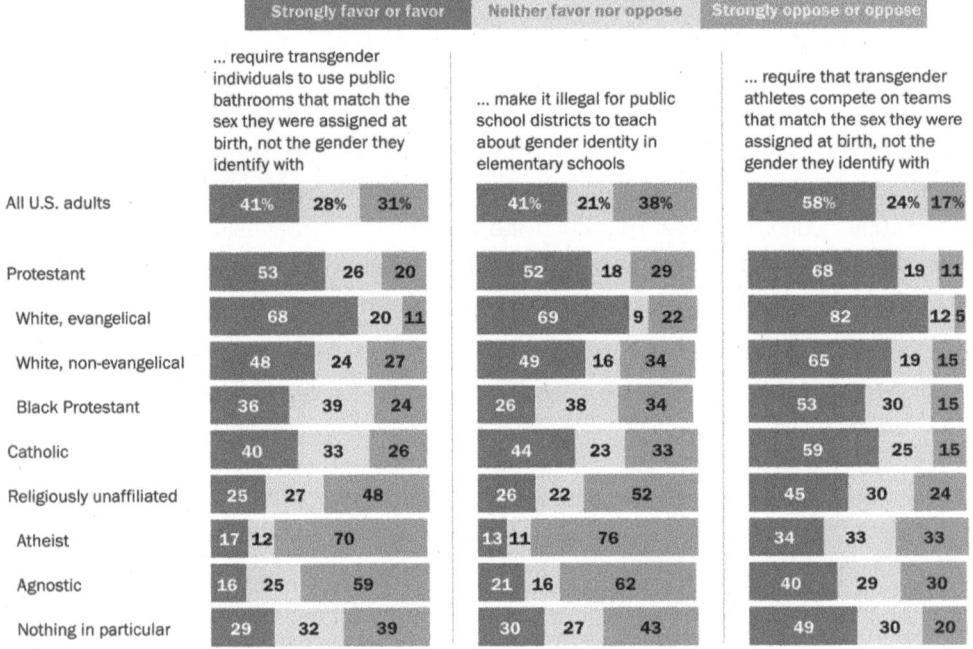

Figure 8.1 Results of 2022 survey on transgender policies conducted by Pew Research Center. This chart organizes responses into overarching categories of Protestant, Catholic, and Religiously Unaffiliated as well as providing a breakdown of subcategories of Protestant (White, evangelical; White, non-evangelical; and Black Protestant) and Religiously Unaffiliated (Atheist, Agnostic, and Nothing in particular). Every category of religion represented tends to favor the requirement of sports participation based on sex assigned at birth more than requiring bathroom use based on sex assigned at birth or banning teaching about gender identity in schools. *Courtesy of Pew Research Center.*

division. During Mack's wrestling competitions, adults in the audience screamed at him to quit wrestling because he did not belong on the girls' team. Similarly, Andraya Yearwood, a trans girl from Connecticut, competed on her high-school's girls' track team and experienced verbal abuse from adults attending her events.[37]

As more stories like this surface and more Americans interact with trans and nonbinary people in their everyday lives, perhaps the political issue of depriving trans people of sports participation will follow the trajectory of homophobic denials of marriage to gay and lesbian adults. If so, the movement toward acceptance of trans individuals is likely to be generational and secular as younger and religiously unaffiliated people are more likely to know and express sympathy for trans discrimination.

Conclusions

A 2022 Pew Research poll investigated stances on policies regarding transgender individuals including requiring individuals to use bathrooms that match the sex they were assigned at birth, making it illegal to teach about gender identity in elementary schools, and requiring that athletes compete on sports teams that match the sex they were assigned at birth. On these issues, white evangelicals demonstrated the highest support for these policies and atheists demonstrated the lowest support.

The issue of sports competition stood out from the other two policies: whereas all groups were consistent in their approaches to the policies regarding bathroom use and elementary-school education on gender, every group demonstrated significantly more support for requiring sports participation to adhere to sex assigned at birth. The percentage of white evangelicals who strongly favored bathroom regulation and regulation of elementary education on gender was 68 percent and 69 percent, respectively; this jumped to 82 percent who strongly favored regulation of sports based on sex assigned at birth. This trend held for all groups surveyed (white evangelical, white non-evangelical, Black Protestant, Catholic, atheist, agnostic, and nothing in particular). Atheists and agnostics, the least likely to favor these policies, still demonstrated a significant difference when it came to the question of sports. On bathroom regulations, only 17 percent of atheists and 16 percent of agnostics strongly favored this policy. On making it illegal to teach about gender identity in elementary schools, 13 percent of atheists and 21 percent of agnostics strongly favored this policy. Both groups demonstrated a significant jump regarding sports: 34 percent of atheists and 40 percent of agnostics strongly favored limiting sports participation based on sex assigned at birth.[38]

Given this survey data, the debate over trans sports participation is likely to continue. Conservative Christians and the Republican party have increasingly focused on anti-trans policies as a provocative wedge issue that functions similarly to their antigay marriage stance. Although we may see eventual increased acceptance of trans and nonbinary individuals along the same trajectory as acceptance of gay marriage, it is likely that the focus on trans women and girls participating in sports will loom large in the immediate future of American politics.

Resources for Further Study

Media
Michael Barnett, dir. *Changing the Game*. 2019; Santa Monica, CA: Hulu.

Online Archive
The findings of the Trevor Project's "2024 National Survey on LGBTQ+ Mental Health" are available for exploration. https://www.thetrevorproject.org/survey-2024/.

Reading
Eric Anderson and Ann Travers, eds., *Transgender Athletes in Competitive Sport* (New York: Routledge, 2017).

Katrina Karkazis and Rebecca M. Jordan-Young, "The Powers of Testosterone: Obscuring Race and Regional Bias in the Regulation of Women Athletes," *Feminist Foundations* 30, no. 2 (2018): 1–39.

Sylvia Tamale, "A Decolonial Analysis of the Phelps/Semenya Conundrum," *Decolonization and Afro-Feminism* (Quebec: Daraja Press, 2020), 105–19.

Chapter 9

Youth Sports

Organized sports for children first emerged in the United States in the late nineteenth century as part of the muscular Christianity's focus on what they called the "boy problem." Concerned that urban, middle-class boys were becoming weak due to their indoor lifestyle and too much time with their mothers and female educators, Protestant reformers turned to organized sports as one method of fostering the rugged male fortitude that they feared was declining with city life. Protestant reformers focused on the boy problem; however, they saw girls as having different needs. Historian Julia Grant has shown that, Protestant reformers believed that "Unlike boys, whose fundamental instincts were thwarted by contemporary civilization, girls' domestic instincts were allowed expression through doll play and caring for younger children."[1] Educators did believe that girls should exercise, but they tended to emphasize activities such as dancing, gymnastics, and swimming that they saw as less strenuous than sports for boys. As boys' organizations and activities emerged, corollaries for girls tended to follow in their wake, but this rarely flowed in the other direction; activities and organizations developed with girls in mind did not develop corollaries for boys. The Young Women's Christian Association (YWCA) began in the United States about a decade after the establishment of the YMCA, and Girl Guides was girls' opportunity for outdoor activities in the vein of the Boy Scouts. As historian Clifford Putney points out, there was no "girl problem," and reformers tended to blame women for exerting too much influence over boys.

In 1995, when sport sociologist Michael Messner enrolled his eldest son in American Youth Soccer Organization (AYSO) soccer at age five, he was told that his son would play on a coed team. However, when he brought his son to practice on the first day, he found that the teams had been segregated by sex. When Messner asked AYSO about this decision, he learned that the organization had based this decision on the inclination of the children to segregate by sex during downtime. Because the children tended to spend halftime divided into girls and boys, AYSO thought team unity would improve with sex-segregation. Messner pointed out that the children also tended to self-segregate along ethnic and racial lines, but the organization was unlikely to initiate racial segregation in the name of team unity.[2] This comparison seemed to fall on deaf ears. Racial segregation of sports strikes many as backward and unfair; in the same vein, segregation of sports based on sex can also raise questions of fairness and progress, especially for children.

Today, with widespread physical education in schools, the passage and implementation of Title IX, and increased attention to children's physical health, American sporting opportunities now target younger and younger athletes, both boys and girls. This chapter examines organized sports for children and shows that the "character building" that muscular Christians promised is accompanied by gendered expectations and may involve severe bodily risk. Although many youth athletes have rewarding sports experiences, sporting activities are not universally good, and youth sporting activities are subject to the same systems of power that govern the worlds of adults. In particular, because many of today's sports are segregated by sex, sports are spaces where children and teens learn to express and evaluate gender. Through an examination of some of the more troubling messages that sports can convey to young athletes, this chapter highlights some downsides of youth sports and raises possibilities for reforming children's athletic experiences.

Gender Narratives and Sports Experiences

A major milestone in girls and women's sports in the United States was the passage of Title IX in 1972. Title IX guaranteed equal funds for men and women in all institutions that receive federal funding. The legislation reads in part, "No person in the United States shall, on the basis of sex, be excluded from participation in, be denied the benefits of, or be subjected to discrimination under any educational programs or activities receiving federal financial assistance." Several factors made Title IX difficult to implement when it came to sports in schools. The most important measure of compliance with Title IX is the measure of an institution's "substantive proportionality." This means that there should be the same ratio of female athletes to female students as there are male athletes to male students. This led many institutions to add more sports teams such as cheerleading, softball, gymnastics, and others aimed at female athletes. Researchers have found that institutions with football teams and with high rates of female enrollment generally have more difficulty complying with Title IX.[3]

Title IX opened opportunities to legally challenge the exclusion of women and girls from sports. For example, the National Organization for Women (NOW) brought a Title IX lawsuit against Little League Baseball (LLB) in 1972. In Hoboken, New Jersey, a girl named Maria Pepe had begun the Little League season playing on the otherwise all-boy team. Pepe's coach reluctantly dropped her from the team after letters from the national organization threatened to revoke the team's charter. In 1973, LLB president Creighton J. Hale argued that boys and girls had biological differences that made boys more inclined toward and better at sports. The case hit the New Jersey Supreme Court in 1974, which ruled in favor of Pepe and mandated that LLB must allow girls to play. Once forced by law to incorporate girls, LLB created Little League Softball. Instead of integrating the sport and letting girls play baseball, they created a parallel infrastructure to manage a significantly

Image 9.1 Maria Pepe poses with a bat at a 1974 baseball game. In 1974, Maria Pepe's legal plea to be included in Little League Baseball was successful, leading to the establishment of Little League Softball as an alternative track for girls. In 2024, Pepe became the eighth woman to receive the highest honor from Little League International: enshrinement in the Hall of Excellence. *Getty Images/Bettmann.*

different game for girls to play. By 2001, LLB president Hale had completely changed his mind. Watching his own granddaughters embrace sport and seeing one of them selected to play on a LLB team in Ohio, he said that inclusion of girls in sport is "one of the best things that happened."[4] Like many men of his generation, personal experience rather than medical science was key to changing his mind.

Basketball was another sport that created different tracks for male and female athletes. Muscular Christians invented basketball in 1891, and women began to play shortly after using modified rules that restricted players to half the court. In the 1960s, the northeast-based Division for Girls' and Women's Sports (DGWS) controlled the rules of women's intercollegiate basketball competition. Like many Protestants, they advocated for a "separate sphere" for women that would emphasize sociability and nurturing skills.[5] DGWS considered contact and competition a threat to feminine nature, so they implemented rules that would limit women's exertion and physicality. Restricting players to half-court was the norm for women's competition until 1971. DGWS rules also restricted the number of times a player could bounce (dribble) the ball before passing. Until 1948, players could bounce the ball once before passing; until the early 1960s, players had two bounces; in 1966, the rules allowed three bounces and one player, called a rover, could play the full court; and in 1971, with the adoption of the full-court game, the women's game adopted the unlimited dribbling rule of the men's game. These gradual rule changes were part of a larger sea change in sports to provide more opportunities for girls and women.

Following his experiences of enrolling his sons in youth sports, sport sociologist Michael Messner analyzed AYSO and Little League Baseball/Softball (LLB/S) in the first decade of the twenty-first century. He asked parents and coaches, was it important that women coached girls or men coached boys? Why? In analyzing the responses he received, he identified three understandings of gender at work. One understanding is equality: treat boys and girls as equal. This outlook advocates for integration of sports but has little power to dismantle the existing segregation of sports by sex. Another understanding is natural difference: treat boys and girls as "hardwired" differently. The assumption that biological differences between male and female bodies lead to male expressions of masculinity and female expressions of femininity is called gender essentialism. Feminism has challenged this essentialism, and empirical evidence shows that girls are interested and skilled at sports. A third understanding is equity with difference. This is the middle ground and the most common response that Messner received. It posits that boys and girls are different but supports equal opportunities for sporting participation. Messner calls this understanding of gender "soft essentialism."[6]

Soft essentialism has several characteristics when it comes to youth sports. Most coaches that Messner interviewed stated that sex-segregated sports were necessary because they assumed that there were natural differences between boys and girls.[7] Many coaches assumed that sports were valuable for girls because sports challenged girls to adopt individualistic, competitive, and aggressive traits counter to their presumed soft, cooperative nature. Meanwhile, coaches assumed that sports were fully consistent with boys' nature; many had never considered whether boys might benefit from a female coach. Messner notes an internal contradiction in their logic:

> On the one hand, adults' narratives tend to view boys as driven by a fairly straightforward natural drive to be competitive, individualist actors in sports and other aspects of public life. But on the other hand, underlying these essentialist constructions of boys are vaguely articulated fears that boys are vulnerable, that they may fail to develop into proper men without adult male role-modeling and leadership.[8]

Although these coaches saw boys as having a competitive and aggressive nature, they also saw a danger of feminization if boys were not "hardened" by the leadership of adult men. This understanding echoes the anxieties of muscular Christians in the late nineteenth and early twentieth centuries explored in chapter two.

Many of the coaches that Messner talked to assumed that boys and girls were essentially different (and boys were essentially better at competition than girls). He reflects on how these assumptions impacted his younger son Miles, who dropped out of organized sports at age nine:

> Miles was the kind of kid who, when the soccer ball came within striking distance, would not automatically go after it; instead he'd hesitate, until another, more aggressive boy went after the ball, and then he'd just move along with the pack of kids, rarely touching the ball. His gentleness and lack of aggressiveness—traits which, incidentally, I see as major attributes that make him a kind and good person—did not serve him well in sports. So, like many boys who don't fit the mold, he opted out of sports early on, thus avoiding the discomfort or even public humiliation that so many boys face as marginal or poor athletes.[9]

Messner points out that coaches' narratives about boys often failed to recognize a range of personalities and instead assumed that boys have a natural affinity for sports—perhaps this is because boys like Miles leave sports, and the boys who stay fit their coaches' assumptions.

Parents and coaches told Messner that they thought it was important to treat girls "fairly" in sport. For many, this meant having parallel tracks of opportunities for boys and girls. AYSO separates boys and girls from its youngest teams, and LLB/S offers sex-integrated T-ball for its youngest participants (four to six years old) and then separates boys into baseball and girls into softball after they have played one season of T-ball and are at least five years old. This means that children in these sports older than five or six years old rarely get an opportunity to play organized coed sports.[10]

One coach told Messner that he coached boys' and girls' teams differently:

> The under-19 boys, we had practice last night, and you know I found myself yelling at a couple of them. Whereas when I coached the high school girls, I never—I won't say never, but almost never—screamed at them. That's just, I find that they kinda go into themselves and it's kind of, uh, it doesn't work out. Whereas the guys you can yell at him, tell him that he's going to do fifty laps and, and they don't hate you. There's no problem, do you know what I mean?[11]

For Messner, coaches who perceived boys as emotionally invulnerable and able to handle being yelled at were missing something important. "What they do not recognize, perhaps, is the many years of gender socialization that nine-year-old boys have already endured—from families, peers, popular culture, and sport—that has taught these boys to hide or repress their emotional and physical pain and not to show their vulnerabilities."[12] Messner's years of observing youth sports have shown him that young boys do have emotional responses to being yelled at, getting injured, or missing a play. The younger boys may cry, but this kind of emotional reaction becomes rare by age eleven or twelve. For Messner, boys do not naturally take well to being yelled at; they are socialized to expect it and socialized on how to react to it. Coaches' narratives about gender difference serve to naturalize the differences that they themselves are constructing.

Troubling Messages for Girls

Prior to the application of Title IX to athletics, cheerleading was often the only organized physical activity that schools offered for girls. When Title IX took effect, many schools sought to establish cheerleading as an official sport to fulfill the law's requirement to provide more sports opportunities for girls. To qualify as a sport under Title IX, the underlying mission of cheerleading could not be showcases at male sporting events and must be regulated competition between cheer squads. Cheerleading took on a judging system similar to competitive gymnastics. Cheerleading is the only sport where athletes compete in their own competitions and are obligated to support other athletic teams. According to sports scholar and critic Steven Overman, "Cheerleading, like beauty pageants, represents versions of ideal womanhood and sends the message that a girl's worth is based primarily on her appearance."[13] However strong and acrobatic cheerleaders are, they still compete in feminine clothing, hair bows, and full makeup. Thirty states recognized competitive cheerleading as a sport in the 2021–2022 school year, though as of 2024, the National Collegiate Athletic Association (NCAA) does not recognize cheerleading as a sanctioned championship sport.

Perhaps the most extreme example of strong, acrobatic girls held to unrealistic beauty standards is elite gymnastics. Journalist Joan Ryan's book, *Little Girls in Pretty Boxes*, draws from nearly one hundred interviews with athletes, coaches, and parents that she conducted in the 1990s. Ryan presents a scathing critique of the industry of elite child athletes and investigates injury, eating disorders, and the myriad ways coaches, parents, and national sports federations exploit child athletes. She calls the treatment of elite gymnasts and figure skaters "legal, even celebrated, child abuse" and argues that the American obsession with winning and fixation on beauty, thinness, and youth have combined to create an environment that decimates young girls' bodies and self-image.[14]

In gymnastics and figure skating, the ideal competitive body is a lean prepubescent body. For the girls that Ryan studied, puberty is an enemy to avoid at all costs, and many undernourish their bodies to prevent the onset of puberty. Starvation to put off puberty combined with strenuous exercise is a dangerous strategy because without menstruation, a girl's body does not produce sufficient estrogen. Low estrogen weakens bones and increases the risk of stress fractures. Most gymnasts do not start menstruating until they retire from the sport. Their careers are short, a matter of five or six years, so they tend to ignore injuries to compete in the window available to them. It was not until 1997 that the International Olympic Committee (IOC) required that female gymnasts be at least sixteen to compete; starting in the 1970s, champion gymnasts tended to be fourteen to seventeen years old. Other sports do not have the same age limitations, and girls as young as thirteen competed in the Tokyo Olympics in 2021.

From the 1950s to the 1990s, Olympic female gymnasts got smaller and smaller and younger and younger: in 1956, the top two female gymnasts were 35 years old and 21 years old; in 1968, individual all-around gold medalist Vera Caslavska was 26 years old, 5'3", and 121 pounds; in 1972, Olga Korbut at 17 years old, 4'11", and 85 pounds began the trend of child gymnasts; in 1976, Nadia Comaneci scored the first perfect 10.0 in Olympic history at 14 years old, 5', and 85 pounds. That same year, the U.S. team averaged 17 1/2 years, 5'3½", and 106 pounds; by 1992, the U.S. team averaged 16 years, 4'9", and 83 pounds.

The trend of "smallification" in gymnastics was a result of both the sport attracting (and coaches recruiting) tiny girls and intensive training stunting their growth. Many of these girls developed an unhealthy relationship with food. According to Ryan,

> Anorexics and bulimics usually are adolescent girls who tend to be perfectionists, who conform and please, who gauge their worth on other people's judgements. They are also girls who have been belittled and humiliated, who believe they are as worthless as the authority figures in their lives say they are. Gymnasts, in general, fit the bill.[15]

A 1992 study at University of Washington of 182 female athletes found that 32 percent practiced disordered eating. Among gymnasts, it was 62 percent.[16] Because these athletes train and undereat, they delay puberty, menstruation, and their final growth spurt, which could be lessened or never occur.

Image 9.2 Shannon Miller with her coach, Steve Nunno, at the 1992 Summer Olympics in Barcelona. Miller was 15, 4'7", and weighed around 70 pounds. At that Olympics, Miller won five medals. *Getty Images/ David Madison.*

Ryan tells the story of Christy Henrich. Going into the 1988 Olympic Games, she missed qualifying by 0.118 of a point. A judge told her that she needed to lose weight if she wanted to make the Olympics, and this set Henrich down a path of disordered eating. She saw losing weight as a serious goal in training for the 1992 Olympics.[17] Henrich ended up quitting gymnastics before then due to a serious struggle with anorexia and bulimia. She was in and out of eating disorder clinics for years. By June 1993, her weight had dropped to 52 pounds, and she was in danger of cardiac arrest. Her mother told Ryan,

> All the strength and determination Christy put into gymnastics, she has now turned against herself. Athletes are very stubborn, very determined, and they can turn all that against themselves. This is a very, very, very hard disease to reverse. She thinks she's not good enough. She thinks she's never been good enough. She's never learned to love herself.[18]

Henrich was able to gain weight through treatment and was up to 70 pounds in the fall of 1993, but, by spring of 1994, she was below 65 pounds again. She said in an interview,

> I still have a hard time with food. In gymnastics, they're always telling you, "Don't eat that, don't eat that." Pretty soon you become so paranoid that everyone is watching what you eat, and you feel everything is bad. You felt like you were really, really doing something wrong if you ate.[19]

That summer, her weight dropped to below 50 pounds, and she died of multiple organ failure.

Although Henrich's story is extreme, undernourishment, disordered eating, and delaying the onset of puberty is still common in sports that emphasize lowering weight. For example, in 2013 sixteen-year-old middle-distance runner Mary Cain began training in a Nike-sponsored program ran by Alberto Salazar, becoming the youngest runner to make the American track and field World Championships team at age seventeen. In the program, the coaching staff prioritized Cain losing weight to increase her competitive advantage. During her time of dieting and strenuous training, Cain stopped menstruating for three years, broke five bones, began self-mutilation, and considered suicide. A runner who trained in the same program under Salazar, Kara Goucher, told the *New York Times*,

> When you're training in a program like this, you're constantly reminded how lucky you are to be there, how anyone would want to be there, and it's this weird feeling of, "Well, then, I can't leave it. Who am I without it?" When someone proposes something you don't want to do, whether it's weight loss or drugs, you wonder, "Is this what it takes? Maybe it is, and I don't want to have regrets." Your careers are so short. You are desperate. You want to capitalize on your career, but you're not sure at what cost.[20]

Cain's public statements on her experience with Nike led to the suspension of Salazar and investigations into the program's training methods. Nike discontinued the program in 2019. In 2023, Nike and Salazar settled in a $20 million lawsuit brought by Cain alleging emotional and physical abuse.

Primary Source

Primary sources provide firsthand accounts of the topic under consideration. They emerge from particular times and places and allow us to imagine the context and thought processes that give rise to a perspective.

Mary Cain's interview with the *New York Times* on November 7, 2019

Courtesy of the New York Times

Context:

- Mary Cain was the fastest runner in a generation at age sixteen, and at seventeen was the youngest runner to make a World Championship team. In this interview with the *New York Times*, she describes training with Nike's Alberto Salazar and how the emphasis on losing weight affected her athletic performance and her well-being.
- In her interview, Mary Cain refers to "RED-S." This is an acronym for Relative Energy Deficiency in Sports, a syndrome of decreased athletic performance usually caused by malnutrition.

Discussion Questions:

- What makes a good coach? If you were a coach, how would you balance care for athletes with training for success?
- Do you agree with Mary Cain's suggestions of how to change the sport of running? Why or why not? If you could make one change in youth sports, what would it be?

The following are excerpts from a transcript originally published in the *New York Times*.

Mary Cain, "I Was the Fastest Girl in America, Until I Joined Nike"[21]

I was the fastest girl in America. I set many national records. And I was a straight-A student. When I was 16, I got a call from Alberto Salazar at Nike. He was the world's most famous track coach and he told me I was the most talented athlete he'd ever seen. During my freshman year in college, I moved out to train with him and his team full-time at Nike world headquarters. It was a team of the fastest athletes in the world. And it was a dream come true.

I joined Nike because I wanted to be the best female athlete, ever. Instead, I was emotionally and physically abused by a system designed by Alberto and endorsed by Nike. This is what happened to me. When I first arrived, an all-male Nike staff became convinced that in order for me to get better, I had to become thinner, and thinner, and thinner... Alberto was constantly trying to get me to lose weight. He created an arbitrary number of 114 pounds, and he would usually weigh me in front of my teammates and publicly shame me if I wasn't hitting weight. He wanted to give me birth control pills and diuretics to lose weight—the latter of which isn't allowed in track and field...

Here's a biology lesson I learned the hard way. When young women are forced to push themselves beyond what they're capable at their given age, they're at risk for developing RED-S. Suddenly, you realize you've lost your period for a couple months. And then a couple months becomes a couple years. And in my case, it was a total of three. And if you're not getting your period, you're not going to be able to have the necessary levels of estrogen to maintain strong bone health. And in my case, I broke five different bones...

I felt so scared. I felt so alone. And I felt so trapped. And I started to have suicidal thoughts. I started to cut myself... Nobody really did anything or said anything. So in 2015, I ran this race, and I didn't run super well. And afterwards, there was a thunderstorm going on. Half the track was under one tent. Alberto yelled at me in front of everybody else at the meet, and he told me that I'd clearly gained five pounds before the race. It was also that night that I told Alberto and our sports psych that I was cutting myself. And they pretty much told me they just wanted to go to bed. And I think for me, that was my kick in the head where I was like, "This system is sick."

... My parents bought me the first plane ride home. And they were like, "Get on that flight. Get the hell out of there." I wasn't even trying to make the Olympics anymore. I was just trying to survive. So I made the painful choice and I quit the team...

There is a systemic crisis in women's sports and at Nike, in which young girls' bodies are being ruined by an emotionally and physically abusive system. That's what needs to change, and here's how we can do it. First, Nike needs to change. In track and field, Nike is all powerful. They control the top coaches, athletes, races, even the governing body. You can't just fire a coach and eliminate a program and pretend the problem is solved. My worry is that Nike is merely going to rebrand the old program and put Alberto's old assistant coaches in charge. Secondly, we need more women in power. Part of me wonders if I had worked with more female psychologists, nutritionists and even coaches where I'd be today. I got caught in a system designed by and for men, which destroys the bodies of young girls. Rather than force young girls to fend for themselves, we have to protect them. I genuinely do have hope for the sport. And I plan to be running for many years to come. And so part of the reason I'm doing this now is I want to end this chapter and I want to start a new one.

Troubling Messages for Boys

Sporting culture has long presented self-sacrifice and "playing with pain" as signs of manliness. According to Messner,

> Athletes who are "playing with pain," "giving up their body for the team," or engaging in obviously highly dangerous plays or maneuvers are consistently portrayed as heroes; conversely, those who remove themselves from games because of injuries raise questions about their character, their manhood.[22]

Many male athletes get the message that their manliness depends on their ability to sacrifice their bodies. This message has drifted younger and younger with the expansion of youth sports and is particularly obvious in the sport of football. In the nineteenth and early twentieth centuries, muscular Christians treated football as masculine character building, while others saw football as necessary for military preparedness following World War I. For example, at the NCAA convention of 1925, Bishop William T. Manning of New York argued, "sports occupied just as important a part of our lives as prayers," and football promoter John L. Griffith argued that maintaining amateur status of college athletes was essential for maintaining the moral education of the game.[23] Football became associated with Thanksgiving around this time, promoting a narrative of national identity and martial strength, and Americans came to see football and physical education for boys as a path to good citizenship.

Critics of football argued that the violence inherent in the sport made it barbaric and savage, but influential Americans such as Theodore Roosevelt celebrated football's roughness and propensity for injury as a martial triumph. Roosevelt helped establish the NCAA to oversee football and other college sports after many schools considered abolishing football in 1905–1906 due to high levels of injuries. The NCAA implemented rule changes intended to cut down on injuries and eliminate the "uncivilized" aspects of the sport.[24]

In the early twentieth century, football expanded into high schools. Concern over injuries led to increased adult supervision of games and practices, dividing the game into four fifteen-minute quarters, and rule changes such as restrictions on pushing and pulling. These did not significantly reduce injuries, but the infrastructure of football expanded anyway. One piece of this infrastructure expansion was the New Deal Works Progress Administration's construction of athletic facilities for high schools across the country in the 1930s. These tended to include a track around a football field. Politicians such as Richard Nixon and Dwight Eisenhower had grown up playing football and promoted the sport as essential to American masculinity and a method of protection from foreign threats.[25] According to Nixon,

> Young Americans need the fighting spirit, the determination, the teamwork and the discipline which competitive athletics inevitably instill... Our young men are going to enter a competitive world where they experience failure as well as success. Let's not kid

ourselves, they won't be properly prepared for life if they have been shielded from the disappointment of failure.[26]

American male leaders envisioned football as a way to instill both cooperation and competitiveness, traits that would benefit American business and national strength. Due to infrastructure, narrative, and colleges desiring feeder programs, high-school football flourished after World War II.

The Pop Warner leagues, named for famed football coach Glenn Scobie "Pop" Warner, emerged in 1930s Philadelphia and provided football league play for boys and men ages 15–30. During World War II, the league shrank significantly with many participants serving in the war. After the war, the Pop Warner leagues began to target boys under fifteen to play football.

At the same time as league football moved younger, the discourse of overprotective mothers common in muscular Christianity reemerged. American author Philip Wylie coined the term "momism," meaning "excessive attachment to, or domination by, the mother."[27] The discourse of momism blamed mothers for standing in the way of their sons playing football and gaining the sport's purported benefits. In this discourse, the father's role was preventing their boys from becoming "sissies" by encouraging them to play football. Coaches and managers in the Pop Warner leagues drew up a code of ethics that included a recommendation against behaviors that would create a "'Momma's boy' stigma by a mother cuddling her son in front of other players and public with words

Image 9.3 Pop Warner Football "Giants" from Warren, Rhode Island, 1960. The boys pictured here are ages ten to twelve. Pop Warner football teams had played in Warren since 1954, and by 1964, boys as young as nine years old were playing in the league. *Courtesy of the Warren Athletic Hall of Fame.*

or gestures."[28] Football was a realm that excluded female influence, participation, and supervision; and therefore supporters of the sport such as Wylie presented it as the ideal sport to turn boys into men.[29] Team doctors and coaches successfully convinced many Americans that football's risks were manageable and that the benefit of cultivating traits of manhood outweighed any safety concerns.

Despite increasing awareness of the dangers of head trauma in tackle football, the sport remains highly popular at the high-school level and younger. Awareness of long-term consequences of repeated head trauma began to emerge in the 1980s. In the 1970s, a concussion without loss of consciousness (often called getting "dinged") was considered mild; therefore, no data was collected on the long-term consequences of mild concussions. A major survey conducted in 1983 revealed that one in five high-school football players likely experienced concussions at least once during a season; and in 1984, the *Journal of the American Medical Association (JAMA)* published findings that a concussion can make athletes more vulnerable to severe consequences if they experience a second brain injury.[30]

Robert Cantu was a neurosurgeon with a young son who played in the Pop Warner leagues. He read the *JAMA* article and developed concussion guidelines in 1986. Cantu's guidelines categorized concussions as Grade 1 (mild), Grade 2 (moderate), and Grade 3 (severe). In the case of a first mild or moderate concussion, Cantu recommended return to play if asymptomatic for one week.[31] For a second mild concussion, he recommended return to play two weeks later if asymptomatic for one week. For a second moderate concussion or a first severe concussion, Cantu recommended a minimum of one month with no football with a possibility of returning to play if asymptomatic for one week. With a second severe concussion or three mild or moderate concussions, Cantu recommended withdrawal of the player for the season. The American Academy of Neurology developed guidelines based on Cantu's recommendations in 1997. However, without significant data, there was still no scientific answer to the question: how many concussions are too many? In addition, the guidelines were contrary to what many parents, players, and coaches wanted—parents did not want their child to lose a spot on the team and the chance for a college scholarship, players wanted to be tough and not admit to injury, and coaches wanted to win with their best players on the field.

Throughout the 1990s, the National Football League (NFL) downplayed concussions as an occupational risk, but this began to change in over the next few decades. In 2002, neuropathologist Bennet Omalu identified evidence of brain damage on the autopsy of Mike Webster, a former NFL player for the Pittsburgh Steelers. He continued his research, and over 2005 and 2006, published his findings in the journal *Neurosurgery*. The NFL denied his finding that Webster's brain damage could be the result of multiple concussions and suggested instead that Webster's brain damage was the result of alcohol, steroid, or illicit drug use. In 2007, a scientific study on high-school football showed that even hits that did not result in concussions affected brain function. A team of Virginia Tech researchers studying young Pop Warner players came to a similar discovery and suggested that just as youth baseball has a "pitch count" (maximum number of pitches per player) to protect players' elbows, youth football should initiate a hit count to protect players' brains. (As of 2024, LLB/S does not provide pitch restrictions for softball despite similar risk of injury for softball players.) Although falling short of implementing a hit limit, Pop Warner did initiate changes in 2012 that limited hard contact to one-third of each practice and forbade drills that involved full-speed, head-on blocking and tackling from players more than three yards apart.

New York Times journalist Alan Schwarz began reporting on Omalu's research in 2007 and published follow-up stories over the next two years. Partly in response to Schwarz's reporting and partly in response to more and more research connecting concussions to long-term consequences, the U.S. House of Representatives held hearings on football head injuries in October 2009 and January 2010. Former NFL player Bernie Parrish called it the "sequel to the tobacco council," implying that just as big tobacco had established its own committee of experts to certify that smoking was not dangerous, the NFL had formed the Mild Traumatic Brain Injury Committee to certify that concussions were not risky. The NFL introduced a training program for youth football in 2012 called "Heads Up Football" meant to educate coaches on safe tackling techniques, but this did not reduce concussions among youth football players.[32]

In both 2000 and 2014, the American Academy of Pediatrics (AAP) recommended against body checking in youth hockey to cut down on concussions. The U.S. Soccer Federation implemented new safety policies in 2015 that prohibited players ten and younger from heading the ball and reduced the number of headers allowed in practice for athletes ages 11–13. Despite widening cultural awareness of the dangers of traumatic brain injuries following the December 2015 release of the movie *Concussion* (starring Will Smith as Bennet Omalu), the AAP has not recommended against tackling in football at any age.[33] Public health scholar Kathleen Bachynski argues that the AAP has dodged this recommendation because, "For over a century, football has been profoundly tied to what it means to be an American man and how to raise boys to meet those ideals."[34] Since football holds a special place in American culture and many families expect and encourage their boys to participate, it is unlikely that research on head injuries will have a significant impact on how football is played or who plays it.

Systemic racial inequalities mean that Black boys especially tend to see football as a path to college and success. With racial integration, football became one opportunity for Black boys to demonstrate value and superiority in previously white-dominated space. However, racially integrated teams still demonstrated racial stereotyping in determining the positions of players. Disproportionately allocating players to positions based on race is called "stacking." White players disproportionately played at quarterback, a position that many coaches saw as an intellectual position, whereas Black players were "stacked" in positions that deliver and receive the most hits (running backs, wide receivers, safeties, and cornerbacks).[35] Although the 2024 NFL season saw the most starting Black quarterbacks to date (fifteen of thirty-two teams), Black players make up 70 percent of the league and as such were still not proportionally represented at quarterback.

Racial integration of high-school sports coincided with the rise of televised football (including the glorification of "big hits" as entertainment value) and with sports scholarships as an increasingly viable path to a college degree and to the NFL. In addition, the death of twelve-year-old Tamir Rice, shot by a Cleveland police office while playing with an air gun on a playground in 2014, drew attention to the dangers of unsupervised play for Black children. According to Bachynski, "When unsupervised children can be perceived as suspicious and dangerous, supervised play in a socially valued sport such as football affords a substantial level of social protection."[36] This social protection is not without risk as we continue to learn about the long-term consequences of repeated head trauma for boys playing football.

Rethinking Youth Sports

What might be different if boys and girls played sports together? In her exploration of gender dynamics on a ten-and-under coed elite swimming team in California, sport sociologist Michela Musto found that boys and girls on the swim team treated each other as peer competitors and evaluated each other's skills based on their swim times, not gender. Boys did not express frustration at losing to girls; instead, they would agree with each other, "Sophia is fast." In setting goals to increase swim speeds, boys and girls would set sights on beating the fastest swimmers regardless of their gender. A swimmer wanted to be the fastest swimmer, not the fastest girl or the fastest boy.

Musto notes that swimmers prepare for team practices in sex-segregated dressing rooms and no policies require boys and girls to interact during unstructured times. During downtime, the team would tend to sex-segregate with the boys spending time with boys and the girls spending time with girls. The interactions between boys and girls during downtime tended to be playfully antagonistic—pouring cold water on each other's heads or splashing with pool noodles—but notably, these interactions did not contribute to a sense of gender hierarchy. The girls were not afraid of the boys, and neither group seemed to assume innate male superiority.[37]

In another rethinking of youth sports, some evangelical Christians have attempted to promote the values of play (creativity, self-discovery, equal opportunity) over the values of sports (competitiveness, obedience, hierarchy). The most prominent example of this is Upward Sports.[38] Caz McCaslin formed Upward Sports in 1995 to provide a noncompetitive sports environment for children to learn about Christianity. Upward's motto is "Every child is a winner," and this philosophy was put into practice by not keeping score and by providing every team member with equal playing time. Coaches rewarded players for good effort, team spirit, and "Christ-likeness" by giving out star stickers for players to wear on their jerseys. Significantly, these awards were not for individual athletic achievement but to recognize players who showcase religious values.

As McCaslin's vision expanded from one basketball league at one church in Spartanburg, South Carolina, to an organization that today involves half a million youth athletes participating in more than two thousand multisport clinics, camps, academies, and leagues in forty-seven U.S. states and seventy-two countries, one defining feature of Upward—not keeping score—disappeared. Upward introduced scorekeeping for athletes older than six so young athletes would learn how to handle winning and losing. Even in the years of not keeping score, there was a tendency for spectators, coaches, and even some players to mentally tabulate scores, so this innovation in youth play proved difficult to fully implement. If Upward was an attempt to embrace the values of play (creative, noncompetitive physical activity), the move to reintroduce scorekeeping brought it firmly back into the realm of sport.

Conclusions

In sex-segregated sports environments, girls and boys can receive troubling messages about their bodies. Some girls who play sports get the message that their bodies must be deprived of food to succeed. Some boys who play sports get the message that their bodies should be sacrificed for the game. These messages can have dire long-term consequences. The muscular Christians who first spearheaded organized sports for children were responding to a problem that they perceived as a failure of boys to develop manliness. This narrative continues to inform the structures, leadership, and implementation of boys' sports. Sports for girls largely emerged as an afterthought predicated on the examples of boys' sports or of cheerleading. Although some instances of sex-integrated sports exist, and there have been experiments with shifting the values of organized sports for children, it is worth considering what we want children to learn from sports and how to reform sports to achieve these goals.

Resources for Further Study
Media
Christopher Bell, dir. *Trophy Kids*. New York: HBO, 2013.

Online Archive

In 2019, Little League launched a media initiative honoring the girls and women who contributed to Little League. More content has been added every March to coincide with Women's History Month. "Girls with Game," https://www.littleleague.org/girls-with-game/.

Reading

Michael A. Messner, *It's All for the Kids: Gender, Families, and Youth Sports* (Berkeley: University of California Press, 2009).

Michela Musto and Michael A. Messner, eds. *Child's Play: Sport in Kids' Worlds* (New Brunswick, NJ: Rutgers University Press, 2016).

Steven J. Overman, *Sports Crazy: How Sports Are Sabotaging American Schools* (Jackson: University Press of Mississippi, 2019).

Chapter 10

Native American Mascots

For decades, Native American activists pressured the Washington, D.C., National Football League (NFL) team to drop the moniker "Redskins" because it is a slur demeaning to Native Americans.[1] Daniel Snyder, who bought the team in 1999, controversially announced in 2013 that the team would never change its name. He told reporters, "We'll never change the name. It's that simple. NEVER—you can use caps."[2] Beginning in 2005, National Collegiate Athletic Association (NCAA) policies led many colleges to rename their sports teams, but professional sports leagues have not adopted practices for monitoring team names, imagery, or mascots. In response to Snyder's comment on never changing its team name, the Oneida Indian Nation launched the "Change the Mascot" campaign, targeting the Washington football team. Over the next few years, the U.S. House and Senate, President Obama, and the United Nations all urged the Washington team to change its name. While the Washington football team held firm, the governor of California signed the California Racial Mascots Act, which eliminated the use of "Redskins" as a mascot in all the state's public schools.[3]

Several years later, amid Black Lives Matter protests erupting across the United States in the aftermath of George Floyd's death on May 25, 2020, at the hands of police officers, the pressure further mounted on the Washington football team. After threats of corporate boycotts, Snyder announced that the team would adopt a new name for the 2021 season and play under the name "Washington Football Team" for the 2020 season. The Navajo Nation released a statement on the name change: "July 13, 2020 is now a historic day for all Indigenous peoples around the world as the NFL Washington-based team officially announced the retirement of the racist and disparaging 'Redskins' team name and logo."[4] The context of the Black Lives Matter protests is important because the use of Native American mascots and imagery relies on understandings of whiteness and, particularly, a European colonial idea of whiteness built on the social, cultural, and religious exclusion of African and Native American residents of the New World.

During the time of contact and European expansion in the Americas, discourses of whiteness, civilization, and Christianity worked together to exclude and dehumanize Africans and Native Americans. This chapter addresses colonial narratives of race, muscular Christianity's use of Native American imagery, and the history of Native American mascots to show that Native American mascotry relies on a stereotype of native savagery that developed alongside the conflation of Christianity and whiteness.[5] Native American mascots emerged in the early twentieth century and remain in use in the twenty-first century, continuing to glorify the idea of native savage violence while holding this violence at arm's length from whiteness. Paying attention to the history of American Christianity helps us understand the rise of Native American mascots as well as the impassioned debates surrounding the use of Native American team names and imagery.

Civilization and Savagery

The concept of "civilization" is essential to understanding European interaction with Native Americans in the colonial era. Europeans saw Christianity as inherent to civilization and sought to remake Native Americans in their image through converting them to both Christianity and to European laws and customs. European colonization of the Americas became destructive to Native American communities by the middle of the seventeenth century. This was the same period in which witchcraft accusations and trials declined in Europe, and historian Ronald Niezen has suggested that European focus on the "lost souls" in the New World replaced their previous focus on internal heresy.[6] For example, the New England Puritans saw Indian rituals as devil worship comparable to English witchcraft. For the Puritans, this confirmed their own sense of moral superiority and justified dispossession and violence toward native populations. From their point of view, both Indian rituals and English witchcraft were instances of manipulating sacred power that existed beyond the bounds of Christian authority. In addition, the English perceived land to be unoccupied if it was uncultivated. New England magistrates vehemently rejected the argument that Indians preserved land for hunting and upheld the legal principle of *vacuum domicilium*, allowing them to seize land not being "used" by the natives. New England Puritans' emphasis on devil worship and *vacuum domicilium* confirmed their ideas: to be civilized required both Christianity and conformity to European norms, such as farming.[7]

European settlement in Virginia provides a further example of conflating civilization and Christianity. Early settlers of Virginia saw Indians as potential Christians who had a connection back to Noah and needed to be taught the error of their ways so that they could be divinely restored and redeemed. Using a few verses from Genesis 9, Europeans developed a theory of a "curse of Ham" that explained human origins and diversity, including skin color. In Genesis 9, Noah is angry at his son Ham and so curses Ham's son, Canaan. For European theologians, Noah's curse explained the existence of heathenism by identifying a lineage of people separated from God. Their theory described Noah's three sons as having distinct lineages: Ham in Africa, Shem in Asia, and Japheth in Europe. Affiliating Africans with the curse of Ham led to a European cultural assumption that people with darker skin were prone to sexual immorality, sin, and heresy. In addition,

Noah's curse positioned the descendants of Ham as servants of the descendants of Shem and Japheth, an arrangement that some used to justify slavery. Prominent English missionaries in the New World included American Indians in the lineage of Ham. Most seventeenth-century English theologians believed that the curse of Ham was reparable and that peoples of Africa could be brought into the fold. As such, Anglo-Virginians originally approached Indians as primitive pagans capable of redemption, but their lived experiences of war, struggle, and starvation soon challenged their vision of a utopian commonwealth where Indians would embrace English cultural, political, and religious forms and become "civilized."

The 1606 charter of the Virginia Company assumed that Christian conversion would naturally follow if Indians adopted the norms of English civilization. For Anglo-Virginians, Indian conversion meant acceptance of the Christian God *and* acceptance of English government and culture. The motley crew of Englishmen voyaging to settle Virginia were not ideal ambassadors for forming relationships with the Indians of the region, and by the end of the summer of 1607, native populations consistently attacked their settlement at Jamestown. By September, only 40 of the original 104 settlers were alive, and they were ill and malnourished. In mid-September, Indians brought corn to the starving settlers. Prominent settler John Smith interpreted this as divine providence: God had put terror into the savages' hearts. However, for the local tribal leader, a gift of food signaled the superiority of the giver, and the settlers' acceptance of the food was a sign of subordination.[8]

Desperate, the English sometimes ate human flesh, both English and Indian. When new Englishmen arrived, they saw this as a "creeping heathenism." Some English also left Jamestown to live among the Indians, who sometimes accepted the English and sometimes killed them. The English had not anticipated desertion of their settlement for Indian living, and they blamed Indians for their fellow countrymen's heathenism, believing there to be powerful witches among the Indians. The idea of creeping heathenism combined with a major Indian attack in 1622 that killed a third of the residents of Jamestown (more than 350 people) led to decreased interest in converting Indians. The Virginia Company officially abandoned any attempts to convert Indians in 1623, and when the company dissolved in 1624, it left behind a legacy that historian Rebecca Goetz called "hereditary heathenism": the idea that heathenism and Christianity are part of one's lineage, not a matter of individual choice or action.[9]

The idea of hereditary heathenism had social implications for both settlers and Indians. One of these was increased regulation of interracial marriage and sexual relationships. Over the mid- and late-seventeenth century, colonial authorities implemented harsher and harsher punishments for English/Indian and English/African fornication (sex outside of marriage). There were also punishments for English/English fornication, but these were not nearly as severe. Authorities relied on a religious justification for the severity of these punishments, claiming that sex with a heathen brought a shame to Christians and hurt the whole community by opening the community to the danger of creeping heathenism.[10]

Virginia's 1705 *Law of Servants and Slaves* conflated Christian with white and non-Christian with Indian and African, making religious presumptions about race explicit. According to Rebecca Goetz,

> The act prohibited the whipping of a "christian white servant naked." This was the first time that Christians were legally and explicitly defined by a physical distinction—skin color—and granted certain privileges based upon color and religious identity. The act also provided for the "christian care and usage of all christian servants" and forbade all "negros, mulattos, or Indians" from owning Christian servants. Christianity was thus strongly equated with whiteness.[11]

The 1705 law culminated a process by which Anglo-Virginians defined themselves by their religion and defined racial others (Africans and Indians) as incapable of it.

During the 1750s, stories of violent Indian attacks began to circulate widely among settlers. These stories described Indians killing families and used similar imagery: scalping, the ripping apart of families (sometimes in the form of a fetus ripped from a pregnant woman's body), and vivid gore of unburied bodies. Historian Peter Silver calls this the "anti-Indian sublime" and noted that as a rhetorical tool, it was effective at uniting English-speaking culture against Indians and against political leaders who might stand in the way of vengeance against Indians.[12] During the Seven Years' War (1756–1763), European settlers in the countryside felt that their only protection against Indian violence was solidarity. Promises to band together to fight the Indian enemy created a feeling of community, and sometimes countrymen would march long distances to come to the aid of other white settlers. The label of "white people" preserved this feeling of unity by relying on the assumption that being "white" affected how one thought and acted regarding the Indian war. "White people" tended to mean "the suffering European inhabitants of the colonies" and became the basis for political unity of settlers.[13] European/Indian relations during this time are important because this moment saw the creation of "whiteness" as well as stereotypes of native savagery that continue to inform debates over Native American mascots today.

Muscular Christianity and Playing Indian

Another important historical moment to consider is the era of muscular Christianity. This time period—the 1880s to the 1920s—is when organized and institutionalized opportunities for white men and boys to "play Indian" first emerged. These decades were a time of Protestant innovation as white Protestant male leaders grappled with their fears of white boys becoming overly feminized. Increasing waves of Jewish and Catholic immigration coupled with the great migration of rural, Black Southerners to the urban North contributed to white Protestant anxiety that these working-class populations were physically stronger. The arrival of these "outsiders" called attention to white Protestants' own physical weakness. This was also the time of the lowest populations of Native Americans in the United States—around two hundred thousand in 1910.[14]

During this era, the field of child psychology embraced a "recapitulation theory" of human development, claiming that as boys grew into men, they recapitulated (or repeated) each stage of humans' historical development from savage to civilized. Under this theory, the boy was a little savage who needed rigorous physical conditioning to develop his moral sense. One early organization that took this mission to heart was the Boy Scouts, founded in England in 1908 and imported to the United States in 1910. Historian Rayna Green has noted the prevalence of playing Indian in the early decades of the Boy Scouts:

> Learning to walk, stalk, hunt, survive like an "Indian," to produce beaded and feathered authentic outfits, to dance and sing authentic music, to produce tools and weapons, are the skills later to become fixed in the Order of the Arrow, Scouting's highest achievement.[15]

These organizations used Indian imagery and mimicry in their mission to move the boy from savage to civilized. "Playing Indian" in boys' organizations lumped all natives into the category of "savage," and this understanding informed their activities.

Image 10.1 The practice of Boy Scouts performing Indian dances continued well into the twentieth century. In this image, a Boy Scout troop from La Junta, Colorado, prepares to perform a "deer dance" for their annual Winter Ceremonial in December 1977. The *Denver Post* published this photo alongside a story on the Scouts' dance performance, wherein the reporter claimed that the Scouts became "as close to being true Indians as any son of modern American culture can."[16] *Getty Images/Ernie Leyba.*

Concurrent with the rise of boys' organizations, "Wild West" shows grew in popularity, cementing the image of the feather headdressed Indian riding into battle. The most famous show by far was Buffalo Bill's Wild West, organized and orchestrated by William Cody, who portrayed Buffalo Bill. Cody hired thirty-six Pawnees from Indian Territory to perform in his first show in Omaha in 1883. A highlight of the show was an Indian attack on the Deadwood mail coach, successfully defended by Buffalo Bill and his partner, sharpshooter Dr. William Frank Carver. According to historian L. G. Moses,

> Audiences thrilled to the Indian's attack on the Deadwood Stage. So entertaining was the Wild West show inspired by Buffalo Bill that within two years of its first appearance in Omaha, nearly fifty circuses, medicine shows, and rival Wild West shows had incorporated, and in some instances copied, many of its features.[17]

Between 1883 and 1933, hired Indians performed across the United States and Europe; each performance added weight to the idea that Native Americans were dangerous

Image 10.2 Lester Leutwiler was the first to portray Chief Illiniwek. He is pictured here next to the University of Pennsylvania mascot, Benjamin Franklin, at the University of Illinois football game against Penn on October 30, 1926. *Courtesy of University of Illinois Archives.*

attackers in elaborate costume and that white men could defeat them. These images endured through Hollywood Westerns and began to emerge in sports contexts.[18]

The use of Native American monikers for sports teams was widespread by the 1920s, and the following decades were the height of popularity for Indian mascotry. One of the early mascots who set the tone for this period was Chief Illiniwek, the mascot for the University of Illinois from 1926 until 2007. The man who first portrayed Chief Illiniwek, Lester Leutwiler, was a white high-school senior who attended nearby Urbana High School. In 1925, Leutwiler had attended a Boy Scout camp operated by Ralph Hubbard, an Indian dance enthusiast, where he learned how to emulate Indian dance movements and make Indian costumes. When Leutwiler returned from camp with his Indian costume, he and his fellow Scouts performed what they had learned for Urbana High School. Leutwiler's dancing led to an invitation to perform at the University of Illinois in October 1926 during the halftime show at their football game against University of Pennsylvania.

During the show, Leutwiler emerged from a hiding place just beyond the stands and led the band down the field, dancing all the way. After bands from both schools performed, Leutwiler as Chief Illiniwek and Penn's mascot met midfield to share a ceremonial catlinite pipe and left the field arm in arm. In this way, the halftime performance succinctly enacted a negotiation between factions that resulted in the Indian leaving the ground of the fight. According to historian Jennifer Guiliano,

> The interplay between Leutwiler and the UPenn mascot can be read as a reenactment of American colonialism that elided actual consequences of violence, disorder, and disruption in favor of a more neutral narrative of equitable relations and white succession... There is no place for the "Indian" to remain in the stadium. He appears only to contextualize white inheritance of the field, the stadium, and the university.[19]

The organizers of the 1926 halftime appearance of Chief Illiniwek intended this to be a one-time performance, but the act so thrilled the fans that Leutwiler reprised Chief Illiniwek periodically during the 1927 season. In the 1928 season, Leutwiler's performances became a regular feature of Illinois football halftime shows. Over the course of the late 1920s and 1930s, colleges and universities across the country adopted the "Illinois model" of a choreographed halftime show featuring mascots and band accompaniment.

The Call to Change the Mascot

In the late 1960s, the American Indian Movement sued to have Native American team names and logos dropped, and since then many Native Americans have continued to protest the use of Native American mascots in sports. Their activism sparked considerable backlash. Historian C. Richard King conjectures that the defense of Native American mascots constituted a defense of white masculinity. He theorizes that the strong response in favor of keeping these mascots was related to white, conservative defensiveness about the meaning of gender and race in the contemporary United States.[20] Similarly, in activist Andrea Smith's writing on white supremacy, she argues that the genocide of native peoples in North America is not separable from the enslavement of African Americans or from the othering of foreign-born American residents.[21] These three ongoing legacies work together to shore up white supremacy by creating an idea of "whiteness" that maintains its own superiority through different but complementary mechanisms. The multivalency of the construct of whiteness held in place by these three pillars can help explain why the debate over Native American mascots and team names became a proxy for debates over political correctness, minority rights, and American identity.

One provocative example is the protests and backlashes in Minneapolis and St. Paul in fall 1991 and winter 1992 when the cities hosted the World Series (Minnesota "Twins" versus Atlanta "Braves") and the Super Bowl (Washington "Redskins" versus Buffalo "Bills"). By the time of these protests, Native American parents had successfully campaigned against Native American mascot usage in Minnesota high schools, and twenty of the fifty schools that previously had Native American mascots/team names in the state had made a change. Police reported approximately three thousand protesters at the Super Bowl, the largest showing of Native American activism since the Wounded Knee protest in 1973. The Super Bowl protesters confronted the thousands of fans who attended the game. Vernon Bellecourt, the director of the American Indian Movement, called for the Washington football team to change its name, saying, "This is 1992. The name of your football team has got to be changed… The chop stops here."[22]

For the most part, the team's fans and administrators seemed bewildered by the protest. Washington's team owner at the time, Jack Kent Cooke, said in a radio interview after Washington's victory, "There is nothing in the world wrong with the name Redskins."[23] Given the prevalence of Western iconography in sports, Cooke may have seen his team's name as appropriate. This iconography is not limited only to Native Americans but also includes pioneers, cowboys, rangers, blazers, mavericks, mustangs, broncos, and buffalo/bison. Sociologist Laurel Davis writes, "In this sports symbolism, parts of the past that were perceived as destroyed or conquered by the colonists, such as buffalos or Native Americans, are now eulogized."[24] In the narrative of Western expansion and manifest destiny, all aspects of the "wilderness" are primitive, and conquering these lands and peoples achieves "civilization." Davis contends that the reason supporters defended the use of Native American iconography is that challenging that iconography hit a "raw nerve" by challenging a cherished version of American masculinity.

From the 1970s to the 1990s, nearly fifteen hundred institutions changed, retired, or reworked their native mascots, but at the end of the twentieth century, sports teams at more than twenty-five hundred schools still used Native American names, imagery, or references, including more than eighty colleges and universities.[25] The University of Illinois, home to Chief Illiniwek, was one of these. Despite protests from Native American students and faculty throughout the 1980s and 1990s, the University of Illinois continued to include

Chief Illiniwek's dance performances in its halftime shows. The University of Illinois did ban Chief Illiniwek's likeness from homecoming parades and was unable to bring him to away games at universities that had banned the presence of Native American mascots on their campuses, such as the University of Minnesota in 1993 and the University of Iowa in 1994.

The documentary film *In Whose Honor?* aired in 1997 and brought national attention to the University of Illinois' decision to continue its Chief Illiniwek tradition.[26] The film focused on Charlene Teters, a Native American graduate student at the University of Illinois in the 1980s who raised significant critiques of Chief Illiniwek. Teters moved to Champaign, Illinois, with her family from Santa Fe, New Mexico, to take a scholarship in the art department. In *In Whose Honor?* she tells her interviewer, "If I knew ahead of time what was ahead of me, I would not have come here, and I certainly would not have brought my kids here." Teters was unprepared for how saturated the town and campus were with images of Chief Illiniwek. She recounts how the head of the art department encouraged her to keep her head down, get her degree, and get out of there.

Teters said that she probably would have followed that advice, except that her children convinced her to take them to a college men's basketball game. She tried to prepare them for what they might see—paint, war chants, feathers, the dancing chief—telling her children to ignore it and just enjoy the game. At the game, when Chief Illiniwek came to the floor to dance wearing buckskin and a long, feathered headdress, Teters watched her children sink in their seats. She becomes emotional in the interview, and her voice cracks as she says, "I saw my daughter try to become invisible and my son try to laugh. It gave me a sadness that still won't leave me… what I saw in my children was a blow to their self-esteem, and it still makes me angry."

Juxtaposed with Teters's recounting of this experience is an interview with University of Illinois Trustee Susan Gravenhorst who suggests that Native Americans who find Chief Illiniwek offensive do not understand the reverence that the community has for the chief. "Perhaps they ought to come to a game," she said, "I can't imagine that—the chief who deports himself, whomever serves as the chief, deports himself with such dignity and such solemnity. I can't imagine that that can be perceived as a racial insult or as a slur on the Native American community. To me, it's a compliment." By placing Gravenhorst's interview directly after Teters's tearful recollection of her and her children's experience at a game, the film nudges the viewer to sympathize with Teters and see the trustee as arrogant and out of touch. Largely because of attention brought to the issue by *In Whose Honor?*, the University Board of Trustees commissioned a report to investigate the positions for and against Chief Illiniwek.

Image 10.3 Chief Illiniwek in 2004. A University of Illinois student portrays Chief Illiniwek at the halftime football show on October 16, 2004, in Champaign, Illinois. The university discontinued Chief Illiniwek performances in 2007. *Getty Images/Jonathan Daniel.*

Primary Source

Primary sources provide firsthand accounts of the topic under consideration. They emerge from particular times and places and allow us to imagine the context and thought processes that give rise to a perspective.

Excerpts from "The Chief Illiniwek Dialogue: Intent and Tradition vs. Reaction and History," Report to the Board of Trustees of the University of Illinois

©*The Board of Trustees of the University of Illinois 2020, all rights reserved. Permission to use these materials may be obtained from the University of Illinois.*

Context:

- In January 2000, the Board of Trustees of the University of Illinois passed a resolution to gather information on the controversy surrounding halftime performances of Chief Illiniwek. For the next several months, they solicited feedback from alumni, students, faculty, staff, and the public. The board appointed Louis B. Garippo to compile a report and present it to the board on August 1, 2000.[27]

What follows is the portion of the report written by John Madigan, the student who portrayed Chief Illiniwek at the time. He describes the origin and nature of the halftime dance.

Discussion Questions:
- How does Madigan support continuing the Chief Illiniwek performance? Do you agree or disagree with his position? Why?
- If you were a board member, what would be your most important priority in deciding whether to keep or discontinue Chief Illiniwek? What information in Madigan's statement would be most useful to you in making your decision? Why?

The Dance
John Madigan, Chief Illiniwek XXXIII
Fancy dancing

The halftime performance of the University of Illinois' Chief Illiniwek takes its movements from the Native American style of dancing called "fancy dancing" or "fancy feather dancing," which is considered the brightest and fastest of Native American dance styles.

Fancy dancing did not originate from any old dance or style. Fancy dancing originated as a method of entertaining visitors at reservations in the early 1920s and to display aspects of Native culture that were not restricted for ceremonial use. The outfit combined the popular bustles of traditional dancers and made them larger, brighter, and more exciting and added feathers, fluffs, and colors wherever they would fit. Today, fancy dancers' regalia contains very intricate feather patterns and colors, including neon colors and other eye-catching patterns. Fancy dancing belongs to no one tribe—it started in Oklahoma and is now all over the country, with some differences in dress and style in the North.

Fancy Dancers dance much faster than all other styles, and it is sometimes freestyle, with dancers doing such wild things as the splits and back flips. Many fancy dancers feel that these movements are necessary to win the top prizes and cash awards at fancy dancing competitions. These movements may be less common due to the level of skill required to perform them.

The dance style is of two types: a basic simple step while dancing around the drum and a "contest" step with fast and intricate footwork combined with a spinning up and down movement of the body…

... many powwows or grounds where fancy dancing competitions are held are athletic fields or similar venues. Fancy dancing troupes travel in the Southwest to perform shows for tourists and visitors.

The Chief dances a fancy dance
The performance of Chief Illiniwek is very similar to fancy dancing seen at powwows today. The basic step in the dance is the double step, which has been part of the performance since its inception. The later part of the dance involves intricate footwork and fast spinning movements. The split jumps and high kicks display the dancer's skill and ability. Just as fancy dancing has changed and evolved since the 1920s, so has the performance of Chief Illiniwek. There is no fault in either one, since this form of dancing was designed as an artistic expression. Artistic expression will vary from individual to individual, and different people will perform different steps or movements completely different. Certain movements in the performance of Chief Illiniwek have stayed the same for the sake of consistency from individual to individual. Because the role of Chief Illiniwek is considered to be bigger than the individual performing, there was a need to be somewhat consistent from year to year and from Chief to Chief. The performance of Chief Illiniwek can neither be classified as "non-authentic" or "authentic," because it has changed and evolved just as fancy dancing has over the past century. Would those who argue that Chief Illiniwek's performance and dress are not authentic also argue that today's fancy dancers who use neon colored feathers and beadwork are not authentic as well?

Native American influence on the Chief's dance
The first three individuals who portrayed Chief Illiniwek (Lester Leutwiler, Webber Borchers, and William Newton) studied Native American dancing (especially fancy dancing) for years before they held the role of Chief Illiniwek. They became interested in Native American culture through their involvement with Eagle Scouts and they all spent time at Ralph Hubbard's summer camp designed to teach and appreciate fancy dancing. Leutwiler used the steps and skills that he learned through studying Native American dancing to help create the performance of Chief Illiniwek. Leutwiler stated, "This performance took place at a time when Native Americans in the West were installed on reservations and struggling for survival. Many in the area of Champaign-Urbana had only heard stories about the… Indians. I simply wanted to prove there was another side to the culture that most people were unaware of… the inspirational side, the beautiful side, the meaningful side." When Webber Borchers traveled to the Pine Ridge Reservation during his tenure as Chief Illiniwek, he spent many hours with several of the Sioux men on the reservation learning and perfecting his dance steps. Upon his departure, they inducted him as an honorary tribal member.

In 2005, the NCAA Executive Committee adopted a new policy that "prohibited NCAA colleges and universities from displaying hostile and abusive racial/ethnic/national origin mascots, nicknames or imagery at any of the eighty-eight NCAA championships."[28] In November 2004, as part of the development of this policy, the NCAA asked thirty-three schools to submit self-evaluations to determine the extent of the use of Native American imagery on their campuses. Fourteen of these schools either decided to remove references to Native Americans or the NCAA determined that they did not use Native American imagery.[29] Most of these had team names such as "Warriors" that could be retained with new mascots and logos.

The NCAA concluded that nineteen colleges including the University of Illinois did not comply with their policy and would be unable to participate in NCAA championships with their current mascots.[30] Through an appeal process where colleges demonstrated that their teams' namesakes were formally condoned by the tribe they named, the NCAA granted waivers to five colleges to retain their use of Native American team names.[31] The University of Illinois successfully appealed to retain the name "Illini" for their sports teams because the name did not refer to a particular tribe, but they discontinued the appearances of Chief Illiniwek in 2007 to comply with NCAA rules.

Unofficial "Chiefs" continued to show up at Illini games, and not until August 2017 did the school officially ban the playing of its "war chant" at games. Earlier that summer, the Unite the Right protest in Charlottesville, Virginia, brought national attention to white supremacy groups. The *Chicago Tribune* interviewed Charlene Teters, the Native American activist who had fought against the use of Chief Illiniwek in the 1980s and 1990s and appeared in *In Whose Honor?*, on her response to the university's retiring of the war chant. She said in the 2017 interview, "It's interesting in light of Charlottesville. The power of imagery can move people. The Confederate flag and swastikas have power. Words have power. These chants are race-based. It's time for the university to move away from it."[32]

For Teters and other activists, Native American mascots are reminders of white supremacist patterns in American society. Mass attention to the Unite the Right rally and the death of protester Heather Heyer during the event brought white supremacy into a national conversation that touched on anti-Black sentiments and antisemitism. Native American activists such as Teters were able to connect this to the racism and white supremacy bound up in Indian mascots and pressure institutions such as the University of Illinois to end practices like its war chant and fans dressing in feathers.

Another major target for Native American activists has been the Washington football team. One challenge to the name "Redskins" came in the form of a legal battle over trademark usage. Since 1946, federal trademark law has included a provision that allowed the government to deny trademarks that are disparaging or offensive to a group of people. In 2015, a federal court upheld the canceling of the Redskins' trademarks due to the court's finding that the name and images were disparaging to a substantial segment of the Native American population. However, in 2017, another court case reached the Supreme Court on a similar matter. The Asian American rock band "The Slants" had its trademarks canceled because its name was a derogatory slur for Asians. In this case, the Supreme Court ruled that The Slants could keep their trademarks because, even though their name was based on a derogatory racist slur, the group employed this term as a method of reclaiming and disarming Asian stereotypes. Daniel Snyder, owner of the Washington football team, saw the case as a victory for his cause, stating that he was "thrilled" by the decision.[33] Although Snyder saw this as a victory, it is unlikely he would have been able to argue that his team's use of a derogatory racist slur was for the purpose of dismantling stereotypes.[34]

A few days before the 2014 Super Bowl, the National Congress of American Indians in association with Change the Mascot released the video "Proud to Be." It did not air on television at the time but had an ad spot during the NBA playoffs that June. The video is a two-minute montage of Native Americans that shows some in tribal dress and others in casual clothing in settings such as classrooms or doctors' offices. The narrator lists a series of one-word labels including names of tribes, careers like "teacher" and "soldier," and adjectives ranging from negative descriptors like "forgotten" to positive descriptors like "resilient." In the closing to the video, the narrator says, "Native Americans call themselves many things. The one thing they don't?" He stops speaking as the image on the screen shows a Washington Redskins helmet.[35]

Image 10.4 Washington Redskins helmet. The Washington, D.C., football team uniforms included helmets featuring a Native American in profile with feathers until the team dropped the moniker "Redskins" in 2021. *Getty Images/Dorling Kindersley.*

In August 2014, the Washington football team released the video "Redskins Is a Powerful Name." It opens on a nearly identical image of the team helmet, zooming in on the icon of an Indian head and feathers. The two-minute video is a montage of interview clips with Native Americans who defend the name "Redskins" as a powerful warrior name. The video points out that the Washington Redskins logo was designed by a Native American and approved by Native American leaders. Native Americans in the video express concerns about other challenges in their communities such as health care, alcoholism, and reservation living conditions. According to one interviewee, "I feel like it's too insignificant to talk about when there's bigger issues in Indian country." And another attests, "If you could help in any other way, it would be greatly appreciated, but the mascot issue isn't an issue for us, not for Native Americans."[36] The video makes the claim that focusing attention on Native American mascots is detrimental because it distracts from more meaningful actions that could improve Native American life.

The closing screen of "Redskins Is a Powerful Name" directs viewers to visit Redskinsfacts.com to learn more. This site is no longer available, but in 2014 the site read:

> Here at RedskinsFacts.com, we're thinking football fans. We're passionate about the game, and even more passionate about the "Burgundy and Gold." None of us believe in offending or discriminating against people of any ethnicity for any reason.
>
> We believe the Redskins name deserves to stay. It epitomizes all the noble qualities we admire about Native Americans—the same intangibles we expect from Washington's gridiron heroes on game day. Honor. Loyalty. Unity. Respect. Courage. And more.[37]

The site made the argument that the name "Redskins" was not offensive because a significant number of Native Americans did not find it offensive and because the team did not intend it to be offensive.

Broadcasting professor Andrew Billings and communication studies professor Jason Black analyzed YouTube comments for "Proud to Be" and "Redskins Is a Powerful Name." In the case of the Washington football team, advocates of changing the team name pointed to America's history of dehumanizing Native Americans and argued that this dehumanization is preserved in names and images that treat Native Americans as objects, not people.[38] Billings and Black recommend increased education in U.S. schools about Native Americans so that residents would be better able to see why these mascots are not just offensive but also stand in the way of cross-cultural understanding. In addition to education, the authors note that economic boycotting of teams, sports journalists and media outlets refusing to say/print derogatory names, and legal challenges to disparaging naming and iconography are opportunities to push for an end to the exploitation and degradation of Native Americans through mascotry.

In the summer of 2020, following weeks of Black Lives Matter protests across the country, the Washington football team announced that it would change its name. The announcement came after significant pressure from FedEx, Nike, and Pepsi, as well as other corporations. FedEx held the naming rights for the stadium in D.C., Nike made the team's uniforms, and Pepsi was their snack and beverage partner. Over June and July 2020, all three companies experienced growing pressure from shareholders to sever ties with the Washington football team if they refused to retire the name "Redskins." The investors' letter to the CEO of FedEx tied their demands to the Black Lives Matter protests sweeping the country. The letter read in part:

> In light of the Black Lives Matter movement that has focused the world's attention on centuries of systemic racism, we are witnessing a fresh outpouring of opposition to the team name. Therefore, it is time for FedEx to meet the magnitude of this moment, to make their opposition to the racist team name clear, and to take tangible and meaningful steps to exert pressure on the team to cease using it.[39]

Summer 2020 saw hundreds of corporations releasing statements pledging to take antiracist actions. Products that relied on Black caricatures such as Aunt Jemina and Uncle Ben began rebranding. Social media platforms were filled with discussions of whether corporate statements were lip service or an indication of changing policies. Accusations of hypocrisy led to corporations taking measures such as making large donations to racial justice organizations, conducting workplace diversity training, making Juneteenth a company holiday, and instituting efforts to decrease discrimination against Black shoppers.

In addition to the financial pressure on the Washington football team, summer 2020 saw a groundswell of sports journalists refusing to use the term "Redskins" in their coverage. Peter King, a longtime NFL reporter for *Sports Illustrated*, had stopped using the name in 2013. He wrote in a note in one of his articles, "Here's what it came down to for me: Did I want to be part of a culture that uses a term that many in society view as a racial epithet? The answer kept coming back no."[40] Others followed suit, and by 2020, many had adopted the practice of referring to the team as "the Washington football team" or "Skins." Snyder's team played the 2021 NFL season under the temporary name "Washington Football Team" and adopted the name "Commanders" in 2022.

Conclusions

A few years before the Washington football team announced its intention to change its name, C. Richard King expressed doubts that such a name change would lead to the end of Native American mascots:

> I worry that the success may not be transferrable precisely because for many the problem is the slur… [I]t is this logic that makes the Blackhawks and the Chiefs seem acceptable to most in the public: the r-word is a slur; it is bad; it must go; however, American Indian mascots can be okay, positive, and defensible. This contradictory thinking, which has its roots in white entitlement, the appropriations of settler colonialism, and erasures and inventions of anti-Indianism, remains undisturbed by the focus on the slur and may make it difficult to harness the momentum…[41]

Time will tell whether Snyder's decision in summer 2020 was a tipping point or an isolated event. Even as Native Americans celebrated the changing of the Washington football team's mascot, activists set their sights on other professional teams that relied on stereotypes of Native Americans such as the Atlanta "Braves" and the Kansas City "Chiefs." The Cleveland "Indians" changed their name to the Cleveland "Guardians" in 2022; shortly after Cleveland's announcement, the Kansas City Chiefs discontinued using the horse "Warpaint" in cheerleading performances but maintained their team name.

The history of Indian mascotry in the United States is tied to a long history of white Americans "playing Indian." Whether through settler violence in the eighteenth century, boys' organizations in the early twentieth century, or halftime entertainment spectacles from the 1920s to today, some white people have enjoyed stereotypes of Native Americans as savage warriors. This is a legacy of European Christian settlement in the Americas. The European conflation of Christianity, civilization, and whiteness created and maintained stereotypes of Native American savagery. To admit that these stereotypes are inaccurate and harmful would be to admit that there was no essential tie between whiteness, Christianity, and civilization; that white dominance was undeserved; and that perhaps Western conquest was itself a savage act.

Resources for Further Study

Media

Jay Rosenstein, dir. *In Whose Honor?* 1997; Beacon, NY: New Day Films.

Online Archive

A time line of the University of Illinois' documents and decisions regarding its mascot is available from the American Indian Studies Program. "Mascot Timeline," https://ais.illinois.edu/resources/mascot-information/mascot-timeline.

Reading

Jennifer Guiliano, *Indian Spectacle: College Mascots and the Anxiety of Modern America* (New Brunswick, NJ: Rutgers University Press, 2015).

C. Richard King, *Redskins: Insult and Brand* (Lincoln: University of Nebraska Press, 2016).

Ellen J. Staurowsky, "American Indian Imagery and the Miseducation of America," *QUEST* 51 (1999): 382–92.

Chapter 11

Doping

On January 18 and 19, 2013, Oprah Winfrey's OWN network aired a two-part interview with Lance Armstrong. In the interview, he admitted for the first time to using banned performance-enhancing techniques in all seven of his Tour de France victories. The setting was the lobby of the Four Seasons Hotel in Austin, Texas, and Winfrey and Armstrong sat in leather chairs angled half toward each other, half toward the camera. Between the two was an end table holding two glasses of water with matching metal straws. Clearly, Winfrey had considered how to make the atmosphere of the interview feel intimate and personal rather than cold and legalistic.

Over the course of two ninety-minute segments, Winfrey asked hard questions, some of which Armstrong answered and some of which he avoided. When Winfrey asked, "Do you owe David Walsh an apology?," Armstrong responded, "That's a good question."

Winfrey pushed, "Do you owe David Walsh an apology who for thirteen years has pursued this story, who wrote for the *Times*, who has now written books about you and this entire process?" To which, Armstrong managed to reply, "I would, I would, I'd apologize to David."[1] Armstrong's tendency to admit that an apology was justified but to not deliver it characterized the interview as a whole. Widely regarded as a partial apology at most, the public expressed disappointment in Armstrong's dodging of responsibility.

This chapter investigates two examples of professional athletes accused of doping and considers their moments of confession: Lance Armstrong and Major League Baseball. Confession is a religious ritual that can provide a way for wrongdoers to achieve redemption in their communities. The performance-enhancement scandals in Major League Baseball and Lance Armstrong's career provide a window on failed confessions, on athletes unable to achieve redemption after disappointing the public. These failed confessions reveal an underlying contradiction: American culture tends to preserve the idea that sport is morally valuable and therefore holds athletes to a high moral standard; however, athletes tend to see doping as a systemic problem, rather than an individual problem, and therefore they are unlikely to take responsibility for their actions.

Historical Understandings of Confession, Sporting Morality, and Doping

Nineteenth-century American Protestantism has influenced our cultural understandings on the importance of public confession and the moral value of sport. Turning to evangelist Charles Finney's innovation, the "anxious bench," we can see how public confessional practices in the early nineteenth century laid the groundwork for American cultural expectations of shame and regret as essential for forgiveness. Finney was a revival preacher and would provide a row of seats between himself and the audience. Finney called for individuals to approach this bench of seats, confess their inner shames and torments, and leave the bench on the right path to salvation. When sinners were on the bench, the preacher prodded them with questions, attempting to reveal the root of their shame and, in so doing, provide a path for confession and redemption. Historian of American religions Kathryn Lofton describes the ritual as such:

> The bench was the climactic site in the revival process, setting sinners physically apart from the audience as symbols of sin, and of their own failure to make a break with their sinful past: they were separated by their failures, and by their failure to cease their failures.[2]

For Finney, all sins were voluntary, meaning they stemmed from the will of the sinner; and because of this, all sinners had the ability to reshape their wills and cease sinful ways. He saw the anxious bench as a tool to accomplish this. Finney's most famous use of the anxious bench was in Rochester, New York, in 1830–1831. Over the course of six months in Rochester, he preached ninety-eight sermons and boasted more than twelve hundred conversions. Inspired by Finney's claims of numerical success, other revivalists adopted his tactics, and features such as emotional public confession became common across New England.[3]

One cultural site that preserved the idea of shamed sinners set apart and forced to name their sins to achieve salvation was the *Oprah Winfrey Show*. Lofton's analysis of Winfrey's interview structure reveals a parallel with the anxious bench.[4] Winfrey's interviews often followed a predictable ritual format: the guest submits to questioning and prodding from Winfrey, reveals wrongdoing and inner torment, and is set free from this pain by Winfrey's therapeutic self-help. Lofton writes, "If Charles Finney was pastor to nineteenth-century America, it is not an overstatement to suggest that Winfrey is his twenty-first-century parallel."[5] Winfrey's successful format widely influenced television programming and remains a staple for interview shows.

A second historical influence to consider is muscular Christianity. As addressed in other parts of this book, muscular Christianity was a movement of Protestant men who defined manliness as a combination of Christian morality and athleticism. Protestant Americans enjoyed the idea that team sports could contribute to spiritual growth. Sports sociologist Jay Coakley summarizes the trend this way: "In large part, organized sports became important because they could be used to train loyal and hardworking people dedicated to achievement and production for the glory of God and country."[6] This sense that sport contributed to one's morality continues to inform popular perceptions of sport and athletes. However, as Coakley has pointed out,

> The mere fact that people do or do not play sports tells us little about their overall lives and how they go about developing their sense of who they are, how they are connected to others, and what is important in their lives. This is why hundreds of studies have not given us the evidence we need to determine whether sports do or do not build character.[7]

The question of whether sport builds character remains unanswered, but American culture tends to adopt the muscular Christian perspective that sport participation is inherently good and moral.

One of the major challenges to the idea that sport is morally good is the prevalence of doping. The term "doping" likely originated with cheating in horse racing by drugging a horse to be slower. Organized criminals were often responsible for horse doping, and this may have led to the association of drug use in competition with criminality, corruption, and disrepute. However, for the first half of the twentieth century, American institutions applauded innovations in drug performance enhancements. For example, in the 1950s, amphetamine use was widespread on both the USSR and USA Olympic teams. Both countries had relied on these drugs for troop invigoration during World War II, and when the war ended, troops returned home and spread the word about "pep pills." It was not until the 1960s that American media and policy makers increasingly connected amphetamines with social degeneracy and counterculture movements. At the same time, the deaths of high-profile Tour de France cyclists who used amphetamines increased concern about the safety of drug use during sport. This contributed to the International Olympic Committee's (IOC) developing a list of banned substances and testing for these directly pre-competition, which they claimed would preserve amateurism and fair play.

In their exploration of how the governing institutions of sport became interested in banning substances, sports historians Paul Dimeo and Verner Møller proposed that those in charge relied on an idealized understanding of sport as a competition between amateurs (not paid professionals) who seek to measure natural talents against each other. The authors point out that this noble understanding of international competition was unrealistic in the 1960s and remains unrealistic today.[8] Sports scientist David Mottram concurs, writing that in the 1960s, "The fear of bringing sport into disrepute meant that many sporting authorities denied the possibility that doping took place, therefore, anti-doping testing was, at best, haphazard."[9] By the mid-1970s, several constituencies emerged with a vested interest in painting doping as a practice condoned by communist countries and opposed by the moral West. As Dimeo puts it, "In the politics of the Cold War the propaganda machine told the public that the communists were all evil, whereas in the West the small minority of wrongdoers did not represent the morality of the people."[10] Dimeo presents this propaganda as disingenuous and critiques anti-doping as moral theater that does not ensure sporting equality.

In the 1970s, the IOC lifted the requirement that an athlete be an unpaid amateur, allowing paid professionals to compete in the Olympics. Over the course of the 1970s and 1980s, another drug replaced amphetamines as the drug of choice for performance enhancement: steroids. Because athletes could use steroids in the off season to produce muscle gains that would impact in-season competition, anti-doping agencies added out-competition testing in an effort to detect steroid use year-round. The IOC began testing for steroids in 1976, but this did not stop doping. As Dimeo put it, "It ended a hundred years of relatively open drug use, and ushered in a new period of deceit, underground innovation, high profile 'catches,' and difficult decisions on borderline drugs."[11]

By investigating the development of anti-doping policies, we can see that the muscular Christian ideas that sport is inherently good and that "pure" sport benefits society still impact institutions today. The primary organization that enforces anti-doping policies in the United States is the U.S. Anti-Doping Agency (USADA), which formed in 2000. According to USADA's website, "Athletes who dope seek to gain an unfair advantage over their competitors, thereby undermining their competitors' hard work and threatening the credibility of their sport. This win-at-all-costs attitude violates the underlying values that make sport meaningful to society."[12] Although USADA does not spell out the "underlying values" that it mentions, its stance seems to infer a muscular Christian understanding of sport as morally valuable.

In USADA's words, winning at all costs is a detriment to sport, but this quality informs sports participation at a basic level. As sport sociologist Shirl Hoffman has noted, to fully engage in sporting competition an athlete must be willing to embrace the "killer instinct," a quality Hoffman defines as "ridding yourself of sympathies for your opponent that might inhibit you in applying your full resources to furthering your own cause."[13] This quality is a major challenge to the idea of sport as morally valuable—is it morally admirable to achieve one's success at the expense of another? Rather than addressing this ethical dilemma built into the structures of sport, anti-doping agencies tend to rely on muscular Christian understandings of sport. As we turn to our case studies, we will see that the muscular Christian association of sport and morality pervades anti-doping actions and that the American public tends to expect an anxious-bench-style confession from athletes caught doping.

Major League Baseball

From 1971 to 1990, seven labor disputes between Major League Baseball's (MLB) players' union and team owners disrupted season play. The 1994 season brought the worst dispute; beginning in August 1994, players went on strike for 234 days, resulting in the only cancellation of the World Series since World War I. Fans, players, journalists, and team administrators all worried that the strike spelled the end of an era for professional baseball. A number of players retired early, Michael Jordan's transition to professional baseball was cut short, and disappointed fans grew cynical over what they saw as rich people arguing about money.

Fast-forward to the summer of 1998 when Mark McGwire and Sammy Sosa were locked in a race to beat Hank Aaron's home-run record, and fans returned to the sport with gusto. The media loved Mark McGwire. As journalists Mark Fainaru-Wada and Lance Williams saw it, "Something about McGwire's appearance—the red hair and the freckled, craggy face that sometimes burst into a winning smile—seemed to invite affectionate hyperbole."[14] Teams set records for attendance at games; McGwire's team, the St. Louis Cardinals, boasted a record-setting attendance of more than three million home tickets for the season.

In August of McGwire's home-run summer, a journalist caught sight of androstenedione, a steroid commonly known as "andro," in McGwire's locker and tried to raise the alarm about potential drug use in Major League Baseball. However, the backlash was not against McGwire but against the reporter, Steve Wilstein. At the time, andro was a legal substance that anyone could buy at a supplement store, but the Olympics and the National Football League had banned the drug. In response to the story, the Cardinals' manager threatened to ban the Associated Press from the clubhouse, and though Commissioner Bud Selig promised an investigation into the health effects of andro, he was clear that no action would be taken against McGwire.

According to MLB player Jose Canseco, steroid use was widespread, and everyone benefited from it—the players, the owners, the fans, and the media. He writes,

> Looking back, I think the country had been in the grip of a collective delusion. People were wondering, foolishly, how the game had become so damn *big*, and they looked everywhere for explanations... The ballparks were smaller, they said. The strike zone was smaller. The bats were better and more powerful... The entire analysis was laughable. The answer was clear and any fool could sum it up in one word. The word was *steroids*.[15]

With fans returning to the sport in record-breaking numbers, Major League Baseball had little motivation to pursue a doping case against McGwire. The success of the 1998 season was a relief after the struggles to appease fans disappointed by the 1994 World Series cancellation.

Inspired by the attention McGwire and Sosa garnered, as well as the common locker-room knowledge that steroids played a part in their success, other players jumped on the steroid train. Barry Bonds showed up to spring training in 1999 with an extra fifteen pounds of muscle, unheard of for an athlete in his mid-thirties. Though some journalists harbored suspicions that Bonds's larger physique was the result of steroids, the example of the nearly banned and reviled Steve Wilstein dissuaded them from investigating Bonds's drug use.[17] That season, Bonds blew out his elbow because he had gained muscle too quickly and overtaxed his tendons. It could have been a career-ending injury, but he was back playing seven weeks later. The media bought the story that the injury was the result of a long baseball career, and coverage did not mention steroids.

Images 11.1 and 11.2 Jose Canseco played Major League Baseball for seventeen seasons and began using steroids in 1984. He is pictured left in the mid-1980s when he played for the Oakland A's and right in 2000 when he played for the Tampa Bay Devil Rays. Canseco wrote about playing baseball in 2005, "If you compare the baseball player of today with the players of twenty years ago, you'll find that now they are bigger, faster, and stronger. The reason for that is simple: Competition is fierce, the money is unbelievable, and a majority of the players have been using steroids."[16] *Getty Images/Rich Pilling.*

Starting in the late 1990s, Victor Conte began providing athletes with undetectable steroids. Conte began supplying professional baseball players just as MLB ramped up its testing initiatives. He produced elaborate calendars for his clients to micromanage their doses of various drugs as well as anticipate testing schedules and make sure athletes tested clean. Conte's organization, the Bay Area Laboratory Co-operative (BALCO), produced a wide array of drugs that were difficult to detect or easy to mask. Among these were human growth hormone (HGH), erythropoietin (commonly known as EPO, a drug that boosts a person's blood hematocrit levels, allowing for increased oxygen circulation and therefore increased stamina), insulin (usually prescribed for diabetes and powerful when combined with other drugs), modafinil (a strong stimulant usually prescribed for narcolepsy), and two designer drugs that became known as "the Clear" and "the Cream." The Clear (norbolethone) was a difficult-to-detect steroid, ensuring that athletes would "clear" their drug tests. The Cream was a topical drug applied to the skin to increase testosterone levels in the body, disguising one telltale sign of steroid use: low testosterone. The human body produces human growth hormone and insulin, making them undetectable. In September of 2003, the IRS and the San Mateo County Narcotics Task Force raided BALCO and discovered that Conte was providing illegal and designer drugs to athletes in an array of sports, including professional baseball players Jason Giambi and Barry Bonds.[18]

On January 20, 2004, in George W. Bush's State of the Union address, the president focused on steroids, saying:

> Athletics play such an important role in our society, but unfortunately, some in professional sports are not setting much of an example. The use of performance-enhancing drugs like steroids in baseball, football and other sports is dangerous and it sends the wrong message: that there are shortcuts to accomplishment and that performance is more important than character. So tonight I call on team owners, union representatives, coaches and players to take the lead, to send the right signal, to get tough and to get rid of steroids now.[19]

The president's use of the term "character" harks back to muscular Christianity's premise that sport holds moral value and that athletes benefit morally from playing sports. Clear also is the president's assumption that athletes have a moral obligation to serve as role models.

A few weeks later, U.S. Attorney John Ashcroft announced a forty-two-count indictment against BALCO and its administrators. And in spring 2004, the Senate held hearings on steroid use in professional baseball. One point of contention was the prevalence of andro, legal for use but banned by the National Football League and the Olympics. The players' union chief, Donald Fehr, testified that he did not see anything wrong with professional baseball players using andro. This angered Senator John McCain, who replied, "Your failure to commit to addressing this issue straight on immediately will motivate this committee to search for legislative remedies. I don't know what they are. But I can tell you, and the players you represent, the status quo is unacceptable."[20] In October, Congress passed the Anabolic Steroid Control Act of 2004; the Act put eighteen performance enhancers, including andro, on the banned substances list.

In March 2005, Jose Canseco was preparing to publish *Juiced: Wild Times, Rampant 'Roids, Smash Hits, and How Baseball Got Big*, his autobiographical account of steroids in professional baseball, and the House Government Reform Committee brought professional baseball players Canseco, Mark McGwire, Sammy Sosa, Rafael Palmeiro, and Curt Schilling to testify on steroid use. An influential voice that emerged through the congressional steroid hearings was Donald Hooton. Hooton's son, Taylor, had committed suicide at age seventeen, and Hooton blamed steroid use for his son's death. Hooton believed that his son took steroids because he admired professional baseball players and wanted to be like them. He told Congress, "Players that are guilty of taking steroids are not only cheaters. You are cowards."[21] Sports ethicist Verner Møller has noted a tendency to expect elite athletes to be role models because young people look up to them. However,

Image 11.3 Mark McGwire swearing in for the 2005 House Government Reform Committee hearings on steroid use in professional baseball. Each player was sworn in separately for the hearing, an unusual practice that heightened the expectation of confession by prolonging the time dedicated to players' promising honesty and truthfulness. *Getty Images/Pool.*

he points out that athletes have no legal obligation to behave this way, and there are many examples of athletes failing to live up to ethical ideals when it comes to drugs, alcohol, smoking, sex and/or violence.

When Mark McGwire delivered his famous line of the hearings, "I'm not here to discuss the past," it was clear that he did not intend to follow the ritual of confession. This was even more apparent when McGwire invoked Fifth Amendment protections. According to Canseco,

> I thought that was a huge mistake. In my opinion, anyone who takes the Fifth is already guilty. And I guess, for once, the sports media agreed with me. For the next few days, everyone's favorite line was "I'm not here to talk about the past." And it was always delivered with a smirk.[22]

By avoiding the ritual of the anxious bench, McGwire and the others who testified that day could not achieve the benefit of forgiveness. Though the hearing was choreographed in a Finney-esque style, the testifying athletes resisted the paradigm, sidestepping accusations and failing to reveal any inner torment over their actions.

Primary Source

Primary sources provide firsthand accounts of the topic under consideration. They emerge from particular times and places and allow us to imagine the context and thought processes that give rise to a perspective.

Congressional Hearing on Steroids in Major League Baseball

Context:

- The Committee on Government Reform of the U.S. House of Representatives held a hearing on March 17, 2005, titled "Restoring Faith in America's Pastime: Evaluating Major League Baseball's Efforts to Eradicate Steroid Use." The Committee subpoenaed five professional baseball players to testify: Jose Canseco, Mark McGwire, Sammy Sosa, Rafael Palmeiro, and Curt Schilling. Also present was Senator Jim Bunning, a former MLB player. The following provides excerpts from the hearing with speakers identified.

Discussion Questions:

- Considering the language that congressional representatives use, what legacies of muscular Christianity do you see?
- Why would Linda Sanchez deem the testimony "disappointing"? What do you think she was expecting?
- What claims in this testimony do you agree with? What do you disagree with?

Restoring Faith in America's Pastime: Evaluating Major League Baseball's Efforts to Eradicate Steroid Use[23]

Mark Souder (senator, R-Indiana): With drastically rising drug abuse among youth in America, baseball needs to come clean. If anyone takes the Fifth Amendment today saying they would incriminate themselves, it would be a terrible additional tragedy. The scourge of all illegal drug abuse tears at the fabric of our Nation. Baseball was once America's pastime and it needs to start today to regain its former glory.

Donald Hooton (president and director, Taylor Hooton Foundation; father of high-school baseball player Taylor Hooton): I am sick and tired of having you tell us that you don't want to be considered role models. If you haven't figured it out yet, let me break the news to you that whether you like it or not, you are role models, and parents across America should hold you accountable for behavior that inspires our kids to do things that puts their health at risk and that teaches them that the ethics we try to teach them around our kitchen table somehow don't apply to them.

John Sweeney (representative, R-New York) questions Mark McGwire:

Sweeney: Mr. McGwire, I have to ask you this question from your statement. In part ten, you essentially say that the impact on children is devastating. You recognize that. And you want people to understand that the use of any performance-enhancing drug can be dangerous. It is rather an infamous occurrence that in the year you were breaking the home run record, a bottle of andro was seen in your locker... [H]ow did you get to that point that was what you were using to prepare yourself to play?

McGwire: Well, sir, I'm not here to talk about the past, I'm here to talk about the positive and not the negative about this issue.

Mark Souder (representative, R-Indiana): And as far as this being about the past, that's what we do. This is an oversight committee. If the Enron people come in here and say, we don't want to talk about the past, do you think Congress is going to let them get away with that?... [H]ow are we supposed to figure out what our obligations are to the taxpayers if you say you won't talk about the past?

William Lacy Clay (representative, D-Missouri) questions Mark McGwire:

Clay: Mr. McGwire, we are both fathers of young children. Both my son and daughter love sports and they look up to stars like you. Can we look at those children with a straight face and tell them that great players like you played the game with honesty and integrity?

McGwire: Like I said earlier, I am not going to go in the past and talk about my past. I am here to make a positive influence on this.

Clay: Mr. McGwire, you have already acknowledged that you used certain supplements, including andro, as part of your training routine. In addition to andro, which was legal at the time that you used it, what other supplements did you use?

McGwire: I am not here to talk about the past.

Clay: Mr. McGwire, let me go back and ask you, would you have been able to perform at that level without using andro?

McGwire: I am not going to talk about the past.

Clay: OK.

Linda Sanchez (representative, D-California): You guys are in the clubhouses. We are not. We do not have access there. We do not know. But we are getting this: hear no evil, see no evil, don't know anything that is going on... I mean, the first step is admitting, hey, there is a problem, next step, how widespread is it? And then the next step is, what do we do to try to combat it. I am not hearing that from you today, and I am very disappointed, I have to say, extremely disappointed in the testimony today.

When Jose Canseco's *Juiced* came out in 2005, it became a best seller. From the first paragraph, Canseco took issue with those who criticized steroid use. He writes, "I'm tired of hearing such short-sighted crap from people who have no idea what they're talking about. Steroids are here to stay. That's a fact. Steroids are the future."[24] In the book, Canseco claimed that approximately 80 percent of professional baseball players were using steroids, and he attested to personally injecting Mark McGwire with steroids.

By late 2005, Major League Baseball could no longer drag its feet on the issue of performance-enhancing drugs. It replaced the policy of suspending a player for ten days on a first offense and for a year on a fourth offense with a stricter policy of a fifty-game suspension for a first positive test, one hundred for a second, and a lifetime ban for a third. In addition, the new policy added amphetamines to the list of banned substances. Although this was a far stricter policy in terms of punishment, the testing itself could not account for players using human growth hormone, insulin, or maskable drugs. It is unlikely that MLB would have changed its policies at all without the BALCO investigation, Jose Canseco's autobiography, and the congressional hearings.

Perhaps Major League Baseball considered its efforts a success because the American public seemed to regard steroid use as more of a cultural phenomenon than the result of tacit encouragement from sports' higher-ups. Late night television host Jay Leno joked during a 2005 opening monologue, "It turns out Pete Rose has been betting on whether or not Barry Bonds used steroids." During that year's Academy Awards, host Chris Rock joked, "We've given out ten awards so far, and not one of the winners has tested positive for steroids."[25] The moment was rife with cynicism, and Barry Bonds expressed his contempt for the moral crusade against steroid use. During 2005 spring training, he told reporters,

> Man, it's not like this is the Olympics. We don't train for four years for, like, a ten second [event]. We go 162 games. You've got to come back day after day. We're entertainers. If I can't go out there [to play], and somebody pays $60 for a ticket, and I'm not in the lineup, who's getting cheated? Not me.[26]

Barry Bonds's critique of MLB's unrealistic expectations for athletes' bodies shows that he may have believed steroids were necessary to do his job.

As we have seen, Major League Baseball players accused of steroid use did not regard it as an individual sin but as a ubiquitous practice stemming from the pressure to perform at their demanding sport. The American public heard the tale of Taylor Hooton's suicide and fell back on the muscular Christian assumption that athletes should be good role models because sport should develop moral character. An anxious-bench-style confession in the Senate hearing room would have further cemented this understanding by showing an inner torment and guilt over the practice of steroid use. But for the players, this ritual did not make sense. They saw no reason to take individual blame for the commonplace practice of using steroids and sidestepped the ritual.

Lance Armstrong

In 1998, Tour de France officials uncovered widespread doping among participants. Tour de France teams have a soigneur, a nonriding member of the team who provides support and transports supplies. During the 1998 Tour, customs agents stopped Willy Voet, the soigneur for the Swiss Festina team, for a routine border search of his car and found a variety of drugs including amphetamines, EPO, steroids, and masking agents. The discovery led officials to investigate other teams, and they uncovered more doping. Some teams protested the excessive searches, and some withdrew from the race. When the riders entered Paris three weeks after the race's start, fewer than half of those who started the race crossed the finish line.

After the scandal, Swiss rider Alex Zülle described the pressure he felt to use EPO: "As a rider, you feel tied into the system. It's like being on the highway. The law says there's a speed limit of 65, but everyone is driving 70 or faster. Why should I be the one who obeys the speed limit?"[27] For many racers, performance-enhancement strategies seemed to level the playing field, not provide an unfair advantage. What became known as the Festina affair was a blemish on the reputation of the Tour de France, and Tour director Jean-Marie Leblanc announced that if any rider or team threatened the reputation of the race during the next year's Tour, the Tour would expel them. The head of corporate operations for the Tour decreed, "We will be absolutely hardnosed. The Tour will never be the symbol of doping but of the fight against doping."[28]

Lance Armstrong finished fourth in the 1998 Tour, his first Tour after completing his cancer treatments. When Armstrong raced in 1999, journalists wanted to tell the story of the man who beat cancer and came back to win the Tour de France. They did not want to notice that the race was faster than 1998, even though it should have slowed down if doping had decreased, and they did not want to listen to cyclists who voiced suspicions about Armstrong and others doping. For example, cyclist Christophe Bassons told one media outlet that he did not think anyone placing in the top ten of the 1999 Tour was riding clean. Journalist David Walsh writes, "In the press room, there was widespread indifference to Bassons. Armstrong was such a better story and any reporting of Bassons's complaints would lessen the feel-good effect of the back-from-cancer hero."[29] In this way, journalists were complicit in the ongoing doping, not wanting to cast a shadow on a good story.

When Armstrong accepted his last yellow jersey (the symbol of the Tour de France leader) after winning in 2005, he said, "I want to send a message to people who do not believe in cycling, the cynics, skeptics. I am sorry that they do not believe in miracles, in dreams. Too bad for them."[30] It was one month later that the French sport daily *L'Equipe* claimed to have proof that Armstrong had used EPO during his victorious Tour in 1999. *L'Equipe*'s reporter had acquired documents from France's anti-doping laboratory that was retesting samples from the 1999 Tour using improved technologies. Although the samples were anonymized, *L'Equipe* claimed to have evidence that Armstrong's samples tested positive for EPO. In response to this story, Tour director Jean-Marie Leblanc told *L'Equipe* that he felt shocked and "morally betrayed" by Armstrong.[31] Because the lab did not follow appropriate regulations when testing the samples, the Tour could not levy any sanctions against Armstrong, who had, in any case, already retired from professional cycling. Armstrong continued to claim that any allegations that he used performance-enhancing drugs were false and part of a "witch hunt" against him by Tour de France organizers, the World Anti-Doping Agency (WADA), and the French press.[32]

For nearly fourteen years, Armstrong denied that he used performance-enhancing drugs in his Tour de France races. He viciously attacked those who made accusations and leveraged several lawsuits against journalists and anti-doping authorities. In response to the USADA charges against him that were proceeding through the courts in 2012, Armstrong said,

> These charges are baseless, motivated by spite and advanced through testimony bought and paid for by the promises of anonymity and immunity. Although USADA alleges a wide-ranging conspiracy extended over more than sixteen years, I am the only athlete it has chosen to charge. USADA's malice, its methods, its star-chamber practices, and its decision of punish first and adjudicate later are all at odds with our ideals of fairness and fair play.[33]

Perhaps because of these adamant denials, it took many by surprise when Armstrong announced two months later that he would accept the USADA findings against him, charges that resulted in disqualification of his seven Tour victories and a lifetime ban from all sanctioned competitive events, cycling or otherwise. Union Cycliste Internationale (UCI), the governing body of international cycling, accepted the USADA report and implemented Armstrong's disqualification.

Over the years that Armstrong denied his drug use, he made many enemies, including Greg and Kathy LeMond. Greg LeMond was one of the first professional cyclists to express doubts that Armstrong's victories were drug-free. Journalist David Walsh interviewed Kathy LeMond on the day that UCI stripped Armstrong of his titles, and she had this to say, "Where's the shame? I don't see any. No apology to all those whose lives and careers were destroyed; people duped for years into believing his story—nothing for them."[34] Kathy LeMond was not alone in her concerns about Armstrong's lack of remorse. The nation expected a full confession when Armstrong announced his interview with Oprah Winfrey that would air in January 2013.

Media studies scholars Steven Thomsen and Harper Anderson studied responses to Armstrong's interview with Winfrey, and they argue that Armstrong failed to achieve redemption among media and fans because he avoided taking personal responsibility. They note that for atonement to come across as sincere, the accused must not only ask for forgiveness, but must also "provide ample evidence that the accused has experienced

Image 11.4 Oprah Winfrey interviews Lance Armstrong. Over two days and 180 minutes, Winfrey questioned Armstrong about his denial of drug use during his seven Tour de France victories. In the interview, Armstrong did admit to doping in the Tour de France, but he framed his actions as outcomes of the pervasive doping culture of cycling and refused to call his actions cheating. *Getty Images/Handout.*

substantial personal suffering as a consequence."[35] Rather than providing this evidence, Armstrong framed doping as a cultural rather than individual problem. In response to Winfrey's question of whether Armstrong thought he could have won without doping, he said, "Not in that generation, and I'm not here to talk about others in that generation. It's been well documented. I didn't invent the culture, but I didn't try to stop the culture, and that's my mistake, and that's what I have to be sorry for." For Armstrong, his drug use did not constitute cheating because, "I didn't have access to anything that nobody else did."[36]

Media coverage following the interview was critical of Armstrong's performance; in general, analysts were not satisfied with his apology. It is possible that Armstrong's status as a cancer survivor with a successful charitable organization made the news of his rule violations feel like betrayal for those who had turned to him for hope.[37] In Thomsen and Anderson's analysis, Armstrong's confession failed because he evaded personal responsibility. They write,

> To repent of a "sin," the accused must actually see the behavior as sinful. Had he publicly acknowledged that his actions had in fact constituted cheating, the apology would likely be perceived as more authentic, rather than continuing the denials that he had made for more than thirteen years.[38]

For these authors, confession looks like Finney's anxious bench, and Armstrong dodged important parts of the ritual: admitting to sin, shame, and personal torment. Lofton writes,

> Whether victim or perpetrator, audience or actor, the occupant of Winfrey's anxious center is there for a reason: to instruct themselves. At the center of her ritual process is the awareness that all of us, no matter our cultural or criminal position, have some sin from which we must, and shall, be released.[39]

Armstrong's choice to have Winfrey as his interviewer led the audience to expect an anxious-bench-style confession: an admission of sin and torment leading to a declaration of how one will do better in the future. This is not what Armstrong delivered, which might explain why those who watched the interview thought that he came across as pompous, arrogant, and unapologetic.[40]

Conclusions

Most ethical assessments of performance enhancement begin with the premise that athletic competition is beneficial for participants. For example, bioethicist Thomas Murray claims that what makes sports fair is not that every competitor is equal; human diversity means that competitors will always be unequal in natural ability. He argues instead that the value of sport is that sport provides an opportunity for humans to demonstrate dedication and courage, and for all of us to witness and celebrate natural talent honed through perseverance.[41] Similarly, Christian theologian Michael Shafer has argued that the reason the American public finds doping distasteful is not about rule breaking or health concerns; he argues that sport is an opportunity for human flourishing sullied by those who reject natural limits on human performance.[42] These perspectives on sport exhibit the muscular Christian understanding that sport is morally valuable in itself and American expectations that athletes who are caught doping should feel shame and confess.

Rather than placing blame on individual athletes, it is worth considering that elite sport itself may be the cause of doping. As Verner Møller has pointed out, seeking to establish a competitive advantage is "the position every athlete attempts to achieve by means of intensive training, strict diets, coaching advice and just about anything else. Doping is one consequence of this striving for advantage."[43] Some of the values of sport (to cause another to suffer, to determine one individual to be better than another, to sacrifice one's body to the project of winning) are not "character building," but push athletes into dubious moral territory. Jay Coakley, writing with Robert Hughes, has called this phenomenon "positive deviance"—athletes striving to succeed at their sport are willing to disregard or reject other social norms and values. Coakley and Hughes point out that conforming to a sporting identity often requires athletes to subordinate other interests, hobbies, and relationships as they strive for distinction in their sport. They are willing to play with pain and refuse to accept limitations on their time, energy, or body. This willingness to overconform to the values of sport can lead to doping and other rule violations. Because illegal performance enhancement can be linked to over-conformity to sports' values, the authors argue that tougher rule enforcement will have limited effect on trying to control this deviance.[44]

Given the prevalence of positive deviance, it is not surprising that athletes turn to doping. Møller drives this point home when he writes, "Concepts such as fair play and the spirit of sport are a linguistic sugar-coating that is applied to the bitter pill of sport for the purpose of reassuring sponsors, officials who do the funding, and others who cannot reconcile themselves to the fact that sport is what it is."[45] And what is sport to Møller? "Sport is a cultivation of the will to win taken to the threshold of evil."[46]

These understandings of sport are useful for understanding why athletes who are caught doping tend to blame the system rather than take personal responsibility. As Jose Canseco provocatively asked in *Juiced*,

> Is it cheating to do what everyone wants you to do? Are players the only ones to blame for steroids when Donald Fehr and the other bosses of the Major League Players' Association fought for years to make sure players wouldn't be tested for steroids? Is it all that secret when the owners of the game put out the word that they want home runs and excitement, making sure that everyone from trainers to managers to clubhouse attendants understands that whatever it is the players are doing to become superhuman, they sure ought to keep it up?[47]

Of course, the implied answer to Canseco's questions is: No, it is not really cheating. For players who take this point of view, there is no inner torment or sin to confess, so rituals based on the anxious bench are unnecessary, embarrassing, and a distraction from systemic causes of doping.

However, for an American public steeped in muscular Christian understandings of sport as morally valuable, the use of performance-enhancing drugs sure seemed like cheating. Muscular Christianity endures today in the common assertion that sport builds character, and it is worth remembering that this assertion is not an essential truth but a historical particularity born of nineteenth-century Protestant anxiety. If we can reimagine sport as not inherently moral, but as a phenomenon that can have both ethical and unethical outcomes, we come closer to understanding why an athlete might sidestep the public expectation of confession. If we also take into account all those who profit from enhanced performance (athletes, teams, owners, sponsors, fans, and sports media, to name a few), we might see that the nineteenth-century ideologies of muscular Christianity and the anxious bench have contributed to unrealistic expectations regarding athletic morality and the necessity of confession.

Resources for Further Study

Media
Christopher Bell, dir. *Bigger, Stronger, Faster.* 2008. East Melbourne, Australia; Madman Films.
Stephen Frears, dir. *The Program.* 2015. London, England; Studio Canal.

Online Archive
The U.S. Anti-Doping Agency provides a library of resources for athletes. "Athlete Guide to Anti-Doping," https://www.usada.org/athletes/antidoping101/athlete-guide-anti-doping/.

Reading
Shaun Assael, *Steroid Nation: Juiced Home Run Totals, Anti-Aging Miracles, and a Hercules in Every High School: The Secret History of America's True Drug Addiction* (New York: ESPN Books, 2007).
Jose Canseco, *Juiced: Wild Times, Rampant 'Roids, Smash Hits, and How Baseball Got Big* (New York: HarperCollins, 2005).
Verner Møller, *The Ethics of Doping and Anti-Doping: Redeeming the Soul of Sport?* (New York: Routledge, 2010).

Chapter 12

College Sports

In 1957, the National Collegiate Athletic Association (NCAA) made a rule that prohibited college athletes from profiting from their name, image, and likeness (NIL), ensuring that college athletes would be unpaid amateurs. The rule stated: "A student-athlete's picture many not be associated with a commercial product in such a way as to imply endorsement, nor may he receive renumeration."[1] Over the past century, colleges, coaches, administrators, athletes, and fans have weighed in on whether amateur status is essential for college athletics. Those who supported the value of amateurism argued that if athletes were paid, this would distort the values of higher education and undermine the ability of student-athletes to be fully students. The counterargument points out that although amateurism may have been defensible previously, televising college sports has meant that student-athletes remained unpaid while everyone else in college sports profited. Through a number of court cases in the 2010s, activists and former athletes succeeded in changing the NCAA's NIL regulations. In June 2021, the NCAA announced that college athletes could profit from their name, image, and likeness in line with their state's laws, a change that many anticipate will dramatically shift the economic landscape of college sports in the coming decades.

In 2021, there were 849 religiously affiliated colleges and universities in the United States, enrolling 1,808,742 students, about 13 percent of college enrollment as a whole.[2] To understand how these institutions are navigating the rapidly changing dynamics of college sports, we will first trace the history of denominational colleges in the United States and consider how and why amateurism became a driving ideal undergirding intercollegiate sports. Turning to activism in the late twentieth and early twenty-first centuries, we can see how the ideal of unpaid amateurism became a capitalist hypocrisy, eventually overturned in the courts. With more changes underway, college sports are undergoing a sea change likely to have wide-ranging ramifications. Focusing on how denominational colleges and Christian sports ministries on college campuses have responded to the changing economic landscape of college sports reveals emerging challenges: how to advise personal branding, how to showcase the value of community in the face of economic profit, and how to understand inequalities between student-athletes exacerbated by social media monetization strategies.

History of Denominational Colleges and Intercollegiate Sports

The first colleges in North America were all Protestant. During the colonial period, 1636–1776, the nine Protestant colleges operating in North America were: Harvard (1636, Puritan), William & Mary (1693, Anglican/Episcopal), Yale (1701, Congregational), Princeton (1746, Presbyterian), Columbia (1754, Episcopal), University of Pennsylvania (1755, Episcopal), Brown (1765, Baptist), Rutgers (1766, Dutch Reformed), and Dartmouth (1769, Congregational/general Protestant). At the time of American independence, these nine institutions had approximately 135 faculty and 1,000 students. All students and faculty were white men, and about half of all graduates entered the ministry. These colleges required students to attend worship services and to take classes on the Bible. At the time, it would have been impossible to imagine a collegiate institution that was not Christian. Today, none of these original nine maintain a religious affiliation. Two of the nine became public institutions (William & Mary and Rutgers); seven remained private.[3]

The first hundred years of European settlement in North America produced nine colleges, but from the Revolutionary War to the Civil War (1776–1865), nearly six hundred colleges appeared across the country. Informed by the religious fervor of the Second Great Awakening and by westward frontier expansion, these colleges were small, often short-lived, and focused on denominational education. Two significant developments marked this era. In 1819, the Supreme Court decided a case between Dartmouth College and the state of New Hampshire. The state of New Hampshire had tried to assert control over the college, and Dartmouth had resisted this interference. The court found in favor of Dartmouth, beginning the distinction between private institutions and public, state-affiliated institutions. The second significant development was the passage of the Morrill Act of 1862, which granted thirty thousand acres to each state for the purpose of founding a public university. Most of these land-grant institutions were in line with mainstream Christianity, but state control of the largest institutions of higher education set in motion a countervailing trend of denominations founding their own explicitly religious, private institutions.

Of the six hundred colleges that opened from 1776 to 1865, 175 still exist today. Whereas all nine of the colonial colleges dropped their religious affiliation, the 175 colleges that survived this period are significantly more diverse. These colleges fall into seven categories: nonreligious, state-sponsored universities such as the University of Georgia and the University of North Carolina; colleges that became affiliated with municipalities such as the College of Charleston and City College of New York; the first Black colleges such as Howard University in Washington, D.C.; smaller liberal-arts colleges that initially had a strong religious affiliation but later became nonsectarian private institutions such as Grinnell College in Iowa or Antioch College in Ohio; small, church-affiliated colleges that evolved into large nonsectarian, private universities such as Duke University in North Carolina; the first Catholic institutions in the United States such as Georgetown University in Washington, D.C.; and colleges that retained a strong Christian identity and are now members of the Council for Christian Colleges & Universities (CCCU).

From the Civil War to World War II (1865–1944), the number of colleges, the number of enrolled students, and the number of faculty increased dramatically. In 1870, 250 institutions with a total faculty of 5,553 professors served approximately 63,000 students. By 1945, there were 1,768 colleges with a total faculty of 150,000 serving more than 1,675,000 students. Over this period, about two-thirds of all college students attended small, denominationally affiliated colleges.[4]

This was also the era of the first intercollegiate athletic competitions. In 1852, on Lake Winnipesaukee in New Hampshire, a railroad superintendent named James Elkins hosted the first known intercollegiate competition: a boat race between Harvard and Yale. Elkins was hoping to boost tourism to the area and thought the competition would be a good draw. He offered Harvard and Yale financial incentives for their participation, and some men who competed in the race that day were not students; they were professionals that the colleges hired for the day.[5] The commercial success of the event and the expansion of higher education led to the development of more intercollegiate sports. Students at Harvard, Yale, Princeton, and a few other northeastern universities organized intercollegiate football in the 1870s. Walter Camp, a Yale student and later football coach, tirelessly promoted football as a modern game that relied on scientific coaching strategies and quarterback leadership.[6] Universities beyond the Northeast tended to see football as barbaric and overly violent, and the game did not spread to the Midwest and South until the 1920s.

In the 1920s, a debate emerged over the role of athletics at institutions of higher education. Although some argued that men's sport participation was essential for moral fortitude and national preparedness for war, others noted changes to intercollegiate sports that they found troubling. For example, Princeton faculty member Robert Kilburn Root noted the increasing crowds gathering for Saturday football viewing and argued that intercollegiate sport had taken on the trappings of professional sport. On Saturday football, he remarked,

> Is it wholesome that these honest lads should be made a spectacle for the gaping multitude at three dollars a seat, that their pictures should fill all the Sunday supplements, that the quivering ether,—if the physicists still believe in ether,—should be syllabling their names and blazoning their every move to the "radio fans" of half the continent?[7]

Princeton alum Alfred S. Dashiell agreed with Root, voicing a fear that football will "be made into a national religion" and grow to disproportional importance, overshadowing and undermining the moral benefits of amateur sport.[8]

The NCAA convention of 1925 took on this debate, and speakers argued for the value of sport. One speaker was Bishop William T. Manning of New York, who praised the NCAA for "rendering a high moral service in the stand which it has and is making in behalf of properly conducted sports, which have both a moral and spiritual value." Manning

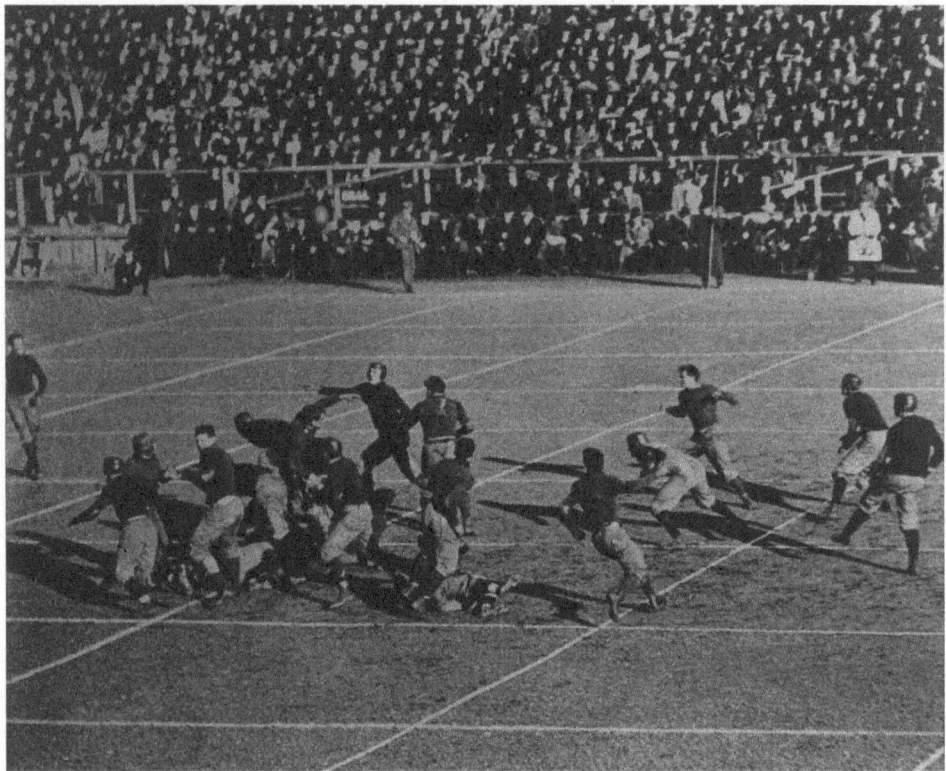

Image 12.1 A football game between Harvard and Yale at Yale's Hamilton Park on November 13, 1875. Football games between elite northeastern colleges became popular spectacles, and by the 1890s crowds grew to the tens of thousands. *Getty Images/Oscar White.*

argued, "There ought to be the closest sympathy between true sportsmanship and true religion, for they are the two great agencies for the development of right living and should work in closest relationship."[9] Manning's vision of the moral qualities of sports carried the day, largely cementing college athletics for men as institutional staples.

The decades following World War II were a tipping point in American higher education. Although student enrollment in 1945 was roughly equal between private and public colleges, by 1975 nearly 80 percent of students attended public institutions. Public colleges dropped behavioral codes and requirements to study the Bible while Christian colleges maintained these. By the 1980s, Christian colleges had either relaxed their religious requirements to appeal to a broader audience or leaned into their religious identity to increase their appeal to a smaller market share of the college student population. The small number of schools that maintained their strong religious identity enjoyed renewed popularity among those who valued a Christian approach to higher education.

From the 1920s to the 1950s, the NCAA was one governing institution among several for college sports and did not hold the extensive power that it does today. Because of this, institutions had a variety of approaches to the question of paying players. For example, the University of Pittsburgh had been regularly paying its athletes a monthly stipend since the 1920s, though this was reduced during the Great Depression. In 1937, football players at Pitt, perhaps inspired by the successful union sit-down strike in Flint, Michigan, used collective bargaining to demand $200 pay and two weeks of vacation if they agreed to play in that year's Rose Bowl. In response, chancellor John Bowman persuaded the board of trustees to eliminate all payments to players and all athletic scholarships, as well as to increase the academic requirements for athletic eligibility. Pitt's football program languished.[10] Some faculty have had a say in the role of sports at their institution. For example, faculty at the University of Chicago were successful in banning football from 1939 to 1969, in large part by portraying football as morally compromising.[11]

Whereas institutions chose whether or not to pay athletes in the first half of the twentieth century, the consolidation of the NCAA as the central authority on college sports in the early 1950s standardized approaches. Throughout its history, the NCAA held strong to one central tenet: college athletes cannot be paid.[12] Restrictions like the NCAA's did not exist for nonathletes in college. Other students on college scholarships have used the talents they were developing while in school to earn money. No oversight institution for students on music scholarships prevented them from being paid musicians or students on theater scholarships from performing in summer theater. Engineering students have paid summer internships; education majors might work at summer camps; and English majors may pick up copyediting or tutoring work. Only athletes were under restrictions regarding earning money for their skills while enrolled in college. By presenting college athletes as essentially amateur, colleges and the NCAA relied on a moral argument that paying athletes would undermine the value of college sport.

Activism and Changes to NCAA Policies

In the early 1980s, television revenues for college sports began to skyrocket. For example, the NCAA brought in $10 million for televising the 1980–1981 men's college basketball season. The 1984 Supreme Court case, *NCAA v. Board of Regents of the University of Oklahoma*, broke the NCAA's monopoly on television profits using antitrust laws. However, the case also emphasized the importance of amateurism in college sports in both the majority opinion and the dissenting opinion. Writing for the majority, Justice John Paul Stevens said, "In order to preserve the character and quality of the 'product,' athletes must not be paid, and must be required to attend class and the like."[13] And writing for the minority, Justice Byron "Whizzer" White declared that the NCAA's television plan preserved amateurism and successfully integrated athletics and education. This continued and affirmed the precedent of amateurism as essential to college sports.

In 2016, economist Dan Rascher estimated that college sports in total generated $13 billion annually, more than the National Football League (NFL). The NCAA generates more than $900 million annually; coaches' salaries can be as high as $10 million (such as that of Mike Krzyzewski, who coached Duke University men's basketball); and ESPN pays billions of dollars for the rights to college sports championships. All this led sports journalist Joe Nocera to this conclusion: "the idea that the players who make all this possible should not get much more than a scholarship isn't just hypocritical. It's offensive."[14]

Former NCAA executive director Walter Byers supported amateurism while he oversaw NCAA operations from the 1960s to the 1980s. He had a change of heart after his retirement, which coincided with the dramatic increase in television revenue from college sports. He wrote in his 1995 memoir, "College amateurism is not a moral issue; it is an economic camouflage for monopoly practice."[15] The 1995 NCAA convention soundly rejected any form of pay for college athletes. The outgoing NCAA president and president of the University of Nevada, Reno, Joseph N. Crowley, declared that the day that colleges pay their athletes would be the day his university would abolish college sports.[16] The head of the NCAA Presidents' Commission, Judith E. N. Albino, president of the University of Colorado, said that paying student-athletes "would fundamentally change what we are about… and put us into a business unrelated to education."[17] The NCAA dug in its heels on the issue and continued to firmly support amateurism.

In 1997, Electronic Arts (EA), maker of the popular video game *Madden NFL*, sought to monetize interest in college sports and negotiated with the NCAA to gain the rights to use likenesses of college players for its game *NCAA Football*. One year later, it also negotiated for the rights to use likenesses of men's college basketball players for *NCAA March Madness* (later changed to *NCAA Basketball*). Ed O'Bannon, a former UCLA basketball player, was surprised to see his likeness used in EA's *NCAA Basketball 09*. O'Bannon had played professional basketball for a short time, but at the time EA released its game, he was working as a car salesman in Nevada. At first, he found it flattering to appear in the game, but then he questioned why EA should profit and he should not. Activists helped O'Bannon organize a legal case against the NCAA, seeking payment for the use of his name, image, and likeness (NIL).

Responses to O'Bannon's lawsuit from college athletic administrations were mixed. Big Ten commissioner Jim Delany predicted that the Big Ten would drop athletic scholarships altogether if O'Bannon succeeded. On the opposite side of the spectrum, former NCAA head Walter Byers supported O'Bannon's cause and used slavery as a metaphor to describe NCAA exploitation of athletes. He wrote that NCAA administrators were "firmly committed to the neoplantation belief that the enormous proceeds from college games belong to the overseers (the administrators) and supervisors (coaches). The plantation workers performing in the arena may receive only those benefits authorized by the overseers."[18] Byers's metaphor is powerful not only in its economic description but also in its implied racial discrimination, referencing the prominence of Black college athletes and white coaches and administrators.

Judge Claudia Wilken was the judge for O'Bannon's case, which came to trial in June 2014. She concluded that rules prohibiting athletes from benefiting from their NIL violated the Sherman Antitrust Act of 1890 as a restraint of trade. The NCAA appealed the

Images 12.2 and 12.3 Ed O'Bannon (left) playing for the UCLA Bruins in 1995. EA Sports released *NCAA Basketball 09* in 2009 featuring an unnamed character in O'Bannon's likeness (right). Although the video game did not use O'Bannon's name, it used his style of left-handed play, his body type, and his UCLA jersey number. *Getty Images/Al Bello; Courtesy of EA Sports.*

decision to the Supreme Court, but their appeal was denied, affirming that the NCAA was subject to antitrust laws. O'Bannon's success paved the way for further lawsuits addressing student-athletes' rights to their name, image, and likeness. Judge Wilken heard a combined class-action lawsuit in 2019 and again ruled against the NCAA, a decision that was upheld by the appellate judges of the Ninth Circuit. Judge Milan Smith wrote that universities have functioned like a cartel to artificially suppress the price that athletes would otherwise receive for their services. He wrote, "Our antitrust laws were originally meant to prohibit exactly this sort of distortion."[19]

In June 2021, the Supreme Court ruled in *NCAA v. Alston* that the NCAA could not limit education-related payments to student-athletes, finding that NCAA limits on scholarships were violations of antitrust law. Although the case did not deal with NIL, Justices Neil Gorsuch and Brent Kavanaugh made clear in their opinion and concurrence, respectively, that other NCAA limitations were likely also violations of antitrust laws. With this, the NCAA decided to defer to state laws regarding NIL. Some states passed laws protecting student-athletes' ability to profit from their NIL, and where these did not exist, colleges put their own rules into effect that served the same purpose. Beginning in 2021, student-athletes could engage in endorsement deals, appear in advertisements, sell memorabilia and autographs, and monetize their social media accounts.

Changes are underway that will further impact college sports. Judicial approval of an NCAA antitrust legal settlement (*House v. NCAA*) in June 2025 will result in the NCAA and Division I colleges paying $2.8 billion over 2025–2035 into a fund to provide back-pay for NCAA student-athletes who were unable to profit from their NIL.[20] The settlement also initiated a profit-sharing model for Division I sports that allows colleges to pay their athletes directly, with a cap set at $20.5 million per school for the first year. Consequently, many Division I schools will limit their rosters for all sports to control their budgets and ensure their ability to offer competitive compensation for players. Most schools initiated roster caps in fall 2025. The federal Department of Education published guidelines in January 2025 requiring colleges to consider revenue sharing as subject to Title IX compliance, meaning that revenue sharing should be divided proportionally between men's and women's sports.[21] A month later, the Trump administration rescinded these guidelines; most Division I colleges with competitive football teams planned to allot 75–85 percent of their $20.5 million revenue-sharing budget to football.[22]

Primary Source

Primary sources provide firsthand accounts of the topic under consideration. They emerge from particular times and places and allow us to imagine the context and thought processes that give rise to a perspective.

The Intercollegiate Tennis Association (ITA) submits a letter of concern to Judge Claudia Wilken regarding the *House v. NCAA* settlement.
Courtesy of the Intercollegiate Tennis Association.

Context:

- In October 2024, Judge Claudia Wilken approved a preliminary plan for a settlement in a case brought by former college athletes against the NCAA. Known as the *House* settlement, the case combined three class-action lawsuits named for key plaintiffs: *House v. NCAA* (named for plaintiff Grant House), *Hubbard v. NCAA* (named for plaintiff Chuba Hubbard), and *Carter v. NCAA* (named for plaintiff DeWayne Carter).
- The preliminary settlement had two major pieces: It provides back pay for former college athletes whom the NCAA denied the ability to profit from their name, image, and likeness. The second piece reorganizes the financial landscape of college athletics by providing revenue sharing for college athletes. Schools can opt in to this model, which eliminates scholarship limits but requires roster limits.
- On January 29, 2025, the Intercollegiate Tennis Association submitted a letter to Judge Claudia Wilken expressing concerns that the revenue-sharing piece of the *House* settlement may have unintended consequences that will undermine non-football and non-basketball college sports.

Discussion Questions:

- What are the concerns that ITA raises in its letter? Do you agree with these concerns? Why or why not?
- What do you think the role of sports at colleges and universities should be? Do you think sports currently fulfill that role? Why or why not?
- What changes would you make to college athletics if you were in charge? What principles and values would guide your decisions? What is at the heart of the matter for you?

Excerpts from Intercollegiate Tennis Association's letter to Judge Claudia Wilken[23]

Settling the *House v. NCAA* case as Presently Contemplated Could Irreparably Damage Varsity College Sports as We Know Them: At this critical and momentous time in varsity college athletics, with tectonic changes already here and apparently more coming, if the proposed settlement of the *House v. NCAA* case were to move forward as currently constituted, it could possibly cause irreparable damage to a very large number of non-football and non-basketball sports programs on college campuses, including tennis. This includes hundreds of thousands of student-athletes and tens of thousands of college coaches.

While we understand and support many of the basic concepts and tenets on which the *House* settlement is based, including, but not limited to, student-athletes benefiting from their Name, Image, and Likeness and sharing in revenues moving forward, we have some serious specific concerns which we raise at this important moment in your deliberations:

- **The Fallacy of Name, Image and Likeness ("NIL"):** We wish that more people would publicly acknowledge that the current flawed and broken NIL system is actually "pay for play" and not truly about "Name, Image, and Likeness." We believe most people involved in varsity college athletics know this to be the case. Schools are aggressively recruiting student-athletes with the clearly recognized purpose of actually paying them to play for the school's competitive benefit, and not for the student-athletes' value for their NIL in the marketplace, heretofore undefined. This situation must be remedied.

- **The Hypocrisy of Amateurism Regarding Prize Money for Elite College Tennis Players:** At the same time when it is reported that the pay of some football players is now three to four, or even six, million dollars per year, tennis players have been told that they may not accept prize money for well-earned victories at the U.S. Open Tennis Championships, a premiere Grand Slam event where the best in the world compete. This is also the case at other professional tennis tournaments. The hypocrisy is maddening. We do not believe that Division

> l athletics can move to a "professional model" where top football stars are being paid millions of dollars per year to compete, while the enterprise tries to hang on to the last thread of "amateurism" in other sports such as tennis. This inequality must also be remedied.
>
> **The Future of All Sports Needs to Be Taken into Account:** We respectfully submit that those responsible for determining and approving the final *House v. NCAA* settlement must more thoroughly contemplate and properly account for the future for all sports and not simply football and basketball. History will not judge well those who may permanently damage a wide array of historically important and globally vital sports that have been an integral part of the varsity college athletic landscape for generations and which deserve to be protected and supported for generations to come.
>
> **Remaining Faithful to the Purposes of Higher Education**
> Intercollegiate athletics have historically held a very important place in American higher education. Together we must conceptualize how to best maintain their rightful place within the new and changing American university and college sports ecosystem. Historically, the role of sports in society has been, in part, to help human beings live richer lives, exploring the fullness of human potential.
>
> Amidst these critical times of important decisions, the resolution of the *House* settlement and related plans for the short-term and longer-term future of college sports must preserve the best that history has taught us, build upon those solid foundations that can continue to support the college sports and higher education enterprises, and represent and ensure the best interest of all sports.

Responses to NIL Changes from Christian Colleges and Sports Ministries

After the ruling in *Alston* in 2021, states and institutions created their own rules regarding what student-athletes can and cannot endorse. From 2009 to 2021, twenty-five states passed laws regarding student-athletes and NIL. All these state laws prohibited student-athletes from endorsing products that would conflict with contracts that their team already had in place and from doing endorsements during team practices and events. Most required that institutions provide financial literacy courses for student-athletes.

Denominationally affiliated colleges tended to further restrict student NIL options. As of 2022, the sixty-four U.S. denominational colleges and universities with Division I sports restricted endorsement opportunities for their athletes along the lines of the school's morality code, such as prohibiting deals with gambling establishments, alcohol brands, tobacco, banned substances, and sexually explicit material. For example, Davidson College (Presbyterian) in North Carolina provided this policy for its athletes:

> Scholar-athletes may not endorse or enter NIL activities in categories that conflict with NCAA legislation (i.e., banned substances and sports wagering) or institutional values (e.g., alcohol, tobacco, gentleman/strip clubs, bail bonds companies, nutritional substances not controlled by the FDA, etc.).[24]

Similarly, Georgetown (Jesuit Catholic) in Washington, D.C., provided these limitations, citing its institutional values:

> Student-athletes may not participate in NIL activities that could harm the University's reputation or would be inconsistent with Georgetown's Catholic and Jesuit identity, including, but not limited to, the promotion of products or services associated with gambling, firearms, adult entertainment, tobacco, and banned substances.[25]

Catholic institutions tended to provide more restrictions than Protestant institutions. For example, Marquette University in Wisconsin included prophylactics as a banned NIL endorsement, and Seton Hall in New Jersey also prohibited endorsing "abortion, artificial contraception and divorce."[26] It is likely that court cases in the coming decades will address the constitutionality of these restrictions as activists are likely to argue that NIL endorsements constitute free speech.

Changes to NIL regulations have resulted in a wave of college athlete endorsement opportunities. According to Jeremiah Donati, Texas Christian University's director of intercollegiate athletics, "It's one of the first questions out of every parent's mouth: What's your NIL strategy? If you don't have an NIL strategy, you're going to get killed in recruiting."[27] Paul Putz, sports historian and assistant director of the Faith and Sports Institute at Baylor University's Truett Seminary, talked with *Christianity Today* about the challenges of NIL deals for Christian athletic programs. He presented the central question as, "If we're an athletic program that wants to be a Christian athletic program, how do we connect what's happening in NIL within a broader structure of a Christian flourishing for student athletes?" and stated, "NIL presents a laboratory space for figuring out those questions."[28]

That laboratory space is not only changing because of the influx of money but because student-athletes hoping for better NIL opportunities have begun to think of college sports as a ladder to climb, transferring from school to school over the course of their college years to maximize their playing time and NIL income. The NCAA provides a transfer portal to facilitate transfers between institutions. The portal launched in 2018, but new rules went into effect in 2021 that allowed athletes to transfer to new institutions without sitting out the year after transfer, making transferring a more appealing option. Combine this with the opportunity to increase NIL income, and more and more student-athletes put themselves up for transfer. In 2021, the first year that the portal was available for all sports, 17,781 Division I athletes and 7,783

Division II athletes entered the transfer portal. By 2023, these numbers had increased to 21,189 Division I athletes and 11,716 Division II athletes, with about half of all transfer portal entrants successfully transferring to another institution.[29]

Tim Sceggel, vice president of athletics at LeTourneau University, a conservative Protestant college in Longview, Texas, told me that he has seen an increase in use of the transfer portal for athletes at his institution. Sceggel's assessment of student-athletes in the 2020s is that this generation of college athletes become overwhelmed more easily than students in the past. "They hit the first roadblock and they give up. They see college athletes on social media making all this NIL money, which may or may not be accurate. Combine that with their lack of resiliency and you see them thinking: I'm having a hard time, I'm transferring."[30] Before 2021, Sceggel would have three or four students total use the transfer portal; in 2023 it was up to three or four athletes per team, with about half transferring. Upon entering the transfer portal, student-athletes rescind any obligation their current school has to keep them, so they risk losing their spot on the team by entering the portal. With roster cuts likely due to the 2025 *House* settlement, transfer spots may become more limited.

A sports minister at a large Division I university told me that the transfer portal has affected her ministry:

> We feel the effects of the increased turnover. It feels like the students make these decisions really fast. I think, who are you even consulting? I saw a coach posting on social media, griping about the portal. He was complaining that every six months people jump ship. Some schools can offer NIL deals that we just can't. This coach was complaining that another school can offer an athlete $100,000 and we can offer her $2,000. I understand that it's frustrating for team dynamics to shift every six months. You feel like you are raising up these kids just to have them jump ship. It feels like a loss of loyalty.[31]

For sports ministers who played college sports themselves before the days of NIL, the new era of college sports is daunting. Brian Smith, director of content for Athletes in Action's Ultimate Training Camps, told me that he thinks coaches will quit because of burnout: "This isn't what they signed up for." He added that he foresaw a future where college sports will become entirely driven by money, including throwing money at young athletes before they have the maturity to handle it. He predicted the end of athletes staying for four years at an institution and therefore the end of forming strong relationships during that time. He told me, "It saddens me. The professional structure is taking over the college space and trickling down to high school and youth athletes. Seems like everyone will be a professional athlete really soon."[32]

Holly McKenzie, director of sports ministry at Baylor, a Division I Baptist university in Texas, has been trying to see opportunities for sports ministry in the age of transfers. She recognized the challenges: "We might have an athlete who's on his third or fourth institution; they lose a sense of community. Sport becomes their job—I know it was always like a job—but they lose their passion for it. I know it takes a toll on mental health. We don't know how much commodification affects their mental health." Although transferring and commodification may constitute challenges to mental health, 61 percent of female athletes and 40 percent of male athletes in 2022 cited mental health as their primary reason for pursuing transferring in the first place.[33] For McKenzie, sports ministry needs to adapt quickly to these new challenges. She told me,

> The reality is that the world of college sports is changing a lot but the needs of the human soul are the same. Sports ministry staff are leaving in frustration because they used to have four years to work with an athlete and now they might not even have one. How does having one year instead of four change what you do?[34]

I asked McKenzie how having one year instead of four with an athlete has changed what she does, and she emphasized that providing athletes with a space of support and belonging is important regardless of turnover.

Social Media and Unintended Consequences

Many NIL deals take place via social media, and college athletes know that having a social media presence is likely to net them more NIL opportunities. To understand the emerging moral dilemmas of NIL monetization, it is worth exploring how social media works and how a person can profit from their social media presence. Several components of social media are important to highlight here. First, social media platforms use algorithms to keep users engaged, and these can have dark consequences. Second, the feedback loop of likes, hearts, and comments on social media has an impact on brain chemistry. Third, race and gender are not neutral on social media (or anywhere) and continue to affect who experiences monetary success on social media platforms.

In the 2010s, most social media platforms developed algorithms intended to increase the amount of time that users spent on their platform. These algorithms became known as "dark patterns," using base human impulses to increase engagement with little attention to the consequences. In the years following their implementation, technology reporter Max Fisher and others researched the consequences of these algorithms. One disturbing trend Fisher and others identified on YouTube was the suggestion of videos of prepubescent girls in swimsuits or underwear if a user was watching content of women discussing sex. The researchers found that videos that contained erotic elements and where women mentioned their ages (usually late teens) led to recommended videos of young women playing at being prepubescent and then to (mostly) home videos of young children caught in moments of unintended nudity or performing gymnastics.[35]

When Fisher published these findings, Congress made some movement toward passing a bill that would require turning off social media algorithms for content featuring children, but this proposal did not get a vote. Fisher concluded his book by describing the wide array of experts who have all arrived at the same conclusion: turning off social media algorithms would result in a safer society. This debate is likely to continue, and although platforms may tweak their algorithms, none have expressed interest in deleting them.[36] This matters in the era of NIL because for student-athletes to increase their followers/views/likes, they are subject to the logic of the algorithms.

Evolutionary psychologists have speculated that humans have developed an innate ability to unconsciously monitor how other people perceive them and that the "like" button plays into that component of our biology. Fisher describes humans' responses to receiving likes: "We process that information in the form of self-esteem and such related emotions as pride, shame, or insecurity. These emotions compel us to do more of what makes our community value us and less of what it doesn't."[37] Because these emotions seem to arise naturally, they have great power over human behavior. Fisher points to neurological studies that show that when a heavy Facebook users experience a like, their brain responds in much the same way as gambling addicts. Most users of social media are probably unaware that their experience of getting likes can result in modifications of day-to-day posts and comments to maximize the feeling of gratification that comes with likes.[38] Turning to social media to establish one's brand as a college athlete embroils these athletes in a system of determining value through numbers of followers and immediate responses.

Aware of the pitfalls of relying on social media, institutions such as Texas Christian University (TCU) began to include modules about social media in their required financial literacy courses for athletes in 2021. According to the dean of TCU's business school, Daniel Pullin, who oversaw the financial literacy workshop curriculum, "Social media can cut both ways. We want to make sure from a wellness perspective that our students are prepared to understand that and deal with that and not be paralyzed by it."[39] Although institutions such as TCU seek to help their athletes navigate social media thoughtfully, they are unlikely to call for changes to social media.

Sports ministers and denominational institutions have begun to think about social media, its uses, and its effects on athletes' well-being, but so far there is limited to no attention to how race and gender matter in these spaces. The trend of sportswomen relying on sex appeal to achieve monetization on algorithmic social media platforms is evident. For example, Olivia "Livvy" Dunne was a gymnast at Louisiana State University when the new NIL regulations went into effect, and by 2022 was making more than $1 million a year in endorsements. Her Instagram feed features mostly sexy pictures of Dunne in swimsuits or short dresses posing provocatively. With eight million followers between Instagram and TikTok, this self-presentation is clearly effective for Dunne. She told the *New York Times* in November 2022, "Seven figures. That is something I'm proud of. Especially since I'm a woman in college sports."[40] Noting that professional athletic opportunities for women are limited after college, Dunne expressed pride in earning money as an athlete. The *New York Times* article also noted that the top female athlete earners via social media monetization are white and heteronormative.

Image 12.4 Livvy Dunne shows off her photo in *Sports Illustrated*'s 2023 Swimsuit Issue at the release party on May 18, 2023. *On3* estimates that Dunne's 2024 NIL earnings were $4.1 million.[41] *Getty Images/ Noam Galai.*

The issue of sportswomen's immodesty on social media to maximize NIL is not lost on denominational institutions. Adam Puckett, athletic director at George Fox University, a Quaker college in Oregon, told me, "I wish it wasn't the case, but they [sportswomen] can gain followers with immodest dress. If you put up two photos, one of a game-winning shot and one in a sports bra, the follow count will go to the sports bra."[42] Holly McKenzie, director of sports ministry at Baylor, agreed. She told me, "For women, NIL is more social media based. We know that social media is not good for self-image, for mental health, for sleep, for academics—is the financial reward worth the consequences?" She shared the story of one athlete at Baylor: "I work with an acro athlete. She is really strong, really muscular. She has the job of lifting other athletes over her head. She struggles with body image, and she does have fewer followers on social media than the teammate that she's lifting up." Sportswomen have long struggled to walk the fine line between feminine appearance and athletic strength. Social media has exacerbated this struggle.

Dani Price, director of softball operations and team chaplain for the softball team at Baylor University, told me, "NIL is still really new in the softball world. These athletes are being fed this idea that if they look a certain way, they might get a deal. They feel pressure to make money because they see their peers making money."[43] One way to make money is to stand out through self-expression strategies such as hair extensions, synthetic nails, and/or elaborate makeup. ESPN broadcasts Division I softball games, so players know that they will see themselves on television. They also are well aware of the media success of softball players such as Michaela Edenfield who wears elaborate eye makeup, different for each game, and was in the top ten of softball NIL earners in 2025.[44]

Changes that allowed student-athletes to make money based on their identity as athletes have raised new moral dilemmas. The structures of social media are not neutral and tend to reflect existing power dynamics of racism, sexism, and heteronormativity. Sports ministry for college athletes and denominational colleges are in the early stages of developing advice for how to navigate NIL monetization from a Christian position, and it is yet unclear what strategies will emerge as the landscape of college athletics continues to change.

Conclusions

College sports are big business. In a 2011 episode of PBS's *Frontline* titled "Money and March Madness," investigative journalism professor Lowell Bergman interviewed NCAA President Mark Emmert. Bergman confronted Emmert with the very high salaries of men's college basketball coaches. He provided the examples of John Calipari, who made $4 million a year at Kentucky, and Bill Self, who made $3 million at Kansas. Bergman asked Emmert if it is fair to pay coaches so much when the players do not make their market value. Emmert dodged the question, saying, "The fact is, they're not employees. They're student-athletes." Bergman pushed back, questioning whether Emmert saw it as a contradiction to have highly paid coaches when athletes were not paid. Emmert responded, "I think what would be utterly unacceptable is, in fact, to convert students to employees."[45] Emmert and others clung to the idea of amateurism to avoid addressing the dramatic financial inequalities between college athletes and everyone else in the industry.

The millions of dollars flowing in college sports are now reaching athletes in a significant way, upending more than fifty years of policies that prevented athletes from sharing in the profits of their labor. A new era of college sports is dawning in the 2020s as court cases and settlements dramatically shift the economic landscape. Although some consequences remain unknown, already apparent are practices of increased transferring between institutions, reliance on social media, and ongoing challenges related to mental health. As these changes continue to unfurl, it is yet unclear how denominational colleges and sports ministries will respond.

Resources for Further Study

Media
Bob DeMars, dir. *The Business of Amateurs*. Austin, TX: Tugg, 2016.

Online Archive
The NCAA provides a searchable online resource page for student-athletes, colleges, and agents with educational material on NIL. NCAA NIL Assist, "Education," https://nilassist.ncaa.org/education/.

Reading
Samuel Schuman, *Seeing the Light: Religious Colleges in Twenty-First-Century America* (Baltimore, MD: Johns Hopkins University Press, 2010).

Andy Schwarz and Jason Belzer, "National Letter of Indenture: How College Athletes Are Similar to, and in Many Ways Worse Off Than, the Indentured Servants of Colonial Times," Appendix 2 in Joe Nocera and Ben Strauss, *Indentured: The Inside Story of the Rebellion against the NCAA* (New York: Penguin, 2016), 349–64.

Ronald A. Smith, *The Myth of the Amateur: A History of College Athletic Scholarships* (Austin: University of Texas Press, 2021).

Notes

Preface

1. Gerald R. Gems, "Sport and the Assimilation of American Catholics," *U.S. Catholic Historian* 36, no. 2 (Spring 2018): 33–54; Julie Byrne, *O God of Players: The Story of the Immaculata Mighty Macs* (New York: Columbia University Press, 2003).
2. Tim Chambers, dir. *The Mighty Macs*. 2009; Los Angeles, CA: Freestyle Releasing, 2011.
3. Hunter Hampton, "Saints Embrace Savagery: BYU Football and the Making of Modern Mormonism," in *The History of American College Football: Institutional Policy, Culture, and Reform*, ed. Christian Anderson and Amber Fallucca (New York: Routledge, 2021), 110–32. For a comparative treatment of denominational colleges' football programs, see Hunter Hampton, *The Gridiron Gospel: Faith and College Football in 20th-Century America* (Champaign: University of Illinois Press, 2025).
4. Paul Putz, *The Spirit of the Game: American Christianity and Big-Time Sports* (New York: Oxford University Press, 2024), 174–202.
5. Onaje Woodbine, *Black Gods of the Asphalt: Religion, Hip-Hop, and Street Basketball* (New York: Columbia University Press, 2018).
6. Richard Light and Louise Kinnaird, "Appeasing the Gods: Shinto, Sumo, and 'True' Japanese Spirit," in *With God on Their Side: Sport in the Service of Religion*, ed. Tara Magdalinski and Timothy Chandler (New York: Routledge, 2002), 139–59. For further scholarship on Asian religions and sport, see Zachary T. Smith, Dennis J. Frost, and Stephen G. Covell, eds., *Religion and Sport in Japan* (Honolulu: University of Hawaii Press, 2024).
7. Ferne Perlstein, dir. *Sumo East and West*. PBS Independent Lens, 2003.
8. Andrea Jain, *Selling Yoga: From Counterculture to Pop Culture* (New York: Oxford University Press, 2015).
9. Joseph Alter, *The Wrestler's Body: Identity and Ideology in North India* (Berkeley: University of California Press, 1992).
10. Philip P. Arnold, *The Gift of Sports: Indigenous Ceremonial Dimensions of the Games We Love* (Solana Beach, CA: Cognella Academic Publishing, 2012); Thomas Vennum, *American Indian Lacrosse: Little Brother of War* (Baltimore, MD: Johns Hopkins University Press, 2008).
11. Rebecca Alpert, *Religion and Sports: An Introduction and Case Studies* (New York: Columbia University Press, 2015).
12. Rebecca Alpert and Art Remillard, eds., *Gods, Games, and Globalization: New Perspectives on Religion and Sport* (Macon, GA: Mercer University Press, 2019); David Torevell, Clive Palmer, and Paul Rowan, eds., *Training the Body: Perspectives from Religion, Physical Culture and Sport* (New York: Routledge, 2022).

13. Jeffrey Scholes and Randall Balmer, eds., *Religion and Sport in North America: Critical Essays for the Twenty-First Century* (New York: Routledge, 2023).
14. Rebecca Alpert, Afe Adogame, and James Deming, eds., *Handbook on Religion and Sport* (New York: Routledge, forthcoming).

Chapter 1

1. Eric Bain-Selbo and D. Gregory Sapp, *Understanding Sport as a Religious Phenomenon* (New York: Bloomsbury Academic, 2016), 2.
2. Paul Myhre, *Introduction to Religious Studies* (Winona, MN: Anselm Academic, 2009), 4.
3. Ibid., 13.
4. Emile Durkheim, *The Elementary Forms of Religious Life*, trans. Karen E. Fields (New York: The Free Press, 1995), 220.
5. David Chidester, "The Church of Baseball, the Fetish of Coca-Cola, and the Potlatch of Rock 'n' Roll," in *Religion and Popular Culture in America*, ed. Bruce David Forbes and Jeffrey H. Mahan (Berkeley: University of California Press, 2005), 221.
6. Joseph L. Price, ed., *From Season to Season: Sports as American Religion* (Macon, GA: Mercer University Press, 2001).
7. Joseph L. Price, "The Super Bowl as Religious Festival," in *Sport and Religion*, ed. Shirl Hoffman (Champaign, IL: Human Kinetics, 1992), 13–15.
8. Catherine L. Albanese, *America: Religions and Religion* (Belmont, CA: Wadsworth, 1992), 9–10.
9. Ibid., 475–7.
10. Michael Novak, "The Natural Religion," in *Sport and Religion*, ed. Shirl Hoffman (Champaign, IL: Human Kinetics Books, 1992), 36.
11. Rudolf Otto, *The Idea of the Holy*, trans. John W. Harvey (Oxford: Oxford University Press, 1981).
12. Paul Tillich, *Dynamics of Faith* (New York: Harper and Row, 1957).
13. Joan M. Chandler, "Sport is Not a Religion," in *Sport and Religion*, ed. Shirl Hoffman (Champaign, IL: Human Kinetics, 1992), 59.
14. Malory Nye, *Religion: The Basics*, 2nd ed. (New York: Routledge, 2008), 3.
15. For an excellent analysis of this, see Winnifred Sullivan, *The Impossibility of Religious Freedom* (Princeton, NJ: Princeton University Press, 2005).
16. Jonathan Z. Smith, *Relating Religion: Essays in the Study of Religion* (Chicago: University of Chicago Press, 2004), 377.
17. Internal Revenue Service, "Definition of a Church," https://www.irs.gov/charities-non-profits/churches-religious-organizations/definition-of-church (accessed December 17, 2024).
18. Craig Martin, *A Critical Introduction to the Study of Religion* (New York: Taylor & Francis, 2017), 3.
19. Ibid., 4.
20. Ibid.
21. Brent Nongbri, *Before Religion: A History of a Modern Concept* (New Haven, CT: Yale University Press, 2013), 6.
22. Martin, *A Critical Introduction to the Study of Religion*, 8.

23. Donald M. Fisher, *Lacrosse: A History of the Game* (Baltimore, MD: Johns Hopkins University Press, 2002), 14–16.
24. "The Game of Lacrosse," *The Graphic*, June 3, 1876, 542.
25. Fisher, *Lacrosse*, 24–34.
26. Jay Coakley, "Assessing the Sociology of Sport: On Cultural Sensibilities and the Great Sport Myth," *International Review for the Sociology of Sport* 50 (2015): 403.
27. Megan Goodwin and Ilyse Morgenstein Fuerst, *Religion Is Not Done with You: or, the Hidden Power of Religion on Race, Maps, Bodies, and Law* (Boston, MA: Beacon Press, 2024), 24.
28. Ibid., 26.
29. Jay Coakley, *Sport in Society: Issues and Controversies*, 7th ed. (Boston, MA: McGraw-Hill, 2001), 20.
30. Religion of Sports, "About," https://www.religionofsports.com/about (accessed March 25, 2025).

Chapter 2

1. William J. Baker, "Introduction," in James Naismith, *Basketball: Its Origin and Development* (Lincoln: University of Nebraska Press, 1996), xii.
2. Quoted in James Wharton, *Crusaders for Fitness: The History of American Health Reformers* (Princeton, NJ: Princeton University Press, 1982), 281.
3. Figures gathered from U.S. Census Data. "1860 Census: Population of the United States," https://www.census.gov/library/publications/1864/dec/1860a.html (accessed November 12, 2024); "1880 Census: Volume 1. Statistics of the Population of the United States," https://www.census.gov/library/publications/1883/dec/vol-01-population.html (accessed November 12, 2024); "1900 Census Bulletin 11: Populations of Cities Having 25,000 Inhabitants or More in 1900," https://www2.census.gov/library/publications/decennial/1900/bulletins/demographic/11-population-cities-25000-inhabitants.pdf (accessed November 12, 2024); "Abstract of the Fourteenth Census of the United States," https://www2.census.gov/library/publications/decennial/1920/abstract/abstract-1920-part2.pdf (accessed November 12, 2024).
4. David G. Schuster, *Neurasthenic Nation: America's Search for Health, Happiness, and Comfort, 1869–1920* (New Brunswick, NJ: Rutgers University Press, 2011), 85–6.
5. Ibid., 89.
6. Theodore Dreiser, *Sister Carrie* (New York: Double Day, Page, and Co., 1900).
7. Schuster, *Neurasthenic Nation*, 93.
8. Diana Martin, "The Rest Cure Revisited," *The American Journal of Psychiatry* 164, no. 5 (May 2007): 737–8.
9. For a fictionalized account of her experience with rest cure for neurasthenia, see Charlotte Perkins Gilman, "The Yellow Wallpaper," *The New England Magazine*, January 1892.
10. James Naismith, *Basketball: Its Origin and Development* (Lincoln: University of Nebraska Press, 1996), 30.
11. Ibid.
12. Ibid., 53–5.
13. Ibid., 120.
14. Eric Anderson, Rory Magrath, and Rachael Bullingham, *Out in Sport: The Experiences of Openly Gay and Lesbian Athletes in Competitive Sport* (London: Routledge, 2016), 25. John Donald

Gustav-Wrathall, in his history of gay cruising at the YMCA, argues that, ironically, the YMCA's increased emphasis on male physique led to men looking on other men's bodies with desire. In addition, the YMCA was one of safest places to pursue homosexual encounters because of its Christian reputation; it was less likely to be raided by the police. This made YMCAs across the country spaces for male sexual encounters from at least the 1880s through the height of gay cruising in the 1940s to the 1960s. As the YMCA shifted its mission to families instead of men and relocated from cities to suburbs in the 1970s, gay cruising declined. After the riots outside the Stonewall gay club in New York City in 1969, it became much harder for police to justify raids on places where gay people congregated. John Donald Gustav-Wrathall, *Take the Young Stranger by the Hand: Same-Sex Relations and the YMCA* (Chicago: University of Chicago Press, 1998).

15. Quoted in Ken Parille, *Boys at Home: Discipline, Masculinity, and "The Boy-Problem" in Nineteenth-Century American Literature* (Knoxville: University of Tennessee Press, 2009), 18.
16. "Against Boys" *The Living Age* 984, no. 77 (April 1863): 85–8.
17. Thomas Hughes, *Tom Brown's School Days* (Cambridge: Macmillan, 1857).
18. Parille, *Boys at Home*, 24.
19. Quoted in Julia Grant, *The Boy Problem: Educating Boys in Urban America, 1870–1970* (Baltimore, MD: Johns Hopkins University Press, 2014), 41.
20. Ibid., 42.
21. Theodore Roosevelt, "What We Can Expect of the American Boy," *St. Nicholas* 27, no. 7 (May 1900): 571–2.
22. Clifford Putney, *Muscular Christianity: Manhood and Sports in Protestant America, 1880–1920* (Cambridge, MA: Harvard University Press, 2001), 111.
23. Quoted in ibid., 104.
24. Ibid., 113–14.
25. Quoted in David L. Witt, *Ernest Thompson Seton: The Life and Legacy of an Artist and Conservationist* (Layton, UT: Gibbs Smith, 2010), 104.
26. William Forbush, *The Boy Problem* (New York: Pilgrim Press, 1901), 15–16.
27. Ibid., 204.
28. Nina Mjagkij, "True Manhood: The YMCA and Racial Advancement, 1890–1920," in *Men and Women Adrift: The YMCA and YWCA in the City*, ed. Nina Mjagkij and Margaret Spratt (New York: New York University Press, 1997), 141.
29. Michelle Alexander has examined the consequences of politics of respectability in the age of mass incarceration, arguing that politics of respectability is doomed to fail not because something is wrong with the Black poor, but simply because nothing is special about them: they break the law just like everyone else but are more likely to suffer because of it. Michelle Alexander, *The New Jim Crow: Mass Incarceration in the Age of Colorblindness* (New York: The New Press, 2010), 216–17.
30. Mjagkij, "True Manhood," 149.
31. Ibid., 141.
32. Ibid., 146.
33. Benjamin René Jordan, *Modern Manhood and the Boy Scouts of America: Citizenship, Race, and the Environment, 1910–1930* (Chapel Hill: University of North Carolina Press, 2016), 198.
34. Quoted in ibid., 204.

35. Ibid., 208.
36. Grant, *The Boy Problem*, 66.
37. Quoted in Putney, *Muscular Christianity*, 11.
38. Yeonsik Jung, "'Our One Great National Malady': Neurasthenia and American Imperial and Masculine Anxiety at the Turn of the Twentieth Century," *Korean Journal of Medical History* 30, no. 2 (August 31, 2021): 393–432.

Chapter 3

1. "The Global Religious Landscape: Jews," Pew Research Center, https://www.pewresearch.org/religion/2012/12/18/global-religious-landscape-jew/ (accessed December 4, 2024).
2. Stephen Prothero, *God Is Not One: The Eight Rival Religions That Run the World* (New York: Harper One, 2010), 265.
3. Peter Levine, *Ellis Island to Ebbets Field: Sport and the American Jewish Experience* (New York: Oxford University Press, 1992), 12–13.
4. Quoted in Ari F. Sclar, "'The Disadvantage Far Outweighs the Benefits': How the Rise and Fall of 'the Jewish Game' at the 92nd Street YMHA Exemplified Jewish Conceptions of Athleticism," in Bruce Zuckerman, Ari F. Sclar, and Lisa Ansell, eds., *Beyond Stereotypes: American Jews and Sports* (West Lafayette, IN: Purdue University Press, 2014), 97.
5. Quoted in ibid., 100.
6. Ibid., 103.
7. Quoted in Linda J. Borish, "Jewish Women in the American Gym: Basketball, Ethnicity, and Gender in the Early Twentieth Century," in *Jews in the Gym: Judaism, Sports, and Athletics*, Leonard J. Greenspoon (Purdue, IN: Purdue University Press, 2012), 227.
8. Daniel Nathan, *Saying It's So: A Cultural History of the Black Sox Scandal* (Champaign: University of Illinois Press, 2002), 38.
9. Levine, *Ellis Island to Ebbets Field*, 103–5.
10. Nathan, *Saying It's So*, 28.
11. Ibid., 36.
12. Leo P. Ribuffo, "Henry Ford and 'The International Jew,'" *American Jewish History* 69, no. 4 (June 1980): 437–77. *The Protocols of the Learned Elders of Zion* remains an influential antisemitic text in the twenty-first-century United States. See Daniel Schulman, "America's Most Dangerous Anti-Jewish Propagandist: Making Sense of Anti-Semitism Today Requires Examining Henry Ford's Outsize Part in its Origins," *The Atlantic*, November 7, 2023, https://www.theatlantic.com/ideas/archive/2023/11/henry-ford-anti-semitism/675911/ (accessed December 28, 2023).
13. "Jewish Gamblers Corrupt American Baseball," *Dearborn Independent*, September 3, 1921, https://chroniclingamerica.loc.gov/lccn/2013218776/1921-09-03/ed-1/seq-8/ (accessed February 12, 2025).
14. "Jewish Degradation of American Baseball," *Dearborn Independent*, September 10, 1921, https://www.loc.gov/item/2013218776/1921-09-10/ed-1/ (accessed December 28, 2023).
15. Mae Ngai, *Impossible Subjects: Illegal Aliens and the Making of Modern America* (Princeton, NJ: Princeton University Press, 2004), 24.
16. "Immigration Law of 1924." Sixty-Eighth Congress, Chapter 190. https://govtrackus.s3.amazonaws.com/legislink/pdf/stat/43/STATUTE-43-Pg153a.pdf (accessed November 7, 2023).

17. Ngai, *Impossible Subjects*, 27.
18. Quoted in Levine, *Ellis Island to Ebbets Field*, 64.
19. Quoted in ibid.
20. Ibid., 65.
21. Quoted in Jeffrey Gurock, *Judaism's Encounter with American Sports* (Bloomington: Indiana University Press, 2005), 88
22. Ibid., 87.
23. Rebecca Alpert, *Out of Left Field: Jews and Black Baseball* (New York: Oxford University Press, 2011), 8.
24. Alan J. Pollock, *Barnstorming to Heaven: Syd Pollock and His Great Black Teams*, ed. James A. Riley (Tuscaloosa: University of Alabama Press, 2006), 49.
25. Quoted in Alpert, *Out of Left Field*, 114.
26. Ibid., 122–30.
27. Rebecca Alpert, *Religion and Sports: An Introduction and Case Studies* (New York: Columbia University Press, 2015), 98.
28. Ibid., 99–100.
29. Quoted in ibid., 102.
30. "Sherrill Rebuffs Olympic Ban Plea: Scores Agitation," *New York Times*, October 22, 1935, https://timesmachine.nytimes.com/timesmachine/1935/10/22/93714412.html (accessed November 7, 2023).
31. Alpert, *Religion and Sports*, 103.
32. Ibid., 105.
33. Raphael Medoff, "American Jewish Responses to the Holocaust," in *The Columbia History of Jews and Judaism in America*, ed. Marc Lee Raphael (New York: Columbia University Press, 2008), 296–9.
34. Ibid., 308.
35. Levine, *Ellis Island to Ebbets Field*, 134–7.
36. Ibid., 245.
37. Ibid., 244–6.

Chapter 4

1. "Christian Employment.com," https://christianjobnet.com/christian-sports/ (accessed October 1, 2024).
2. "NCCAA Career Hub," https://thenccaa.org/sports/2016/6/29/NCCAA_Career_Hub.aspx (accessed October 1, 2024).
3. This chart includes data from 2019 instead of 2020 because the COVID-19 pandemic resulted in the cancellation of FCA camps during 2020. Fellowship of Christian Athletes, "One Heart at a Time: Ministry Report '05," https://www.fca.org/docs/default-source/default-document-library/About/annual-reports/2005-ministry-report.pdf (accessed October 1, 2024); Fellowship of Christian Athletes, "Ignite the World of Sports for Jesus Christ: 2010 Ministry Report," https://www.fca.org/docs/default-source/default-document-library/About/annual-reports/fca-ministry-report-lg-2010-b.pdf (accessed October 1, 2024); Fellowship of Christian Athletes, "Undefeated: 2015 Ministry Report," https://www.fca.org/fca-in-action/blog-detail/2016/02/01/2015-ministry-report (accessed October 1,

2024); Fellowship of Christian Athletes, "Let's Go: 2019 Ministry Report," https://web.archive.org/web/20201203000754/https://2019.fca.org/ (accessed October 1, 2024); Fellowship of Christian Athletes, "Ministry Impact 2024," https://media.fca.org/m/56178be9c83dc1c8/original/FCA-Ministry-Impact-2024.pdf (accessed February 3, 2025).

4. Wayne Atcheson, *Impact for Christ: How FCA Has Influenced the Sports World* (Grand Island, NE: Cross Training Publishing, 1994), 158.
5. Campus Crusade for Christ decided in 2011 to use the name "Cru" for its ministries in the United States and to maintain its original title for its international ministries. The U.S. leadership of the organization began reevaluating the organization's name in 2009 and chose "Cru" after extensive research. Many chapters of Campus Crusade for Christ had been using the nickname "Cru" since the mid-1990s. Part of the decision to reevaluate the organization's U.S. name was a realization that Americans have a negative association with the word "crusade." "Frequently Asked Questions," Cru, http://www.cru.org/about-us/donor-relations/our-new-name/qanda.htm#1 (accessed August 2, 2013).
6. In the early 2000s, Cru retitled the text "Would You Like to Know God Personally?" and changed the language from "laws" to "principles." Cru, "Would You Like to Know God Personally?" https://www.cru.org/us/en/how-to-know-god/would-you-like-to-know-god-personally.html (accessed October 1, 2024).
7. Quoted in Travis Vogan, *ABC Sports: The Rise and Fall of Network Sports Television* (Berkeley: University of California Press, 2018), 25.
8. Joe Smalley, *More Than a Game* (San Bernadino, CA: Here's Life Publishers, 1981), 31, 26.
9. Quoted in Paul Putz, *The Spirt of the Game: American Christianity and Big Time Sports* (New York: Oxford University Press, 2024), 116.
10. Ibid., 119.
11. Frank Deford, "The Word According to Tom," *Sports Illustrated*, April 26, 1976, 55. This was part of a three-article series on "Sportianity." The other two articles were: Frank Deford, "Religion and Sport," *Sports Illustrated*, April 19, 1976, 88–102; and Frank Deford, "Reaching for the Stars," *Sports Illustrated*, May 3, 1976, 42–60.
12. Deford, "The Word According to Tom," 65.
13. Deford, "Religion and Sport," 100.
14. Ibid., 102.
15. Jerry Pile, "Sports and War," *The Christian Athlete*, January 1972, 2–8.
16. Quoted in Putz, *The Spirt of the Game*, 214.
17. Deford, "The Word According to Tom," 56.
18. Quoted in Annie Blazer, *Playing for God: Evangelical Women and the Unintended Consequences of Sports Ministry* (New York: NYU Press, 2015), 61.
19. Wes Neal, *The Handbook on Athletic Perfection: A Training Manual for Christian Athletes* (Prescott, AZ: Institute for Athletic Perfection, 1975), 43.
20. Ibid., 20.
21. Ibid., 20.
22. Quoted in Blazer, *Playing for God*, 63.
23. Susan K. Cahn, *Coming on Strong: Gender and Sexuality in Twentieth-Century Women's Sport* (New York: The Free Press, 1994), 250.
24. Leslie Heywood and Shari L. Dworkin, *Built to Win: The Female Athlete as Cultural Icon* (Minneapolis: University of Minnesota Press, 2003), xxi.

25. "FIFA Women's World Cup—USA 1999," http://www.fifa.com/tournaments/archive/tournament=103/edition=4644/overview.html (accessed July 1, 2007).
26. Lori Rentzel, *Emotional Dependency and How to Keep Your Friendships Healthy* (Downers Grove, IL: InterVarsity Press, 1984). Pat Griffin's work includes an account of distribution of this pamphlet at FCA and AIA events for female coaches. Pat Griffin, *Strong Women, Deep Closets* (Champaign, IL: Human Kinetics, 1998), 109–32.
27. Deb Hoffman, Julie Caldwell, and Kathy Schultz, *Experiencing God's Power for Female Athletes: How to Compete Knowing and Doing the Will of God* (Grand Island, NE: Cross Training Publishing, 1999), 133.
28. Ibid., 3.
29. Excerpted from ibid., 138–42.
30. Melissa Wilcox, *Coming Out in Christianity: Religion, Identity, and Community* (Bloomington: Indiana University Press, 2003); Michelle Wolkomir, *Be Not Deceived: The Sacred and Sexual Struggles of Gay and Ex-Gay Christian Men* (New Brunswick, NJ: Rutgers University Press, 2006).
31. Candace Chellew-Hodge, *Bulletproof Faith: A Spiritual Survival Guide for Gay and Lesbian Christians* (San Francisco, CA: Jossey-Bass, 2008), 171.
32. Ibid., 7.
33. Ibid., xi–xii.
34. Interview by author.
35. Mary Jackson, "Taking Sides: A Growing Divide over the Theology of Sexual Brokenness Threatens to Tear Evangelical Institutions Apart," *World News Group*, February 22, 2024, https://wng.org/articles/taking-sides-1708229211 (accessed March 21, 2025).
36. See Sprinkle's response to Rosaria Butterfield. Sprinkle, "Responding to Rosaria Butterfield's Claims About Preston Sprinkle and The Center," The Center for Faith, Sexuality, and Gender, November 29, 2023, https://www.centerforfaith.com/blog/responding-to-rosaria-butterfield-s-claims-about-preston-sprinkle-and-the-center (accessed February 11, 2025).
37. Tony Mator, "Cru Discontinues LGBTQ Training Program for Staff," *Ministry Watch,* October 14, 2024, https://ministrywatch.com/cru-discontinues-lgbtq-training-program-for-staff/ (accessed February 7, 2025).
38. Interview by author.
39. Interview by author.
40. Kelsey Davis and Georgia McKee, "The CAC Story," Christian Athlete Circles, https://christianathletecircles.org/our-story (accessed February 28, 2025).
41. Interview by author.
42. Shirl Hoffman, "Sports Fanatics: How Christians Have Succumbed to the Sports Culture—And What Might Be Done About It," *Christianity Today*, February 2010, http://www.christianitytoday.com/ct/2010/february/3.20.html (accessed February 12, 2025).
43. John F. Harris, "God Gave Us 'What We Deserve,' Says Falwell," *Washington Post*, September 14, 2001, https://www.washingtonpost.com/archive/lifestyle/2001/09/14/god-gave-us-what-we-deserve-falwell-says/ef3e322e-03e0-453e-b8ea-b8bc592a6479/ (accessed February 12, 2025); Jefferson Walker, "God, Gays, and Voodoo: Voicing Blame after Katrina," *Communication and Theater Association of Minnesota Journal* 41, no. 1 (November 2015): 29–48.

Chapter 5

1. Ellen W. Gorsevski and Michael L. Butterworth, "Muhammad Ali's Fighting Words: The Paradox of Violence in Nonviolent Rhetoric," *Quarterly Journal of Speech* 97, no. 1 (February 2011): 59. Thomas Hauser, a biographer of Ali, suggests that Ali simply lost the gold medal. Hauser, *Muhammad Ali: His Life and Times* (New York: Simon & Schuster, 1991).
2. Stephen C. Finley, *In and Out of This World: Material and Extraterrestrial Bodies in the Nation of Islam* (Durham, NC: Duke University Press, 2022), 19.
3. Elijah Muhammad, *Message to the Blackman in America* (Phoenix, AZ: Secretarius MEMPS Publications, 1973); 116.
4. Louis Lomax, dir. *The Hate That Hate Produced*, 1959.
5. Malcolm X and Alex Haley, *The Autobiography of Malcolm X* (New York: Ballantine Books, 1964; 2015 mass market edition), 250, emphasis in original.
6. Ibid., 258–60, emphasis in original.
7. Maureen Smith, "*Muhammad Speaks* and Muhammad Ali: Intersections of the Nation of Islam and Sport in the 1960s," in *With God on Their Side: Sport in the Service of Religion*, ed. Tara Magdalinski and Timothy J. Chandler (New York: Routledge, 2002), 180.
8. Henry Machirella, "Cassius In, Meets with Muslim," *New York Daily News*, March 2, 1964.
9. Quoted in Walter Dean Myers, *The Greatest: Muhammad Ali* (New York: Scholastic Press, 2001), 54.
10. Quoted in Howard Bingham and Max Wallace, *Muhammad Ali's Greatest Fight: Cassius Clay vs. the United States of America* (New York: M. Evans and Company, 2000), 105.
11. Quoted in Grant Farred, *What's My Name? Black Vernacular Intellectuals* (Minneapolis: University of Minnesota Press, 2003), 38.
12. Hamilton Gregory, *McNamara's Folly: The Use of Low-IQ Troops in the Vietnam War* (Conshohocken, PA: Infinity Publishing, 2015); Kirklin J. Bateman, "Project 100,000: New Standards Men and the U.S. Military in Vietnam" (PhD diss., George Mason University, 2014), https://www.proquest.com/dissertations-theses/project-100-000-new-standards-men-u-s-military/docview/1617970765/se-2 (accessed November 20, 2024).
13. Bingham and Wallace, *Muhammad Ali's Greatest Fight*, 112.
14. Karl Evanzz, "The FBI and the Nation of Islam," in *The FBI and Religion: Faith and National Security Before and After 9/11*, ed. Sylvester A. Johnson and Steven Weitzman (Berkeley: University of California, 2017), 162–3.
15. Ibid., 162.
16. Muhammad Ali, Part 1 of 4, 34. https://vault.fbi.gov/muhammad-ali/Muhammad%20Ali%20Part%2001%20of%2004/view (accessed November 18, 2024).
17. Bingham and Wallace, *Muhammad Ali's Greatest Fight*, 115.
18. Dawn-Marie Gibson, "Making Original Men: Elijah Muhammad, the Nation of Islam, and the Fruit of Islam," *Journal of Religious History* 44, no. 3 (September 2020): 319–37.
19. Muhammad Ali, Part 1 of 4, 9. https://vault.fbi.gov/muhammad-ali/Muhammad%20Ali%20Part%2001%20of%2004/view (accessed November 18, 2024).
20. Ibid., 56.
21. Jack Olsen, "A Case of Conscience," *Sports Illustrated*, April 11, 1966, 89.

22. Quoted in Bingham and Wallace, *Muhammad Ali's Greatest Fight*, 130.
23. Quoted in ibid., 131.
24. Quoted in Mike Marqusee, *Redemption Song: Muhammad Ali and the Spirit of the Sixties* (New York: Verso, 1999), 214–15.
25. Martin Luther King Jr., "Beyond Vietnam," April 4, 1967.
26. Quoted in Bingham and Wallace, *Muhammad Ali's Greatest Fight*, 127.
27. Muhammad Ali, Part 2 of 4, 241. https://vault.fbi.gov/muhammad-ali/Muhammad%20Ali%20Part%2002%20of%2004/view (accessed November 18, 2024). It was not until the early 1970s that Congress became aware of counterintelligence tactics at home and abroad and launched an investigation into the nation's intelligence complex. The U.S. Senate "Church Committee," named for Senator Frank Church from Idaho, was the most significant of these investigatory enterprises and soon revealed that the FBI, CIA, and other intelligence institutions were regularly violating constitutional rights of American citizens. The most notable of these was the FBI's Counterintelligence Operation (COINTELPRO). In response to the congressional investigation, the U.S. Congress passed the Foreign Intelligence and Surveillance Act of 1978, which included protocols to protect constitutional rights of Americans. The Justice Department also assured the American public that COINTELPRO had been formally dismantled and ceased to operate in 1971.
28. Bingham and Wallace, *Muhammad Ali's Greatest Fight*, 127.
29. Quoted in ibid., 146.
30. Ibid., 151–2.
31. Smith, "*Muhammad Speaks* and Muhammad Ali," 183.
32. Quoted in Robert Lipsyte, "Clay Refuses Army Oath; Stripped of Boxing Crown," *New York Times*, April 29, 1967, https://archive.nytimes.com/www.nytimes.com/books/98/10/25/specials/ali-army.html (accessed November 20, 2024).
33. Gorsevski and Butterworth, "Muhammad Ali's Fighting Words," 57.
34. Bob Woodward and Scott Armstrong, *The Brethren: Inside the Supreme Court* (New York: Avon Books, 1979), 157–8.
35. Ibid., 159.
36. Ibid., 159–60.
37. Michael Ezra, *Muhammad Ali: The Making of an Icon* (Philadelphia, PA: Temple University Press, 2009).
38. Elijah Muhammad, "Clarification of Actions Taken by Messenger Muhammad Against Muhammad Ali's Action," *Muhammad Speaks*, April 11, 1969, 2.
39. Associated Press, "Bush Presents Ali with Presidential Medal of Freedom," *ESPN*, November 9, 2005. https://www.espn.com/sports/boxing/news/story?id=2219166 (accessed November 21, 2024).
40. *New York Times*, "Obama Remembers Ali as a 'Personal Hero,'" June 10, 2016. https://www.nytimes.com/video/us/100000004464075/obama-remembers-ali-as-a-personal-hero.html (accessed November 21, 2024).

Chapter 6

1. Steve Muhammad and Donnie Williams, *BKF Kenpo: History and Advanced Strategic Principles* (Burbank, CA: Unique Publications, 2002), 4.
2. Stephen Prothero, *God Is Not One: The Eight Rival Religions That Run the World* (New York: Harper One, 2010), 101–30.
3. Ibid., 169–201.
4. Udo Moenig, *Taekwondo: From a Martial Art to a Martial Sport* (New York: Routledge, 2015), 150–1.
5. Nitobe Inazō, *Bushido: The Soul of Japan* (1900), https://www.gutenberg.org/cache/epub/12096/pg12096-images.html#BUSHIDO (accessed September 26, 2024).
6. Moenig, *Taekwondo*, 153.
7. Shohei Sato, "The Sportification of Judo: Global Convergence and Evolution," *Journal of Global History* 8 (2013): 303.
8. Kano Jigorō, *Jūdō*, November 1917, quoting the official translation from Kodokan, "Reigi: Dignity of the Judoka," http://Kodokanjudoinstitute.org/en/courtesy/grace (accessed January 10, 2024).
9. Quoted in Paul Droubie, "Judo as Authentic Fake: Debates over the Sacred and Profane," in *Religion and Sport in Japan*, ed. Zachary Smith, Stephen Covell, and Dennis Frost (Honolulu: University of Hawai'i Press, 2024), 96.
10. Moenig, *Taekwondo*, 163.
11. Quoted in ibid., 156.
12. Quoted in ibid., 158.
13. Eric Madis, "The Evolution of Taekwondo from Japanese Karate," in *Martial Arts in the Modern World*, ed. Thomas A. Green and Joseph R. Svinth (Westport, CT: Praeger, 2003), 185–207.
14. Quoted in Michel Brousse and David Matsumoto, *Judo in the U.S.: A Century of Dedication* (Berkeley, CA: North Atlantic Books, 2005), 31.
15. Quoted in ibid., 53.
16. Duncan Ryūken Williams, *American Sutra: A Story of Faith and Freedom in the Second World War* (Cambridge, MA: The Belknap Press of Harvard University, 2019), 3.
17. Ibid., 86.
18. Eric L. Muller, *American Inquisition: The Hunt for Japanese American Disloyalty in World War II* (Chapel Hill: University of North Carolina Press, 2007), 32.
19. Quoted in ibid., 33.
20. Ibid., 36–7.
21. Brian Masaru Hayashi, *Democratizing the Enemy: The Japanese American Internment* (Princeton, NJ: Princeton University Press, 2004), 200–204.
22. Williams, *American Sutra*, 238–41.
23. Quoted in Brousse and Matsumoto, *Judo in the U.S.*, 90.
24. Quoted in George Rego and Abdul Rashid, *The Founding of Jujutsu and Judo in America* (Independently Published, 2022), 170–1.
25. Quoted in ibid., 175.
26. Zachary F. Price, *Black Dragon: Afro Asian Performance and the Martial Arts Imagination* (Columbus: The Ohio State University Press, 2022), 4.
27. Quoted in ibid., 14.

28. Quoted in James Halpin, "The Little Dragon: Bruce Lee (1940–1973)," in *Martial Arts in the Modern World*, ed. Thomas A. Green and Joseph R. Svinth (Westport, CT: Praeger, 2003), 122.
29. "Conversation with Teacher," Robert Clouse, dir. *Enter the Dragon*. 1973; Hong Kong: Concord Production, Inc., and Warner Bros.
30. Muhammad and Williams, *BKF Kenpo*, 47–51.
31. Ibid., 84.
32. Ibid., 67.
33. Interview by author.
34. James Tremayne, "Karate's Last Angry Man," *Karate Illustrated*, May 1974, 13–17.
35. Interview by author.
36. Muhammad and Williams, *BKF Kenpo*, 86–7.
37. Ibid., 85–6.
38. Ibid., 58.
39. Jon Shirota, "An Equal Opportunity Sensei," *Karate Illustrated*, January 1973, 16.
40. Interview by author.
41. Muhammad and Williams, *BKF Kenpo*, 68.
42. Interview by author.
43. Price, *Black Dragon*, 59.

Chapter 7

1. Interview by author.
2. Steven Fink, *Dribbling for Dawah: Sports Among Muslim Americans* (Macon, GA: Mercer University Press, 2016), 65.
3. Michael Sells, *Approaching the Qur'an: The Early Revelations*, 3rd ed. (New York: One World Academic, 2023).
4. Besheer Mohamed and Jeff Diamant, "Black Muslims Account for a Fifth of All U.S. Muslims, and About Half Are Converts to Islam," Pew Research Center, January 17, 2019, https://www.pewresearch.org/short-reads/2019/01/17/black-muslims-account-for-a-fifth-of-all-u-s-muslims-and-about-half-are-converts-to-islam/ (accessed March 6, 2025).
5. Leila Ahmed, *Women and the Rise of Islam* (New Haven, CT: Yale University Press, 1992), 55–6.
6. Leila Ahmed, *A Quiet Revolution: The Veil's Resurgence, from the Middle East to America* (New Haven, CT: Yale University Press, 2011), 68–92.
7. Bozena C. Welborne, Aubrey Westfall, Özge Çelik Russell, and Sarah A. Tobin, *The Politics of the Headscarf in the United States* (Ithaca, NY: Cornell University Press, 2018), 25.
8. Ahmed, *A Quiet Revolution*, 204.
9. Ibid., 207–9.
10. Associated Press, "Iran Women's Soccer Team Thwarted by Hijab Ban," *CBS News*, June 7, 2011, https://www.cbsnews.com/news/iran-womens-soccer-team-thwarted-by-hijab-ban/ (accessed March 10, 2025).
11. Full text of the article is available. Julie Kimball and Tahrier Walid Sub Laban, "Muslim Women's Swimwear at the University of California, Santa Cruz," *Swimming World News*, March 23, 2007, https://www.swimmingworldmagazine.com/news/

muslim-womens-swimwear-at-the-university-of-california-santa-cruz/ (accessed October 22, 2024).
12. Interview by author.
13. Kulsoom Abdullah, "Presentation to the IWF June 2011," YouTube Video, 6:13, June 25, 2011, https://www.youtube.com/watch?v=2b0Z7qf0Pko (accessed March 24, 2025).
14. Interview by author.
15. Interview by author.
16. Interview by author.
17. Alaa Elassar, "This Muslim Basketball Player Refused to Take off Her Hijab, Opening New Doors for Athletes of Other Faiths," *CNN*, November 7, 2020, https://www.cnn.com/2020/11/07/us/bilqis-abdul-qaadir-basketball-hijab-trnd/index.html (accessed October 7, 2024).
18. Laura Yuen, "Amaiya Zafar Wants to Box Competitively, and Modestly," *MPR News*, September 23, 2015, https://www.mprnews.org/story/2015/09/23/muslim-boxer (accessed October 23, 2024); Cindy Boren, "A Muslim Girl Wasn't Allowed to Box in a Hijab, so Her Opponent Shared Victory with Her," *Washington Post*, November 22, 2016, https://www.washingtonpost.com/news/early-lead/wp/2016/11/22/a-muslim-girl-wasnt-allowed-to-box-in-a-hijab-so-her-opponent-shared-victory-with-her/ (accessed October 23, 2024).
19. Boren, "A Muslim Girl Wasn't Allowed to Box in a Hijab, so Her Opponent Shared Victory with Her."
20. Alaa Elassar, "A Muslim Athlete Was Disqualified from Her High School Volleyball Match for Wearing a Hijab," *CNN*, September 27, 2020, https://www.cnn.com/2020/09/27/us/hijab-volleyball-disqualified-nashville-trnd/index.html (accessed October 2, 2024).
21. Karissa Niehoff, "NFHS Playing Rules Committees Address Religious, Cultural Concerns of Participants," *NFHS News*, June 2, 2021, https://www.nfhs.org/articles/nfhs-playing-rules-committees-address-religious-cultural-concerns-of-participants/ (accessed March 24, 2025).
22. Dalia Fahmy, "How Common Is Religious Fasting in the United States?" Pew Research Center, April 25, 2024, https://www.pewresearch.org/short-reads/2024/04/05/how-common-is-religious-fasting-in-the-united-states/ (accessed March 24, 2025).
23. Ron Synovitz, "Muslim Olympians Face Ramadan Fasting Choices," *Voice of America*, June 12, 2012, https://www.voanews.com/a/muslim-olympians-ramadan-fasting/1208050.html (accessed January 8, 2024).
24. Sam Borden, "Observance of Ramadan Poses Challenges to Muslim Athletes," *New York Times*, July 31, 2012, https://www.nytimes.com/2012/08/01/sports/olympics/ramadan-poses-challenges-for-muslims-at-the-olympics.html (accessed March 24, 2025).
25. Interview by author.
26. Hamza Abdullah, "Coach Hamza's Guide for Athlete's in Ramadan," https://drive.google.com/file/d/14dZVQGAelvKDSNWyuHHARwkusKmgVue4/view (accessed March 12, 2025).
27. Tribune News Service, "Kyrie Irving Lights Up Barclays Center Despite Challenge of Playing During Ramadan," *Denver Post*, April 12, 2022, https://www.denverpost.com/2022/04/12/kyrie-irving-lights-up-barclays-center-despite-challenge-of-playing-during-ramadan-to-play-an-nba-game-like-that-hes-different/amp/ (accessed January 16, 2025).
28. Aminah Malik, "Faith, Fasting, and Football: Muslim Student Athletes During Ramadan," *Georgetown Voice*, April 27, 2024, https://georgetownvoice.com/2024/04/27/faith-fasting-and-football-muslim-student-athletes-during-ramadan/ (accessed February 17, 2025).

29. University Athletic Association, "Fasting for Faith: UAA Student-Athletes Observe Ramadan," March 28, 2024, https://uaasports.info/news/2024/3/27/general-uaa-student-athletes-find-strength-in-observing-ramadan.aspx (accessed February 20, 2024).
30. Adam Rossow, "No Food, No Water for 14 Hours a Day: Inside a Muslim Runner's Daily Ramadan Routine at Texas," *Spectrum News*, April 29, 2022, https://spectrumlocalnews.com/tx/south-texas-el-paso/news/2022/04/28/texas-longhorns--muslim--runner--ramadan (accessed January 28, 2025).
31. Mike Massaro, "UConn Players Inspire Muslim Community by Observing Ramadan at Final Four," *NBC Connecticut*, April 3, 2023, https://www.nbcconnecticut.com/news/sports/dog-house/uconn-players-inspire-muslim-community-by-observing-ramadan-at-final-four/3006968/ (accessed January 30, 2025); Kelly Lu, "Fasting for Ramadan Doesn't Slow Down Northwestern Athletes," *Daily Northwestern*, April 4, 2024, https://dailynorthwestern.com/2024/04/04/campus/fasting-for-ramadan-doesnt-slow-down-northwestern-athletes/(accessed February 13, 2025).
32. Jack Jenkins, "U.S. Soccer Leagues Add Game Breaks for Players Fasting During Ramadan," *Religion News Service*, April 4, 2023, https://religionnews.com/2023/04/04/u-s-soccer-leagues-add-game-breaks-for-players-fasting-during-ramadan/(accessed February 11, 2025).
33. Kevin Reynolds, "BYU Doesn't Have to Play on Sundays. So Should the NCAA Better Accommodate Muslim Athletes During Ramadan?" *Salt Lake Tribune*, March 21, 2024, https://www.sltrib.com/sports/byu-cougars/2024/03/21/byu-doesnt-have-play-sundays-so/(accessed February 12, 2025).
34. Shara Talia Taylor and Eryn Mathewson, "'I'm Not a Model. I'm an Athlete and People Should Focus More on My Athleticism Rather Than My Clothes,'" *CNN*, March 21, 2023, https://www.cnn.com/2023/01/16/sport/muslim-women-athletes-spt-intl/index.html (accessed October 16, 2024).
35. Taylor Vortherms, "Deering High May Be First U.S. School to Offer Athletic Hijabs," *The Portland Press Herald*, May 21, 2017, https://www.centralmaine.com/2017/05/21/deering-high-may-be-the-first-school-in-the-u-s-to-offer-athletic-hijabs/(accessed October 9, 2024).
36. Interview by author.
37. Interview by author.
38. Besheer Mohamed, "New Estimates Show U.S. Muslim Population Continues to Grow," Pew Research Center, https://www.pewresearch.org/short-reads/2018/01/03/new-estimates-show-u-s-muslim-population-continues-to-grow/ (accessed March 24, 2025).

Chapter 8

1. Quoted in Maggie Mertens, "Separating Sports by Sex Doesn't Make Sense," *The Atlantic*, September 17, 2022, https://www.theatlantic.com/culture/archive/2022/09/sports-gender-sex-segregation-coed/671460/ (accessed December 24, 2024).
2. Quoted in ibid.
3. "Gender Neutral Sports Regulation Delayed," *The Post-Journal,* September 10, 2024, https://www.post-journal.com/news/top-stories/2024/09/gender-neutral-sports-regulation-delayed/ (accessed December 24, 2024).
4. Kay Ivey, Twitter post, April 9, 2022, https://x.com/kayiveyforgov/status/1512779927694753795 (accessed June 6, 2024).

5. In using the language of "women with high testosterone" or "women with intersex variations," I follow the practice of women, gender, and sexuality scholar Valerie Moyer. She notes that this language is imperfect but is the "most respectful way to refer to women athletes who have been non-consensually revealed to have intersex traits, yet identify as women, not as intersex." Valerie Moyer, "Revising Trans-Exclusionary Narratives in Women's Sports Activism: Who Are the 'Women' of Women's Athletics?," in *Athlete Activism: Contemporary Perspectives*, ed. Rory Magrath (New York: Routledge, 2022), 96n1.
6. Judith Butler, *Bodies That Matter: On the Discursive Limits of "Sex"* (New York: Routledge, 1993).
7. Different studies have come to different conclusions on the rate of intersexed births by using broader or narrower understandings of what constitutes intersexed. A 2000 study by Brown University biologist Anne Fausto-Sterling found the birth rate of intersexed people to be 1.7 percent worldwide. Fausto-Sterling's broad definition of intersexed included conditions that do not usually result in atypical genitalia like Klinefelter syndrome (males that have an extra X chromosome), Turner syndrome (females with one X chromosome), and late-onset adrenal hyperplasia (overproduction of androgen). This broad understanding of intersexed placed the percentage of babies born intersexed on par with the percentage of babies born with red hair. Anne Fausto-Sterling, *Sexing the Body: Gender Politics and the Construction of Sexuality* (New York: Basic Books, 2000). Physician Leonard Sax has argued against this broad definition, stating, "If the term *intersex* is to retain any meaning, the term should be restricted to those conditions in which chromosomal sex is inconsistent with phenotypic sex, or in which the phenotype is not classifiable as either male or female." Using his narrower definition that focuses on atypical genitalia, the percentage of the global population born intersexed is much lower, 0.018 percent. Leonard Sax, "How Common Is Intersex? A Response to Anne Fausto-Sterling," *Journal of Sex Research* 39, no. 3 (2002): 174–8.
8. Elizabeth Reis and Suzanne Kessler, "Why History Matters: Fetal Dex and Intersex," *American Journal of Bioethics* 10, no. 9 (2010): 58–9.
9. Paisley Currah, *Sex Is as Sex Does: Governing Transgender Identity* (New York: NYU Press, 2022), 44–5.
10. Jon Benzinger, "Thinking Through the Lia Thomas Controversy (Christian Perspective)," YouTube Video, 4:32, April 19, 2022, https://www.youtube.com/watch?v=iCVi7Z3trJo (accessed June 17, 2025).
11. Quoted in Jacob Levy, "16 UPenn Swimmers Ask School Not to Challenge Transgender Policy That Could Block Teammate Lia Thomas from Competing," *CNN*, February 4, 2022, https://www.cnn.com/2022/02/04/us/lia-thomas-ncaa-transgender-policy-letter (accessed June 17, 2025).
12. Vanessa Heggie, "Testing Sex and Gender in Sports: Reinventing, Reimagining and Reconstructing Histories," *Endeavor* 34, no. 4 (2010): 163.
13. Deborah Larned, "The Femininity Test: A Woman's First Olympic Hurdle," *Womensports* 3 (1976): 8–11.
14. Jaime Schultz, "Disciplining Sex: 'Gender Verification' Policies and Women's Sport," in *The Palgrave Handbook of Olympic Studies*, ed. Helen Lenskyj and Stephen Wagg (New York: Palgrave Macmillan, 2012), 455n25.
15. Polish Olympic Committee, "Ewa Klobukowska," https://olimpijski.pl/olimpijczycy/ewa-klobukowska/ (accessed July 8, 2024).
16. World Athletics, "Eligibility Regulations for the Female Classification (Athletes with Differences of Sex Development)," adopted March 31, 2023, 2.

17. Joseph Hooper, "Get into Olympic Shape with Michael Phelps," *Men's Journal*, August 3, 2017, https://www.mensjournal.com/sports/get-into-olympic-shape-with-michael-phelps-20120803 (accessed June 6, 2023).
18. Sylvia Tamale, *Decolonization and Afro-Feminism* (Quebec: Daraja Press, 2020), 111.
19. Bianna Golodryga, Ben Church, and Henry Hullah, "Caster Semenya Says She Went through 'Hell' Due to Testosterone Limits Imposed on Female Athletes," *CNN Sports*, November 6, 2023, https://www.cnn.com/2023/11/06/sport/caster-semenya-totestosterone-limits-world-athletics-spt-intl/index.html (accessed July 3, 2024).
20. Ben Morse, "Caster Semenya Wins European Court of Human Rights Appeal over 'Discriminatory' Testosterone Limit," *CNN Sports*, July 11, 2023, https://www.cnn.com/2023/07/11/sport/caster-semenya-wins-appeal-discriminatory-testosterone-limit-spt-intl/index.html (accessed July 3, 2024).
21. Adam Nagourney and Jeremy W. Peters, "How a Campaign Against Transgender Rights Mobilized Conservatives," *New York Times*, April 16, 2023, https://www.nytimes.com/2023/04/16/us/politics/transgender-conservative-campaign.html (accessed June 6, 2023).
22. There is no empirical evidence that conversion therapy is effective and ample evidence that conversion therapy causes harm to individuals including mental health concerns and increased likelihood of suicide attempts. See Douglas C. Haldeman, ed. *The Case Against Conversion "Therapy": Evidence, Ethics, and Alternatives* (Washington, D.C.: American Psychological Association, 2022).
23. Exodus International, "What 'Cures' Homosexuality?" http://exodus.to/content/view/505/186/ (accessed April 12, 2008).
24. Kristine Stolakis, dir. *Pray Away*. 2021; Los Gatos, CA: Netflix.
25. Pat Griffin, "Changing the Game: Homophobia, Sexism and Lesbians in Sport," in *Gender and Sport: A Reader*, ed. Sheila Scranton and Anne Flintoff (New York: Routledge, 2002), 196.
26. Alan Chambers, "I Am Sorry," June 19, 2013, http://exodusinternational.org/2013/06/i-am-sorry/ (accessed August 15, 2013).
27. Pew Research Center, "Majority of Public Favors Same-Sex Marriage, but Divisions Persist," May 14, 2019, https://www.pewresearch.org/politics/2019/05/14/majority-of-public-favors-same-sex-marriage-but-divisions-persist/ (accessed June 6, 2023).
28. Pew Research Center, "Attitudes on Same-Sex Marriage," May 14, 2019, https://www.pewresearch.org/religion/fact-sheet/changing-attitudes-on-gay-marriage/ (accessed June 6, 2023).
29. Kim Parker, Nikki Graf, and Ruth Igielnik, "Generation Z Looks a Lot Like Millennials on Key Social and Political Issues," Pew Research Center, January 17, 2019, https://www.pewresearch.org/social-trends/2019/01/17/generation-z-looks-a-lot-like-millennials-on-key-social-and-political-issues/ (accessed June 6, 2023).
30. Tom Rosentiel, "Trends in Attitudes Toward Religion and Social Issues: 1987–2007," Pew Research Center, October 15, 2007, https://www.pewresearch.org/2007/10/15/trends-in-attitudes-toward-religion-and-social-issues-19872007/ (accessed June 6, 2023); Gregory Smith, "About Three-in-Ten U.S. Adults Are Now Religiously Unaffiliated," Pew Research Center, December 14, 2021, https://www.pewresearch.org/religion/2021/12/14/about-three-in-ten-u-s-adults-are-now-religiously-unaffiliated/ (accessed June 6, 2023).
31. Robert Putnam and David Campbell, *American Grace: How Religion Divides and Unites Us* (New York: Simon & Schuster, 2010), 128–9.

32. U.S. Congress, House, *Defense of Marriage Act*, HR 3396, 104th Cong., introduced in House May 7, 1996, https://www.congress.gov/bill/104th-congress/house-bill/3396 (accessed July 9, 2024).
33. Full language of the Executive Order is available. Presidential Actions, "Defending Women from Gender Ideology Extremism and Restoring Biological Truth to the Federal Government," January 20, 2025, https://www.whitehouse.gov/presidential-actions/2025/01/defending-women-from-gender-ideology-extremism-and-restoring-biological-truth-to-the-federal-government/ (accessed January 24, 2025).
34. Trevor Project, "2024 National Survey on LGBTQ+ Mental Health," https://www.thetrevorproject.org/survey-2024/ (accessed January 24, 2025).
35. John Bel Edwards, "Veto Message," Louisiana Senate Bill 156, June 29, 2021, https://www.legis.la.gov/legis/BillInfo.aspx?s=21RS&b=SB156&sbi=y (accessed May 25, 2023).
36. Anna Brown, "About 5% of Young Adults in the U.S. Say Their Gender Is Different from Their Sex Assigned at Birth," Pew Research Center, June 7, 2022, https://www.pewresearch.org/short-reads/2022/06/07/about-5-of-young-adults-in-the-u-s-say-their-gender-is-different-from-their-sex-assigned-at-birth/ (accessed June 7, 2023).
37. Michael Barnett, dir. *Changing the Game*. 2019; Santa Monica, CA: Hulu.
38. Michael Lipka and Patricia Tevington, "Attitudes About Transgender Issues Vary Widely Among Christians, Religious 'Nones' in U.S." Pew Research Center, July 7, 2022, https://www.pewresearch.org/short-reads/2022/07/07/attitudes-about-transgender-issues-vary-widely-among-christians-religious-nones-in-u-s/ (accessed June 6, 2023).

Chapter 9

1. Julia Grant, *The Boy Problem: Educating Boys in Urban America, 1870–1970* (Baltimore, MD: Johns Hopkins University Press, 2014), 61.
2. Michael Messner, "Barbie Girls Versus Sea Monsters," *Gender & Society* 14, no. 6 (December 2000): 773.
3. Deborah J. Anderson, John J. Cheslock, and Ronald G. Ehrenberg, "Gender Equity in Intercollegiate Athletics: Determinants of Title IX Compliance," *Journal of Higher Education* 77, no. 2 (March/April 2006): 225–50.
4. Michael Messner, *It's All for the Kids: Gender, Families, and Youth Sports* (Berkeley: University of California Press, 2009), 153.
5. Julie Byrne, *O God of Players: The Story of the Immaculata Mighty Macs* (New York: Columbia University Press, 2003), 81.
6. Messner, *It's All for the Kids*, 141.
7. Ibid., 152.
8. Ibid., 163.
9. Ibid., 161.
10. Ibid., 156.
11. Quoted in ibid., 166.
12. Ibid., 166–7.

13. Steven J. Overman, *Sports Crazy: How Sports Are Sabotaging American Schools* (Jackson: University Press of Mississippi, 2019), 106.
14. Joan Ryan, *Little Girls in Pretty Boxes: The Making and Breaking of Elite Gymnasts and Figure Skaters* (New York: Doubleday, 1995), 4.
15. Ibid., 59.
16. Ibid., 63.
17. Ibid., 58–9.
18. Quoted in ibid., 83.
19. Quoted in ibid., 93.
20. Lindsay Crouse, "I Was the Fastest Girl in America, Until I Joined Nike," *New York Times*, November 7, 2019, https://www.nytimes.com/2019/11/07/opinion/nike-running-mary-cain.html (accessed August 13, 2021).
21. Full transcript available at Mary Cain, "I Was the Fastest Girl in America, Until I Joined Nike," video transcript, *New York Times* (November 7 2019), https://www.nytimes.com/2019/11/07/opinion/nike-running-mary-cain.html (accessed August 13, 2021)
22. Michael Messner, *Taking the Field: Men, Women, and Sports* (Minneapolis: University of Minnesota Press, 2002), 120–1.
23. Matthew Lindaman, *Fit for America: Major John L. Griffith and the Quest for Athletics and Fitness* (Syracuse, NY: Syracuse University Press, 2018), 78–9.
24. Kathleen Bachynski, *No Game for Boys to Play: The History of Youth Football and the Origins of a Public Health Crisis* (Chapel Hill: University of North Carolina Press, 2019), 13–19.
25. Ibid., 19–35.
26. Ibid., 36.
27. Ibid., 39.
28. Quoted in ibid., 45.
29. For analysis of the cultural consequences of this, see Mariah Burton Nelson, *The Stronger Women Get, the More Men Love Football: Sexism and the American Culture of Sports* (New York: Harcourt, 1994).
30. Bachynski, *No Game for Boys to Play*, 183–4.
31. Cantu defined asymptomatic as "no headaches, dizziness, or impaired orientation, concentration, or memory during rest or exertion." Quoted in ibid., 186.
32. Alan Schwarz, "N.F.L.-Backed Youth Program Says It Reduced Concussions. The Data Disagrees," *New York Times*, July 27, 2016, https://www.nytimes.com/2016/07/28/sports/football/nfl-concussions-youth-program-heads-up-football.html (accessed August 16, 2021).
33. Peter Landesman, dir. *Concussion*. Culver City, CA: Columbia Pictures, 2015.
34. Bachynski, *No Game for Boys to Play*, 213.
35. Ibid., 179.
36. Ibid., 180.
37. Michela Musto, "Athletes in the Pool, Girls and Boys on Deck: The Contextual Construction of Gender in Coed Youth Swimming," in *Child's Play: Sport in Kids' Worlds*, ed. Michela Musto and Michael A. Messner (New Brunswick, NJ: Rutgers University Press, 2016), 125–43.
38. "Home," Upward Sports, https://www.upward.org/ (accessed June 20, 2025).

Chapter 10

1. Some scholars have made the choice to use "R-dskins" in their writing. For this chapter, I have chosen to use the term unmodified when the term itself is under consideration and to use "Washington football team" in other instances. I include the term unmodified in all quotations and publication titles. I also use the terms "Native American" and "Indian" interchangeably.
2. Erik Brady, "Daniel Snyder Says Redskins Will Never Change Name," *USA Today Sports*, May 10, 2013, https://www.usatoday.com/story/sports/nfl/redskins/2013/05/09/washington-redskins-daniel-snyder/2148127/ (accessed August 13, 2020).
3. "History of Progress," Change the Mascot, https://www.changethemascot.org/history-of-progress (accessed August 12, 2020). The California Racial Mascots Act affected four high schools that used the moniker "Redskins."
4. Quoted in Rosa Sanchez, "NFL's Washington Redskins to Change Name Following Years of Backlash," *ABC News*, July 13, 2020, https://abcnews.go.com/US/washington-redskins-change-years-backlash/story?id=71744369 (accessed August 12, 2020).
5. Stereotypes of Native Americans proliferate in American culture and range from intriguing beauties, peaceful land guardians, and childlike innocents to drunkards and savages (noble or ignoble). This chapter focuses on the most common stereotype employed in mascotry: the savage. For treatment of other stereotypes, see S. Elizabeth Bird, ed., *Dressing in Feathers: The Construction of the Indian in American Popular Culture* (Boulder, CO: Westview Press, 1996).
6. Ronald Niezen, *Spirit Wars: Native North American Religions in the Age of Nation Building* (Berkeley: University of California Press, 2000), 13–14.
7. Ibid., 33.
8. Rebecca Goetz, *The Baptism of Early Virginia: How Christianity Created Race* (Baltimore, MD: John Hopkins University Press, 2012), 35–6.
9. Ibid., 42–5, 59–60.
10. Ibid., 72–4.
11. Ibid., 137.
12. Peter Silver, *Our Savage Neighbors: How Indian War Transformed Early America* (New York: Norton, 2008).
13. Ibid., 114.
14. Rayna Green, "The Tribe Called Wannabee: Playing Indian in America and Europe," *Folklore* 99, no. 1 (1988): 37.
15. Ibid., 40.
16. Glenn Giffin, "Koshare Scouts Dance in the New Year," *Denver Post*, December 31, 1977.
17. L. G. Moses, *Wild West Shows and the Images of American Indians, 1883–1933* (Albuquerque: University of New Mexico Press, 1996), 23.
18. For analyses of portrayals of Native Americans in Hollywood Westerns, see Jon Tuska, *The American West in Film: Critical Approaches to the Western* (Westport, CN: Greenwood Press, 1985); Andrew Brodie Smith, *Shooting Cowboys and Indians: Silent Western Films, American Culture, and the Birth of Hollywood* (Boulder: University Press of Colorado, 2004).
19. Jennifer Guiliano, *Indian Spectacle: College Mascots and the Anxiety of Modern America* (New Brunswick, NJ: Rutgers University Press, 2015), 40–1. Guiliano points out that many historians have misidentified the University of Pennsylvania's mascot as William Penn, largely due

to misreporting in the Illinois student newspaper at the time. She argues, "The conjoined representations of William Penn, as the colonial founder, and Benjamin Franklin, as the University of Pennsylvania founder, suggest an elaborately constructed convergence where UPenn legitimated its existence through historical genealogies of founding and state formation." Ibid., 124n59.

20. C. Richard King, *Unsettling America: The Uses of Indianness in the 21st Century* (New York: Rowman & Littlefield, 2013), 27–42.
21. Andrea Smith, "Heteropatriarchy and the Three Pillars of White Supremacy: Rethinking Women of Color Organizing," in *Color of Violence*, ed. INCITE! (Durham, NC: Duke University Press, 2016), 66–73. On Smith's claimed racial identity and controversy, see Sarah Viren, "The Native Scholar Who Wasn't," *New York Times Magazine*, May 25, 2021, https://www.nytimes.com/2021/05/25/magazine/cherokee-native-american-andrea-smith.html (accessed September 30, 2024).
22. Ken Denlinger, "Protest of 'Redskins' Draws 2,000 at Stadium," *Washington Post*, January 27, 1992, https://www.washingtonpost.com/archive/sports/1992/01/27/protest-of-redskins-draws-2000-at-stadium/39e3ab8d-791f-4531-98ee-e11d7acceb66/ (accessed October 23, 2020).
23. Quoted in ibid.
24. Laurel R. Davis, "Protest Against the Use of Native American Mascots: A Challenge to Traditional American Identity," *Journal of Sport and Social Issues* 17, no. 1 (April 1993): 17.
25. King, *Unsettling America*, 30–1.
26. Jay Rosenstein, dir. *In Whose Honor?* 1997; Beacon, NY: New Day Films.
27. The full report to the Board of Trustees is available through the Program in American Indian Studies at the University of Illinois. "Dialog Report," https://ais.illinois.edu/system/files/2020-11/Dialogue_Report.pdf (accessed October 1, 2024).
28. National Collegiate Athletic Association, "NCAA News Release: NCAA Executive Committee Issues Guidelines for Use of Native American Mascots at Championship Events," August 5, 2005, http://fs.ncaa.org/Docs/PressArchive/2005/Announcements/NCAA%2BExecutive%2BCommittee%2BIssues%2BGuidelines%2Bfor%2BUse%2Bof%2BNative%2BAmerican%2BMascots%2Bat%2BChampionship%2BEvents.html (accessed August 12, 2020).
29. These fourteen colleges were California State-Stanislaus University (Warriors), Lycoming College (Warriors), Winona State University (Warriors), Hawaii-Manoa University (Rainbow Warriors), Eastern Connecticut State University (Warriors), East Stroudsburg University (Warriors), Husson College (Braves, changed to Eagles), Merrimack College (Warriors), Southeast Missouri State University (Indians, changed to Redhawks), State University of West Georgia (Braves, changed to Wolves), Stonehill College (Chieftains, changed to Skyhawks), San Diego State University (Aztec Warriors), Wisconsin Lutheran College (Warriors), and the University of North Carolina-Pembroke (Braves/Bravehawks). In addition, the College of William and Mary (Indians) recieved an extension to complete its self-study on the mascot issue.
30. These nineteen colleges were Alcorn State University (Braves), Arkansas State University (Indians), Bradley University (Braves), Carthage College (Redmen), Catawba College (Indians), Central Michigan University (Chippewas), Chowan College (Braves), Florida State University (Seminoles), Indiana University-Pennsylvania (Indians), McMurry University (Indians), Midwestern State University (Indians); Mississippi College (Choctaws), Newberry College (Indians), Southeastern Oklahoma State University (Savages), University of Illinois-Champaign

(Illini), University of Louisiana Monroe (Indians), University of Utah (Utes), and University of North Dakota (Fighting Sioux). When the College of William and Mary completed its self-assessment and changed its team name from "Indians" to "The Tribe," the NCAA denied them compliance because they continued to use feathers in their imagery. They subsequently dropped the use of feathers.

31. These five colleges were Catawba College (Catawba Indians), Central Michigan University (Chippewas), Florida State University (Seminoles), Mississippi College (Choctaws), and University of Utah (Utes).
32. Shannon Ryan, "Illinois Must Finally Remove All Links to Chief Illiniwek," *Chicago Tribune*, August 26, 2017, https://www.chicagotribune.com/sports/college/ct-illinois-chief-illiniwek-ryan-spt-0827-20170826-column.html (accessed August 12, 2020).
33. Erik Brady, "Redskins' Daniel Snyder 'THRILLED' with Supreme Court Ruling," *USA Today*, June 19, 2017, https://www.usatoday.com/story/sports/nfl/redskins/2017/06/19/supreme-court-ruling-victory-redskins/408845001/ (accessed August 12, 2020).
34. Andrew Billings and Jason Black, *Mascot Nation: The Controversy over Native American Representations in Sports* (Urbana: University of Illinois Press, 2018), 187–92.
35. National Congress of American Indians, "Proud to Be," YouTube Video, 2:00, January 27, 2014, https://www.youtube.com/watch?v=mR-tbOxlhvE (accessed August 12, 2020).
36. Redskins Facts, "Redskins Is a Powerful Name," YouTube Video, 1:51, August 13, 2014, https://youtu.be/40SFqadRTQ0 (accessed August 12, 2020).
37. Redskins Facts, "The Facts," https://web.archive.org/web/20140812013623/http://www.redskinsfacts.com/facts (accessed August 12, 2020).
38. Billings and Black, *Mascot Nation*, 50–61.
39. Quoted in Alison Kosik, "FedEx Asks the Washington Redskins to Change Their Name After Pressure from Investor Groups," *CNN Business*, July 3, 2020, https://www.cnn.com/2020/07/02/business/fedex-washington-redskins/index.html (accessed August 13, 2020).
40. Peter King, "No. 10, 10 Years In," *Sports Illustrated NFL*, September 6, 2013, https://www.si.com/nfl/2013/09/06/eli-manning-new-york-giants-dallas-cowboys (accessed August 13, 2020).
41. C. Richard King, *Redskins: Insult and Brand* (Lincoln: University of Nebraska Press, 2016), 166–7.

Chapter 11

1. "Oprah's interview with Lance Armstrong," Part II, OWN Network, January 19, 2013. David Walsh was a reporter who followed Armstrong's career for years and was one of the first to raise suspicions about his performance-enhancement strategies. See Pierre Ballester and David Walsh, *L.A. Confidentiel: Les Secrets de Lance Armstrong* (France: La Martiniè, 2004); and David Walsh, *Seven Deadly Sins: My Pursuit of Lance Armstrong* (New York: Atria Books, 2013).
2. Kathryn Lofton, "Public Confessions: Oprah Winfrey's American Religious History," *Women & Performance: A Journal of Feminist Theory* 18 (2008): 56.
3. Marianne Perciaccante, *Calling Down Fire: Charles Grandison Finney and Revivalism in Jefferson County, New York, 1800–1840* (New York: SUNY Press, 2003).
4. Kathryn Lofton, *Oprah: The Gospel of an Icon* (Berkeley: University of California Press, 2011).

5. Lofton, "Public Confessions: Oprah Winfrey's American Religious History," 59.
6. Jay Coakley, *Sport in Society: Issues and Controversies*, 7th edition (Boston, MA: McGraw-Hill, 2001), 72.
7. Ibid., 93.
8. Paul Dimeo and Verner Møller, *The Anti-Doping Crisis in Sport: Causes, Consequences, Solutions* (New York: Routledge, 2018).
9. David R. Mottram, "A Historical Perspective of Doping and Anti-Doping in Sport," in *Drugs in Sport*, 5th ed., ed. David R. Mottram (New York: Routledge, 2011), 24.
10. Paul Dimeo, *A History of Drug Use in Sport 1876–1976* (New York: Routledge, 2007), 121.
11. Ibid., 106.
12. USADA, "Choose USADA: Why Clean Sport Matters," https://www.usada.org/choose-usada/choose-usada-why-clean-sport-matters/ (accessed November 12, 2020).
13. Shirl Hoffman, *Good Game: Christianity and the Culture of Sports* (Waco, TX: Baylor University Press, 2010), 149.
14. Mark Fainaru-Wada and Lance Williams, *Game of Shadows: Barry Bonds, BALCO, and the Steroids Scandal That Rocked Professional Sports* (New York: Gotham Books, 2006), xi.
15. Jose Canseco, *Vindicated: Big Names, Big Liars, and the Battle to Save Baseball* (New York: Simon & Schuster, 2008), 86–7, emphasis in original.
16. Jose Canseco, *Juiced: Wild Times, Rampant 'Roids, Smash Hits, and How Baseball Got Big* (New York: HarperCollins, 2005), 178.
17. Fainaru-Wada and Williams, *Game of Shadows*, 72.
18. Howard Bryant, *Juicing the Game: Drugs, Power, and the Fight for the Soul of Major League Baseball* (New York: Viking, 2005), 303–17.
19. George W. Bush, "Text of President Bush's 2004 State of the Union Address," *Washington Post*, January 20, 2004, https://www.washingtonpost.com/wp-srv/politics/transcripts/bushtext_012004.html (accessed November 12, 2020).
20. Quoted in Shaun Assael, *Steroid Nation: Juiced Home Run Totals, Anti-Aging Miracles, and a Hercules in Every High School: The Secret History of America's True Drug Addiction* (New York: ESPN Books, 2007), 238.
21. Quoted in ibid., 258.
22. Canseco, *Vindicated*, 62.
23. Full text of the hearing is available. *Restoring Faith in America's Pastime: Evaluating Major League Baseball's Efforts to Eradicate Steroid Use*, 109th Cong., March 17, 2005, https://www.govinfo.gov/content/pkg/CHRG-109hhrg23038/html/CHRG-109hhrg23038.htm (accessed March 25, 2025).
24. Canseco, *Juiced*, 1. Canseco changed his tune in his second book, *Vindicated*. In this book, he claimed that his earlier autobiography was an attempt to shed light on steroid use run amok and force the powers of Major League Baseball to clean up the sport.
25. Quoted in Fainaru-Wada and Williams, *Game of Shadows*, 266.
26. Quoted in ibid., 268.
27. Quoted in Daniel M. Rosen, *Dope: A History of Performance Enhancement in Sports from the Nineteenth Century to Today* (Westport, CN: Praeger, 2008), 101.
28. Quoted in ibid.
29. Walsh, *Seven Deadly Sins*, 52.

30. Quoted in Rosen, *Dope*, 155.
31. Quoted in ibid.
32. Ibid., 158.
33. Quoted in Walsh, *Seven Deadly Sins*, 388.
34. Quoted in ibid., 401.
35. Steven R. Thomsen and Harper Anderson, "Using the Rhetoric of Atonement to Analyze Lance Armstrong's Failed Attempt at Redeeming His Public Image," *Journal of Sports Media* 10 (2015): 82.
36. Quoted in ibid., 86.
37. Andrew Meyer, "Redemption of 'Fallen' Hero-Athletes: Lance Armstrong, Isaiah, and Doing Good While Being Bad," *Religions* 10 (2019): 486.
38. Thomsen and Anderson, "Using the Rhetoric of Atonement to Analyze Lance Armstrong's Failed Attempt at Redeeming His Public Image," 93.
39. Lofton, *Oprah*, 99.
40. Thomsen and Anderson, "Using the Rhetoric of Atonement to Analyze Lance Armstrong's Failed Attempt at Redeeming His Public Image," 93.
41. Thomas H. Murray, *Good Sport: Why Our Games Matter—And How Doping Undermines Them* (New York: Oxford University Press, 2018).
42. Michael Shafer, *Well Played: A Christian Theology of Sport and the Ethics of Doping* (Cambridge: Lutterworth Press, 2015).
43. Verner Møller, "The Anti-Doping Campaign" in *Doping and Public Policy*, ed. John Hoberman and Verner Møller (Odense: University Press of Southern Denmark, 2004), 152–3.
44. Robert Hughes and Jay Coakley, "Positive Deviance Among Athletes: The Implications of Overconformity to the Sport Ethic," *Sociology of Sport Journal* 8 (1991): 322.
45. Møller, "The Anti-Doping Campaign," 153.
46. Verner Møller, *The Ethics of Doping and Anti-Doping: Redeeming the Soul of Sport?* (New York: Routledge, 2010), 24.
47. Canseco, *Juiced*, 9.

Chapter 12

1. Quoted in Ronald A. Smith, *The Myth of the Amateur: A History of College Athletic Scholarships* (Austin: University of Texas Press, 2021), 193. For further analysis of the NCAA's manufacture of consent to amateurism, see Richard M. Southall and Ellen J. Staurowsky, "Cheering on the Collegiate Model: Creating, Disseminating, and Imbedding the NCAA's Redefinition of Amateurism," *Journal of Sport and Social Issues* 37, no. 4 (November 2013): 315–429.
2. Digest of Education Statistics, Table 303.90, "Fall Enrollment and Number of Degree-Granting Postsecondary Institutions, by Control and Religious Affiliation of Institution: Selected years, 1980 through 2021," National Center for Education Statistics, https://nces.ed.gov/programs/digest/d22/tables/dt22_303.90.asp (accessed February 27, 2025).
3. Samuel Schuman, *Seeing the Light: Religious Colleges in Twenty-First Century America* (Baltimore, MD: Johns Hopkins University Press, 2010), 21–27.

4. Ibid., 28–33.
5. Shaun R. Harper and Jamel K. Donnor, "Bad Sportsmanship: Why College Sports Are so Scandalous," in *Scandals in College Sports*, ed. Shaun R. Harper and Jamel K. Donnor (New York: Routledge, 2017), 2.
6. Michael Oriard, *Bowled Over: Big-Time College Football from the Sixties to the BCS Era* (Chapel Hill: University of North Carolina Press, 2009), 21–23.
7. Quoted in Matthew Lindaman, *Fit for America: Major John L. Griffith and the Quest for Athletics and Fitness* (Syracuse, NY: Syracuse University Press, 2018), 75.
8. Quoted in ibid.
9. Quoted in ibid., 79.
10. Smith, *The Myth of the Amateur*, 181–2.
11. Harper and Donnor, "Bad Sportsmanship," 5.
12. The NCAA was inconsistent in its policies regarding payment for athletes when it comes to the Olympics. The U.S. Olympic Committee regularly pays medalists through its Operation Gold program. For the 2018 and 2020 Olympics, Operation Gold paid each gold medalist $37,500; each silver medalist, $22,500; and each bronze medalist, $15,000. Operation Gold also regularly pays athletes who win other international competitions. When these Olympians were college athletes, the NCAA did not enforce its policy that college athletes could not receive any payments for their athletic performance. Brandon Penny, "U.S. Olympic Committee Significantly Increases Payments to Athletes for Olympic/Paralympic, World Medals," *Team USA News*, December 13, 2016, https://www.teamusa.org/News/2016/December/13/US-Olympic-Committee-Significantly-Increases-Payments-To-Athletes-For-Olympic-World-Medals (accessed December 29, 2022).
13. Quoted in Smith, *The Myth of the Amateur*, 191.
14. Joe Nocera and Ben Strauss, *Indentured: The Inside Story of the Rebellion Against the NCAA* (New York: Penguin, 2016), 3.
15. Walter Byers and Charles Hammer, *Unsportsmanlike Conduct: Exploiting College Athletes* (Ann Arbor: University of Michigan Press, 1995), 376.
16. Ibid., 372.
17. Quoted in ibid.
18. Quoted in Smith, *The Myth of the Amateur*, 199.
19. Quoted in ibid., 217.
20. Nicole Auerbach and Justin Williams, "What to Know About House v. NCAA Settlement and a Historic Day for College Sports," *New York Times*, May 24, 2024, https://www.nytimes.com/athletic/5517461/2024/05/24/ncaa-lawsuit-house-paying-players/(accessed February 26, 2025). In the days following the final approval of the House settlement, eight female athletes appealed the payout portion of the settlement on the grounds of Title IX compliance. At the time of writing, this appeal was in progress. See Lindsey Schnell and Ralph D. Russo, "Appeal Alleging House v. NCAA Settlement 'Ignored' Title IX Will Pause Back Pay Plans," *New York Times*, June 11, 2025, https://www.nytimes.com/athletic/6419483/2025/06/11/house-ncaa-settlement-appeal-title-ix/ (accessed June 25, 2025).
21. Pete Nakos, "Department of Education States Revenue Sharing Payments Must Follow Title IX," *On3*, January 16, 2025, https://www.on3.com/nil/news/department-of-education-states-revenue-sharing-payments-must-follow-title-ix/ (accessed February 26, 2025).

22. Pete Nakos, "Department of Education Rescinds Rev-Share Title IX Guidance," *On3*, February 12, 2025, https://www.on3.com/nil/news/department-of-education-rescinds-rev-share-title-ix-guidance/ (accessed February 26, 2025).
23. Full text of ITA's letter is available at ITA Tennis, "ITA Submits a Letter of Concern to Judge Claudia Wilken Regarding the *House v. NCAA* Settlement," January 29, 2025, https://wearecollegetennis.com/2025/01/29/ita-submits-a-letter-of-concern-to-judge-claudia-wilken/ (accessed February 25, 2025).
24. Davidson College, "Scholar-Athlete Name, Image, and Likeness (NIL) Policy," July 1, 2021, https://davidsonwildcats.com/documents/2021/6/30/NIL_Policy_PDF.pdf (accessed December 15, 2022), 3.
25. Georgetown University Athletics Department, "University NIL Policy," https://guhoyas.com/feature/blueprint (accessed December 15, 2022).
26. Marquette University Intercollegiate Athletics, "Student Athlete Name, Image and Likeness Policies," July 2, 2021, https://gomarquette.com/documents/2021/9/30/Marquette_NIL_Policy_July_2_2021.pdf (accessed December 15, 2022), 3; Seton Hall University, "Seton Hall University Image, Name, and/or Likeness Policy," November 2022, https://www.shu.edu/policies/seton-hall-university-image-name-and-or-likeness-policy.cfm (accessed December 15, 2022).
27. Texas Christian University, "Changing the Game: How One University Is Teaching Students to Tackle NIL," *Inside Higher Ed Narratives*, https://narratives.insidehighered.com/texas-christian-teaching-students-name-image-likeness-rules/index.html (accessed September 2, 2024).
28. Quoted in Emily Belz, "Christian Athletes Know How to Build Platforms for Jesus. Can They Brand Themselves?," *Christianity Today*, April 24, 2024, https://www.christianitytoday.com/news/2024/april/christian-athletes-nil-deals-ncaa.html (accessed August 20, 2024).
29. NCAA, "Transfer Portal Data: Division II Student-Athlete Transfer Trends," February 21, 2023, https://www.ncaa.org/sports/2023/2/21/transfer-portal-data-division-ii-student-athlete-transfer-trends.aspx (accessed February 26, 2025).
30. Interview by author.
31. Interview by author.
32. Interview by author.
33. Greg Johnson, "2022 Transfer Trends Released for Divisions I and II," NCAA Media Center, February 21, 2023, https://www.ncaa.org/news/2023/2/21/media-center-2022-transfer-trends-released-for-divisions-i-and-ii.aspx (accessed February 26, 2025).
34. Interview by author.
35. Max Fisher, *The Chaos Machine: The Inside Story of How Social Media Rewired Our Minds and Our World* (New York: Little, Brown and Co., 2022), 289.
36. Ibid., 339.
37. Ibid., 29.
38. Ibid., 31.
39. Texas Christian University, "Changing the Game."
40. Quoted in Kurt Streeter, "New Endorsements for College Athletes Resurface an Old Concern: Sex Sells," *New York Times*, November 8, 2022, https://www.nytimes.com/2022/11/08/sports/ncaabasketball/olivia-dunne-haley-jones-endorsements.html (accessed December 23, 2022).
41. "Livvy Dunne," *On3*, https://www.on3.com/db/livvy-dunne-162353/ (accessed February 26, 2025).

42. Interview by author.
43. Interview by author.
44. David Suggs, "Inside Michaela Edenfield's Makeup Routine: The Story of FSU Softball Catcher's Unique Gameday Tradition," *The Sporting News*, June 8, 2023, https://www.sportingnews.com/us/other-sports/news/michaela-edenfield-makeup-fsu-softball/a0spvj9hnmxon3tkqele-2qvt (accessed February 26, 2025); "College Softball NIL Valuations," *On3*, February 26, 2025, https://www.on3.com/nil/rankings/player/college/softball/ (accessed February 26, 2025).
45. Quoted in Ed O'Bannon and Michael McCann, *Court Justice: The Inside Story of My Battle Against the NCAA* (New York: Diversion Books, 2018), 85.

Selected Bibliography

Ahmed, Leila. *A Quiet Revolution: The Veil's Resurgence, from the Middle East to America*. New Haven, CT: Yale University Press, 2011.
Ahmed, Leila. *Women and the Rise of Islam*. New Haven, CT: Yale University Press, 1992.
Albanese, Catherine L. *America: Religions and Religion*. Belmont, CA: Wadsworth, 1992.
Alexander, Michelle. *The New Jim Crow: Mass Incarceration in the Age of Colorblindness*. New York: New Press, 2010.
Alpert, Rebecca. *Out of Left Field: Jews and Black Baseball*. New York: Oxford University Press, 2011.
Alpert, Rebecca. *Religion and Sports: An Introduction and Case Studies*. New York: Columbia University Press, 2015.
Alpert, Rebecca, and Art Remillard, eds. *Gods, Games, and Globalization: New Perspectives on Religion and Sport*. Macon, GA: Mercer University Press, 2019.
Alter, Joseph. *The Wrestler's Body: Identity and Ideology in North India*. Berkeley: University of California Press, 1992.
Anderson, Deborah J., John J. Cheslock, and Ronald G. Ehrenberg. "Gender Equity in Intercollegiate Athletics: Determinants of Title IX Compliance." *Journal of Higher Education* 77, no. 2 (March/April 2006): 225–50.
Anderson, Eric, Rory Magrath, and Rachael Bullingham. *Out in Sport: The Experiences of Openly Gay and Lesbian Athletes in Competitive Sport*. London: Routledge, 2016.
Anderson, Eric, and Ann Travers, eds. *Transgender Athletes in Competitive Sport*. New York: Routledge, 2017.
Assael, Shaun. *Steroid Nation: Juiced Home Run Totals, Anti-Aging Miracles, and a Hercules in Every High School: The Secret History of America's True Drug Addiction*. New York: ESPN Books, 2007.
Atcheson, Wayne. *Impact for Christ: How FCA Has Influenced the Sports World*. Grand Island, NE: Cross Training Publishing, 1994.
Arnold, Philip P. *The Gift of Sports: Indigenous Ceremonial Dimensions of the Games We Love*. Solana Beach, CA: Cognella Academic Publishing, 2012.
Bachynski, Kathleen. *No Game for Boys to Play: The History of Youth Football and the Origins of a Public Health Crisis*. Chapel Hill: University of North Carolina Press, 2019.
Bain-Selbo, Eric. *Game Day and God: Football, Faith, and Politics in the American South*. Macon, GA: Mercer University Press, 2009.
Bain-Selbo, Eric, and D. Gregory Sapp, *Understanding Sport as a Religious Phenomenon*. New York: Bloomsbury Academic, 2016.
Ballester, Pierre, and David Walsh. *L.A. Confidentiel: Les Secrets de Lance Armstrong*. France: La Martiniè, 2004.

Selected Bibliography

Bateman, Kirklin J. "Project 100,000: New Standards Men and the U.S. Military in Vietnam." PhD diss., George Mason University, 2014.

Bingham, Howard, and Max Wallace. *Muhammad Ali's Greatest Fight: Cassius Clay vs. the United States of America*. New York: M. Evans, 2000.

Billings, Andrew, and Jason Black. *Mascot Nation: The Controversy over Native American Representations in Sports*. Urbana: University of Illinois Press, 2018.

Bird, S. Elizabeth, ed. *Dressing in Feathers: The Construction of the Indian in American Popular Culture*. Boulder, CO: Westview Press, 1996.

Blazer, Annie. *Playing for God: Evangelical Women and the Unintended Consequences of Sports Ministry*. New York: NYU Press, 2015.

Borish, Linda J. "Jewish Women in the American Gym: Basketball, Ethnicity, and Gender in the Early Twentieth Century." In *Jews in the Gym: Judaism, Sports, and Athletics*, ed. Leonard J. Greenspoon, 213–38. Purdue, IN: Purdue University Press, 2012.

Bowman, Paul. *The Invention of Martial Arts: Popular Culture Between Asia and America*. New York: Oxford University Press, 2021.

Brousse, Michel, and David Matsumoto. *Judo in the U.S.: A Century of Dedication*. Berkeley, CA: North Atlantic Books, 2005.

Bryant, Howard. *Juicing the Game: Drugs, Power, and the Fight for the Soul of Major League Baseball*. New York: Viking, 2005.

Bundgaard, Axel. *Muscle and Manliness: The Rise of Sport in American Boarding Schools*. Syracuse, NY: Syracuse University Press, 2005.

Butler, Judith. *Bodies That Matter: On the Discursive Limits of "Sex."* New York: Routledge, 1993.

Byers, Walter, and Charles Hammer. *Unsportsmanlike Conduct: Exploiting College Athletes*. Ann Arbor: University of Michigan Press, 1995.

Byrne, Julie. *O God of Players: The Story of the Immaculata Mighty Macs*. New York: Columbia University Press, 2003.

Cahn, Susan K. *Coming on Strong: Gender and Sexuality in Twentieth-Century Women's Sport*. New York: Free Press, 1994.

Canseco, Jose. *Juiced: Wild Times, Rampant 'Roids, Smash Hits, and How Baseball Got Big*. New York: HarperCollins, 2005.

Canseco, Jose. *Vindicated: Big Names, Big Liars, and the Battle to Save Baseball*. New York: Simon & Schuster, 2008.

Chellew-Hodge, Candace. *Bulletproof Faith: A Spiritual Survival Guide for Gay and Lesbian Christians*. San Francisco, CA: Jossey-Bass, 2008.

Chidester, David. "The Church of Baseball, the Fetish of Coca-Cola, and the Potlatch of Rock 'n' Roll." In *Religion and Popular Culture in America*, ed. Bruce David Forbes and Jeffrey H. Mahan, 213–32. Berkeley: University of California Press, 2005.

Coakley, Jay. "Assessing the Sociology of Sport: On Cultural Sensibilities and the Great Sport Myth." *International Review for the Sociology of Sport* 50 (2015): 402–6.

Coakley, Jay. *Sport in Society: Issues and Controversies*. 7th edition. Boston, MA: McGraw-Hill, 2001.

Currah, Paisley. *Sex Is as Sex Does: Governing Transgender Identity*. New York: NYU Press, 2022.

Davis, Laurel R. "Protest Against the Use of Native American Mascots: A Challenge to Traditional American Identity." *Journal of Sport and Social Issues* 17, no. 1 (April 1993): 9–22.

Deford, Frank. "Reaching for the Stars." *Sports Illustrated*, May 3, 1976.

Deford, Frank. "Religion and Sport." *Sports Illustrated*, April 19, 1976.

Deford, Frank. "The Word According to Tom." *Sports Illustrated*, April 26, 1976.

Dimeo, Paul. *A History of Drug Use in Sport 1876–1976*. New York: Routledge, 2007.

Dimeo, Paul, and Verner Møller. *The Anti-Doping Crisis in Sport: Causes, Consequences, Solutions*. New York: Routledge, 2018.

Durkheim, Emile. *The Elementary Forms of Religious Life*. Trans. Karen E. Fields. New York: Free Press, 1995.

Evanzz, Karl. "The FBI and the Nation of Islam." In *The FBI and Religion: Faith and National Security Before and After 9/11*, ed. Sylvester A. Johnson and Steven Weitzman, 148–67. Berkeley: University of California, 2017.

Ezra, Michael. *Muhammad Ali: The Making of an Icon*. Philadelphia, PA: Temple University Press, 2009.

Fainaru-Wada, Mark, and Lance Williams. *Game of Shadows: Barry Bonds, BALCO, and the Steroids Scandal that Rocked Professional Sports*. New York: Gotham Books, 2006.

Farred, Grant. *What's My Name? Black Vernacular Intellectuals*. Minneapolis: University of Minnesota Press, 2003.

Fausto-Sterling, Anne. *Sexing the Body: Gender Politics and the Construction of Sexuality*. New York: Basic Books, 2000.

Fink, Steven. *Dribbling for Dawah: Sports Among Muslim Americans*. Macon, GA: Mercer University Press, 2016.

Finley, Stephen C. *In and Out of This World: Material and Extraterrestrial Bodies in the Nation of Islam*. Durham, NC: Duke University Press, 2022.

Fisher, Donald M. *Lacrosse: A History of the Game*. Baltimore, MD: Johns Hopkins University Press, 2002.

Fisher, Max. *The Chaos Machine: The Inside Story of How Social Media Rewired Our Minds and Our World*. New York: Little, Brown and Co., 2022.

Forbush, William. *The Boy Problem*. New York: Pilgrim Press, 1901.

Gems, Gerald R. "Sport and the Assimilation of American Catholics." *U.S. Catholic Historian* 36, no. 2 (Spring 2018): 33–54.

Gibson, Dawn-Marie. "Making Original Men: Elijah Muhammad, The Nation of Islam, and The Fruit of Islam." *Journal of Religious History* 44, no. 3 (September 2020): 319–37.

Goetz, Rebecca. *The Baptism of Early Virginia: How Christianity Created Race*. Baltimore, MD: John Hopkins University Press, 2012.

Goodwin, Megan, and Ilyse Morgenstein Fuerst. *Religion Is Not Done with You: Or, the Hidden Power of Religion on Race, Maps, Bodies, and Law*. Boston, MA: Beacon Press, 2024.

Gorsevski, Ellen W., and Michael L. Butterworth. "Muhammad Ali's Fighting Words: The Paradox of Violence in Nonviolent Rhetoric." *Quarterly Journal of Speech* 97, no. 1 (February 2011): 50–73.

Grant, Julia. *The Boy Problem: Educating Boys in Urban America, 1870–1970*. Baltimore, MD: Johns Hopkins University Press, 2014.

Green, Rayna. "The Tribe Called Wannabee: Playing Indian in America and Europe." *Folklore* 99, no. 1 (1988): 30–55.

Gregory, Hamilton. *McNamara's Folly: The Use of Low-IQ Troops in the Vietnam War*. Conshohocken, PA: Infinity Publishing, 2015.

Griffin, Pat. "Changing the Game: Homophobia, Sexism and Lesbians in Sport." In *Gender and Sport: A Reader*, ed. Sheila Scranton and Anne Flintoff, 193–208. New York: Routledge, 2002.

Griffin, Pat. *Strong Women, Deep Closets*. Champaign, IL: Human Kinetics, 1998.
Guiliano, Jennifer. *Indian Spectacle: College Mascots and the Anxiety of Modern America*. New Brunswick, NJ: Rutgers University Press, 2015.
Gurock, Jeffrey. *Judaism's Encounter with American Sports*. Bloomington: Indiana University Press, 2005.
Gustav-Wrathall, John Donald. *Take the Young Stranger by the Hand: Same-Sex Relations and the YMCA*. Chicago: University of Chicago Press, 1998.
Haldeman, Douglas C., ed. *The Case Against Conversion "Therapy": Evidence, Ethics, and Alternatives*. Washington, D.C.: American Psychological Association, 2022.
Halpin, James. "The Little Dragon: Bruce Lee (1940–1973)." In *Martial Arts in the Modern World*, ed. Thomas A. Green and Joseph R. Svinth, 111–28. Westport, CT: Praeger, 2003.
Hampton, Hunter. *The Gridiron Gospel: Faith and College Football in 20th-Century America*. Champaign: University of Illinois Press, 2025.
Hampton, Hunter. "Saints Embrace Savagery: BYU Football and the Making of Modern Mormonism." In *The History of American College Football: Institutional Policy, Culture, and Reform*, ed. Christian Anderson and Amber Fallucca, 110–32. New York: Routledge, 2021.
Harper, Shaun R., and Jamel K. Donnor, eds. *Scandals in College Sports*. New York: Routledge, 2017.
Hauser, Thomas. *Muhammad Ali: His Life and Times*. New York: Simon & Schuster, 1991.
Hayashi, Brian Masaru. *Democratizing the Enemy: The Japanese American Internment*. Princeton, NJ: Princeton University Press, 2004.
Heggie, Vanessa. "Testing Sex and Gender in Sports: Reinventing, Reimagining and Reconstructing Histories." *Endeavor* 34, no. 4 (2010): 157–63.
Heywood, Leslie, and Shari L. Dworkin. *Built to Win: The Female Athlete as Cultural Icon*. Minneapolis: University of Minnesota Press, 2003.
Hoffman, Deb, Julie Caldwell, and Kathy Schultz. *Experiencing God's Power for Female Athletes: How to Compete Knowing and Doing the Will of God*. Grand Island, NE: Cross Training Publishing, 1999.
Hoffman, Shirl. *Good Game: Christianity and the Culture of Sports*. Waco, TX: Baylor University Press, 2010.
Hoffman, Shirl, ed. *Sport and Religion*. Champaign, IL: Human Kinetics, 1992.
Hughes, Robert, and Jay Coakley. "Positive Deviance Among Athletes: The Implications of Overconformity to the Sport Ethic." *Sociology of Sport Journal* 8 (1991): 307–25.
Hughes, Thomas. *Tom Brown's School Days*. Cambridge: Macmillan, 1857.
Jain, Andrea. *Selling Yoga: From Counterculture to Pop Culture*. New York: Oxford University Press, 2015.
Jordan, Benjamin René. *Modern Manhood and the Boy Scouts of America: Citizenship, Race, and the Environment, 1910–1930*. Chapel Hill: University of North Carolina Press, 2016.
Jung, Yeonsik. "'Our One Great National Malady': Neurasthenia and American Imperial and Masculine Anxiety at the Turn of the Twentieth Century." *Korean Journal of Medical History* 30, no. 2 (August 2021): 393–432.
Karkazis, Katrina, and Rebecca M. Jordan-Young. "The Powers of Testosterone: Obscuring Race and Regional Bias in the Regulation of Women Athletes." *Feminist Foundations* 30, no. 2 (2018): 1–39.
King, C. Richard. *Redskins: Insult and Brand*. Lincoln: University of Nebraska Press, 2016.

King, C. Richard. *Unsettling America: The Uses of Indianness in the 21st Century*. New York: Rowman & Littlefield, 2013.

Levine, Peter. *Ellis Island to Ebbets Field: Sport and the American Jewish Experience*. New York: Oxford University Press, 1992.

Light, Richard and Louise Kinnaird. "Appeasing the Gods: Shinto, Sumo, and 'True' Japanese Spirit." In *With God on Their Side: Sport in the Service of Religion*, ed. Tara Magdalinski and Timothy Chandler, 139–59. New York: Routledge, 2002.

Lindaman, Matthew. *Fit for America: Major John L. Griffith and the Quest for Athletics and Fitness*. Syracuse, NY: Syracuse University Press, 2018.

Lofton, Kathryn. *Oprah: The Gospel of an Icon*. Berkeley: University of California Press, 2011.

Lofton, Kathryn. "Public Confessions: Oprah Winfrey's American Religious History." *Women & Performance: A Journal of Feminist Theory* 18 (2008): 51–69.

Madis, Eric. "The Evolution of Taekwondo from Japanese Karate." In *Martial Arts in the Modern World*, ed. Thomas A. Green and Joseph R. Svinth, 185–207. Westport, CT: Praeger, 2003.

Marqusee, Mike. *Redemption Song: Muhammad Ali and the Spirit of the Sixties*. New York: Verso, 1999.

Martin, Craig. *A Critical Introduction to the Study of Religion*. New York: Taylor & Francis, 2017.

Martin, Diana. "The Rest Cure Revisited." *American Journal of Psychiatry* 164, no. 5 (May 2007): 737–8.

Medoff, Raphael. "American Jewish Responses to the Holocaust." In *The Columbia History of Jews and Judaism in America*, ed. Marc Lee Raphael, 291–312. New York: Columbia University Press, 2008.

Messner, Michael. "Barbie Girls Versus Sea Monsters." *Gender & Society* 14, no. 6 (December 2000): 765–84.

Messner, Michael. *It's All for the Kids: Gender, Families, and Youth Sports*. Berkeley: University of California Press, 2009.

Messner, Michael. *Taking the Field: Men, Women, and Sports*. Minneapolis: University of Minnesota Press, 2002.

Meyer, Andrew. "Redemption of 'Fallen' Hero-Athletes: Lance Armstrong, Isaiah, and Doing Good While Being Bad." *Religions* 10 (2019): 486.

Mjagkij, Nina. "True Manhood: The YMCA and Racial Advancement, 1890–1920." In *Men and Women Adrift: The YMCA and YWCA in the City*, ed. Nina Mjagkij and Margaret Spratt, 138–59. New York: NYU Press, 1997.

Moenig, Udo. *Taekwondo: From a Martial Art to a Martial Sport*. New York: Routledge, 2015.

Møller, Verner. "The Anti-Doping Campaign." In *Doping and Public Policy*, ed. John Hoberman and Verner Møller, 145–60. Odense: University Press of Southern Denmark, 2004.

Møller, Verner. *The Ethics of Doping and Anti-Doping: Redeeming the Soul of Sport?* New York: Routledge, 2010.

Moses, L. G. *Wild West Shows and the Images of American Indians, 1883–1933*. Albuquerque: University of New Mexico Press, 1996.

Mottram, David R., ed. *Drugs in Sport*. 5th edition. New York: Routledge, 2011.

Moyer, Valerie. "Revising Trans-Exclusionary Narratives in Women's Sports Activism: Who Are the 'Women' of Women's Athletics?" In *Athlete Activism: Contemporary Perspectives*, ed. Rory Magrath, 88–98. New York: Routledge, 2022.

Muhammad, Elijah. *Message to the Blackman in America*. Phoenix, AZ: Secretarius MEMPS Publications, 1973.

Muhammad, Steve, and Donnie Williams. *BKF Kenpo: History and Advanced Strategic Principles*. Burbank, CA: Unique Publications, 2002.

Muller, Eric L. *American Inquisition: The Hunt for Japanese American Disloyalty in World War II*. Chapel Hill: University of North Carolina Press, 2007.

Murray, Thomas H. *Good Sport: Why Our Games Matter—And How Doping Undermines Them*. New York: Oxford University Press, 2018.

Musto, Michela, and Michael A. Messner, eds. *Child's Play: Sport in Kids' Worlds*. New Brunswick, NJ: Rutgers University Press, 2016.

Myers, Walter Dean. *The Greatest: Muhammad Ali*. New York: Scholastic Press, 2001.

Myhre, Paul. *Introduction to Religious Studies*. Winona, MN: Anselm Academic, 2009.

Naismith, James. 1941. Reprinted with introduction. *Basketball: Its Origin and Development*. Lincoln: University of Nebraska Press, 1996.

Nathan, Daniel. *Saying It's So: A Cultural History of the Black Sox Scandal*. Champaign: University of Illinois Press, 2002.

Neal, Wes. *The Handbook on Athletic Perfection: A Training Manual for Christian Athletes*. Prescott, AZ: Institute for Athletic Perfection, 1975.

Nelson, Mariah Burton. *The Stronger Women Get, the More Men Love Football: Sexism and the American Culture of Sports*. New York: Harcourt, 1994.

Ngai, Mae. *Impossible Subjects: Illegal Aliens and the Making of Modern America*. Princeton, NJ: Princeton University Press, 2004.

Niezen, Ronald, *Spirit Wars: Native North American Religions in the Age of Nation Building*. Berkeley: University of California Press, 2000.

Nocera, Joe, and Ben Strauss. *Indentured: The Inside Story of the Rebellion Against the NCAA*. New York: Penguin, 2016.

Nongbri, Brent. *Before Religion: A History of a Modern Concept*. New Haven, CT: Yale University Press, 2013.

Nye, Malory. *Religion: The Basics*. 2nd edition. New York: Routledge, 2008.

O'Bannon, Ed, and Michael McCann. *Court Justice: The Inside Story of My Battle Against the NCAA*. New York: Diversion Books, 2018.

Oriard, Michael. *Bowled Over: Big-Time College Football from the Sixties to the BCS Era*. Chapel Hill: University of North Carolina Press, 2009.

Otto, Rudolf. *The Idea of the Holy*. Trans. John W. Harvey. Oxford: Oxford University Press, 1981.

Overman, Steven J. *Sports Crazy: How Sports Are Sabotaging American Schools*. Jackson: University Press of Mississippi, 2019.

Oxenham, Gwendolyn. "Play Away the Gay." In *Under the Lights and in the Dark: Untold Stories of Women's Soccer*, 109–36. London: Icon Books, 2017.

Parille, Ken. *Boys at Home: Discipline, Masculinity, and "The Boy-Problem" in Nineteenth-Century American Literature*. Knoxville: University of Tennessee Press, 2011.

Perciaccante, Marianne. *Calling Down Fire: Charles Grandison Finney and Revivalism in Jefferson County, New York, 1800–1840*. New York: SUNY Press, 2003.

Pollock, Alan J. *Barnstorming to Heaven: Syd Pollock and His Great Black Teams*, ed. James A. Riley. Tuscaloosa: University of Alabama Press, 2006.

Price, Joseph L., ed. *From Season to Season: Sports as American Religion*. Macon, GA: Mercer University Press, 2001.

Price, Zachary F. *Black Dragon: Afro Asian Performance and the Martial Arts Imagination*. Columbus: Ohio State University Press, 2022.

Prothero, Stephen. *God Is Not One: The Eight Rival Religions That Run the World*. New York: Harper One, 2010.

Putnam, Robert, and David Campbell. *American Grace: How Religion Divides and Unites Us*. New York: Simon & Schuster, 2010.

Putney, Clifford. *Muscular Christianity: Manhood and Sports in Protestant America, 1880–1920*. Cambridge, MA: Harvard University Press, 2001.

Putz, Paul. *The Spirit of the Game: American Christianity and Big-Time Sports*. New York: Oxford University Press, 2024.

Rego, George, and Abdul Rashid. *The Founding of Jujutsu and Judo in America*. Independently Published, 2022.

Reis, Elizabeth, and Suzanne Kessler. "Why History Matters: Fetal Dex and Intersex." *American Journal of Bioethics* 10, no. 9 (2010): 58–9.

Rentzel, Lori. *Emotional Dependency and How to Keep Your Friendships Healthy*. Downers Grove, IL: InterVarsity Press, 1984.

Ribuffo, Leo P. "Henry Ford and 'The International Jew'." *American Jewish History* 69, no. 4 (June 1980): 437–77.

Riess, Steven A., ed. *Sports and the American Jew*. Syracuse, NY: Syracuse University Press, 1998.

Rosen, Daniel M. *Dope: A History of Performance Enhancement in Sports from the Nineteenth Century to Today*. Westport, CN: Praeger, 2008.

Ryan, Joan. *Little Girls in Pretty Boxes: The Making and Breaking of Elite Gymnasts and Figure Skaters*. New York: Doubleday, 1995.

Sato, Shohei. "The Sportification of Judo: Global Convergence and Evolution." *Journal of Global History* 8 (2013): 299–317.

Sax, Leonard. "How Common Is Intersex? A Response to Anne Fausto-Sterling." *Journal of Sex Research* 39, no. 3 (2002): 174–8.

Scholes, Jeffrey, and Randall Balmer, eds. *Religion and Sport in North America: Critical Essays for the Twenty-First Century*. New York: Routledge, 2023.

Schultz, Jaime. "Disciplining Sex: 'Gender Verification' Policies and Women's Sport." In *The Palgrave Handbook of Olympic Studies*, ed. Helen Lenskyj and Stephen Wagg, 443–60. New York: Palgrave Macmillan, 2012.

Schuman, Samuel. *Seeing the Light: Religious Colleges in Twenty-First-Century America*. Baltimore, MD: Johns Hopkins University Press, 2010.

Schuster, David G. *Neurasthenic Nation: America's Search for Health, Happiness, and Comfort, 1869-1920*. New Brunswick, NJ: Rutgers University Press, 2011.

Sclar, Ari F. "'The Disadvantage Far Outweighs the Benefits': How the Rise and Fall of 'the Jewish game' at the 92nd Street YMHA Exemplified Jewish Conceptions of Athleticism." In *Beyond Stereotypes: American Jews and Sports*, ed. Bruce Zuckerman, Ari F. Sclar, and Lisa Ansell, 95–128. West Lafayette, IN: Purdue University Press, 2014.

Sells, Michael. *Approaching the Qur'an: The Early Revelations*. 3rd edition. New York: One World Academic, 2023.

Shafer, Michael. *Well Played: A Christian Theology of Sport and the Ethics of Doping*. Cambridge: Lutterworth Press, 2015.

Shoemaker, Terry. *Religions and Sports: The Basics*. New York: Routledge, 2024.

Silver, Peter. *Our Savage Neighbors: How Indian War Transformed Early America*. New York: Norton, 2008.

Smalley, Joe. *More Than a Game*. San Bernadino, CA: Here's Life Publishers, 1981.

Smith, Andrea. "Heteropatriarchy and the Three Pillars of White Supremacy: Rethinking Women of Color Organizing." In *Color of Violence*: The INCITE! Anthology, 66–73. Durham, NC: Duke University Press, 2016.

Smith, Andrew Brodie. *Shooting Cowboys and Indians: Silent Western Films, American Culture, and the Birth of Hollywood*. Boulder: University Press of Colorado, 2004.

Smith, Jonathan Z. *Relating Religion: Essays in the Study of Religion*. Chicago: University of Chicago Press, 2004.

Smith, Maureen. "*Muhammad Speaks* and Muhammad Ali: Intersections of the Nation of Islam and Sport in the 1960s." In *With God on Their Side: Sport in the Service of Religion*, ed. Tara Magdalinski and Timothy J. L. Chandler, 177–96. New York: Routledge, 2002.

Smith, Ronald A. *The Myth of the Amateur: A History of College Athletic Scholarships*. Austin: University of Texas Press, 2021.

Smith, Zachary T., Dennis J. Frost, and Stephen G. Covell, eds. *Religion and Sport in Japan*. Honolulu: University of Hawaii Press, 2024.

Southall, Richard M., and Ellen J. Staurowsky. "Cheering on the Collegiate Model: Creating, Disseminating, and Imbedding the NCAA's Redefinition of Amateurism." *Journal of Sport and Social Issues* 37, no. 4 (November 2013): 315–429.

Staurowsky, Ellen J. "American Indian Imagery and the Miseducation of America." *QUEST* 51 (1999): 382–92.

Sullivan, Winnifred. *The Impossibility of Religious Freedom*. Princeton, NJ: Princeton University Press, 2005.

Tamale, Sylvia. *Decolonization and Afro-Feminism*. Quebec: Daraja Press, 2020.

Thomsen, Steven R., and Harper Anderson. "Using the Rhetoric of Atonement to Analyze Lance Armstrong's Failed Attempt at Redeeming His Public Image." *Journal of Sports Media* 10 (2015): 79–99.

Tillich, Paul. *Dynamics of Faith*. New York: Harper and Row, 1957.

Torevell, David, Clive Palmer, and Paul Rowan, eds. *Training the Body: Perspectives from Religion, Physical Culture and Sport*. New York: Routledge, 2022.

Tuska, Jon. *The American West in Film: Critical Approaches to the Western*. Westport, CN: Greenwood Press, 1985.

Vennum, Thomas. *American Indian Lacrosse: Little Brother of War*. Baltimore, MD: Johns Hopkins University Press, 2008.

Vogan, Travis. *ABC Sports: The Rise and Fall of Network Sports Television*. Berkeley: University of California Press, 2018.

Walker, Jefferson. "God, Gays, and Voodoo: Voicing Blame After Katrina." *Communication and Theater Association of Minnesota Journal* 41, no. 1 (November 2015): 29–48.

Walsh, David. *Seven Deadly Sins: My Pursuit of Lance Armstrong*. New York: Atria Books, 2013.

Welborne, Bozena C., Aubrey Westfall, Özge Çelik Russell, and Sarah A. Tobin. *The Politics of the Headscarf in the United States*. Ithaca, NY: Cornell University Press, 2018.

Wharton, James. *Crusaders for Fitness: The History of American Health Reformers*. Princeton, NJ: Princeton University Press, 1982.

Wiggins, David. "Victory for Allah: Muhammad Ali, the Nation of Islam, and American Society." In *Muhammad Ali, the People's Champ*, ed. Elliot J. Gorn, 88–116. Champaign: University of Illinois Press, 1998.

Wilcox, Melissa, *Coming Out in Christianity: Religion, Identity, and Community*. Bloomington: Indiana University Press, 2003.

Williams, Duncan Ryūken. *American Sutra: A Story of Faith and Freedom in the Second World War*. Cambridge, MA: Belknap Press of Harvard University, 2019.

Witt, David L. *Ernest Thompson Seton: The Life and Legacy of an Artist and Conservationist*. Layton, UT: Gibbs Smith, 2010.

Wolkomir, Michelle. *Be Not Deceived: The Sacred and Sexual Struggles of Gay and Ex-Gay Christian Men*. New Brunswick, NJ: Rutgers University Press, 2006.

Woodbine, Onaje. *Black Gods of the Asphalt: Religion, Hip-Hop, and Street Basketball*. New York: Columbia University Press, 2018.

Woodward, Bob, and Scott Armstrong. *The Brethren: Inside the Supreme Court*. New York: Avon Books, 1979.

X, Malcolm, and Alex Haley. *The Autobiography of Malcolm* X. New York: Ballantine Books, 1964.

Index

Abdul-Qaadir, Bilqis 115–16
Abdullah, Hamza 106, 117–18, 121
Abdullah, Kulsoom 113–14
AIDS crisis 136, 139
African Americans 167
    and 1936 Olympics 51
    and Boy Scouts 33–5
    and college sports 200–1, 210
    and football 156–7
    and martial arts 88, 98, 100–4
    stereotyped as primitive 28, 33, 161–3
    and YMCA 32–3
Alcott, Bronson 26
Ali, Muhammad 16, 71
    American hero 86
    FBI surveillance 77, 79
    and NOI 75–85
    and Vietnam War 77–9, 82–5
Aqeel, Najah 116
amateur sports 123, 180, 195, 199, 203, 210. *See also* college sports, youth sports
American Indians. *See* Native Americans
American Youth Soccer Organization (AYSO) 143, 146–7
amphetamines. *See under* doping
androstenedione (andro). *See under* doping
antisemitism 16, 21, 37–53
anxious bench 179, 185, 188, 192–3
Arledge, Roone 56–7
Armstrong, Lance 178, 189–192
Asian Americans 16. *See also* Japanese internment
    and martial arts 98–9
Athletes in Action (AIA) 54, 57–8, 60–1, 64, 68, 206

baby boomers 136, 139
baseball (sport) 14. *See also* LLB/S, MLB
    Black baseball 37, 48–9, 52
    Jewish players 52–3
basketball (sport) 24–5, 39, 46–7, 158, 115–16, 200–1. *See also* FIBA, NBA, WNBA
    different rules for women and girls 145–6
Bassons, Christophe 189

Bay Area Laboratory Co-operative (BALCO) 183–4, 188
Beers, George 10
Beggs, Mack 139–140
Black Americans. *See* African Americans
Black Karate Federation (BKF) 88, 100–4
    in *Enter the Dragon* 100
Black Lives Matter 160, 175
Black Protestants 32–3, 140–1
Black Muslims 16, 109. *See also* NOI
Black Sox scandal 41–4
Bonds, Barry 182, 184, 188
boy problem 26–32, 143
Boy Scouts of America (BSA) 143
    Black troops 33–6
    and playing Indian 29, 164, 166, 171
boxing (sport) 116. *See also* IBA
Brundage, Avery 50, 131
Buddhism 88–91, 93–4, 96, 100, 104, 110
Bush, George W. 86, 184
Butterfield, Rosaria 67
Byers, Walter 200

Cain, Mary 150–2
Camp, Walter 197
Campus Crusade for Christ (Cru) 56, 66–8
Canseco, Jose 182–6, 193
Cantu, Robert 155
Carter, Jimmy 85
Caslavska, Vera 148
Catholicism 19–21, 109, 140–1, 196, 205
Cates, Ernie 97–8
Chambers, Alan 135
character building 19, 36, 184
    critique of 144, 178–9, 192–3
cheerleading (sport) 48, 148
Chelette, Ricky 134–5
Chicago Race Riot of 1919 35
children 207. *See also* youth sports
Chief Illiniwek 165–172
Christianity 19–20, 108, 160–3. *See also* Black Protestants, Catholicism, evangelicalism, Protestantism, white Protestants
Christian Athlete Circles (CAC) 68–9

civilization 160–3, 176
Clay, Cassius. *See* Muhammad Ali
Clay, William Lacy 187
Clinton, Bill 86, 136
Cody, William 165
Cold War 131, 180
college sports 25, 123, 195. *See also* NCAA
    at denominational colleges 195, 204–7
    origins 197–8;
    and paying players 199, 202 (*see also* NIL)
colonialism 8–9
    North America 9–11, 160–3, 176
Comaneci, Nadia 150
confession 178–9, 185, 188, 190–3. *See also* anxious bench
Confucianism 88–91, 100, 104
Conscientious Objection (CO) 77–84
Conte, Victor 183
conversion therapy 134–5
COVID-19 pandemic 104, 125
curse of Ham 161–2
cycling (sport) 178, 180, 189–191. *See also* Tour de France, UCI

Davis, Kelsey 68–9
Dearborn Independent 42–4
Deford, Frank 58–60
desegregation 74, 156–7
    of Boy Scouts 33, 35
Diggs, Kelly "Khadijah" 114–15, 121
disordered eating 148–152
Division for Girls' and Women's Sports (DGWS) 145–6
doping 123. *See also* USADA, WADA
    amphetamines 180–1, 189
    androstenedione (andro) 182, 184
    erythropoietin (EPO) 183, 189–190
    human growth hormone (HGH) 183
    and MLB 181–188, 193
    and Olympics 180–1
    origins of 180
    steroids 181–9, 193
    and Tour de France 178, 180, 189–192
Duncan, Ron 98
Dunne, Olivia 208–9

Edenfield, Michaela 210
Edwards, John Bel 139
Eisenhower, Dwight 153
Electronic Arts (EA) 200–1
Eliot, Charles 39–40
erythropoietin (EPO). *See under* doping
Ethiopian Clowns (baseball team) 48–9

eugenics 45
evangelicalism 16, 20
    and sports (*see* sports ministry)
    theology 55, 61
    views on homosexuality and gay marriage 134–6, 140
    views on transsexuality 129, 140–1
Exodus International 134–5
ex-gay ministry 66–7, 134–5

Fard, W. D. 72
Federal Bureau of Investigation (FBI) 103–4
    and Japanese internment 93
    and Muhammad Ali 77, 79
Fédération Internationale de Football Association (FIFA) 14, 62–3, 110–11, 118
Fellowship of Christian Athletes (FCA) 54–6, 58, 60, 64, 68
fencing (sport) 120
field hockey (sport) 125–6
figure skating (sport) 148
Finney, Charles 179, 192
Floyd, George 160
football (sport) 106, 125, 131, 144, 153–7. *See also* NFL, Pop Warner, Super Bowl
    intercollegiate 197–9, 202, 204
Ford, Henry 42
Fruit of Islam (FOI). *See under* NOI

Gabbard, Tulsi 126
gay marriage 127, 135–7, 141
gender 123, 126–130, 137–8, 208–9
    education about 140–1
    norms 63, 146–7
    pronouns 68
    soft essentialism 146–7
    and youth sports 144–158
generation Z 135, 139
Giambi, Jason 184
Girl Guides 143
great migration 21, 37, 96, 163
great sport myth 13–14
Greenberg, Hank 52
Griffith, John L. 153
Gulick, Luther 24
gymnastics (sport) 148–150, 208–9

Hannah, Dave 57–8
heathenism 162–3
Henrich, Christy 150
high school sports 25, 116. *See also* youth sports
hijab. *See* veiling

Index

Hitler, Adolf 49–50
hockey (sport) 156
homophobia 26, 55, 63–70, 126–7, 133
    and conservative Christianity 134–8, 141
Hooten, Donald 184, 186–7
Hooten, Taylor 184, 186–8
House v. NCAA 201–4
human growth hormone (HGH). *See under* doping

immigration 16, 19, 21
    1924 Immigration Law 21, 36, 45–6
    Catholic 45, 163
    Chinese 45
    Jewish 37, 39, 163
    Muslim 109–110
Indians. *See* Native Americans
industrialization 19, 24–6
Intercollegiate Tennis Association (ITA) 202–4
International Association of Athletics Federation (IAAF, now World Athletics) 131–2
    and sex testing 131–3
International Basketball Federation (FIBA) 115–16
International Boxing Association (IBA) 116
International Olympic Committee (IOC) 49–50, 148, 180–1. *See also* Olympic Games
    and sex testing 131–2
International Weightlifting Federation (IWF) 113–14
intersexuality 126–7
Irving, Kyrie 118–19
Islam 16, 72, 85, 107–9
Ironman 114–15
Ivey, Kay 126

Japanese internment. *See under* World War II
Jewish Community Center (JCC) 40. *See also* YMHA, YWHA
Jones, KC 101, 103–4
Jordan, Michael 181
Judaism 21, 37–8, 110
judo (martial art/sport) 88, 90–4, 96, 104
    in U.S. military 97–9
jujutsu (martial art) 88, 90, 93, 98

Kano, Jigori 88, 90–3
karate (martial art/sport) 88, 91, 100–4
King, Martin Luther Jr. 77, 83
Klobukowska, Ewa 131
Kodokan 88, 90–1
Korbut, Olga 148
Koufax, Sandy 52

kung fu (martial art/sport) 88, 99, 104
    movie industry 16, 99–100, 104

lacrosse (sport) 9–11
Leblanc, Jean-Marie 189–190
Lee, Bruce 88, 99–100, 103
LeMond, Kathy 190
Leno, Jay 188
Leutwiler, Lester 165–6, 171
LGBTQIA+ 66–9, 134–141
Little League Baseball/Softball (LLB/S) 144–7, 156, 159
Living Hope Ministries 134–5

Madigan, John 170–1
Mann, Horace 26
Major League Baseball (MLB) 37, 41–4, 49
    and doping 178, 181–8, 193
Major League Soccer (MLS) 119–120
martial arts 88–105
    and Black Americans 88, 100–4
    and Hollywood 99–100
    in Japan 89–91
    and Japanese internment 94–5
    in Olympics 104
    in U.S. military 16, 97–9
Martínez–Patiño, Maria José 131
McCain, John 184
McClanen, Don 55–6
McGwire, Mark 182, 183–8
McKee, Georgia 68–9
McKenzie, Holly 206–7, 209
millennials 135, 139
Miller, Shannon 150
modest clothing 16, 109–116. *See also* veiling
Muslim Americans 106–9. *See also* NOI
    and Ramadan 117–121
    and September 11, 2001 106–8
    U.S. population 109
    and veiling 109–116, 120–1
Muhammad, Elijah 72–5, 78–82, 84–5
Muhammad, Ibtihaj 120
Muhammad, Steve 88, 100–4
Muhammad, W. D. 85
muscular Christianity 17, 19, 123, 179–181, 184, 192–3
    and African Americans 32–5
    and boys 27–32, 143–4, 158
    and football 153–4
    invention of basketball 24–5, 39
    and martial arts 91
    playing Indian 164–5
    YMCA 23–6

Naismith, James 24–5, 39
name, image, and likeness (NIL) 195, 200–210
Nation of Islam (NOI) 71–5, 88, 110
    and CO 84
    Fruit of Islam (FOI) 78–9
National Basketball Association (NBA) 46, 118–19
National Collegiate Athletic Association (NCAA) 57, 115, 120, 129, 148, 151, 197–205, 211
    Native American mascots 160, 172
    NIL 195, 200–10
    transfer portal 205–7
National Football League (NFL) 117–18, 121, 155–7, 160, 182, 184
Native Americans 9–11, 161–3
    activism 161, 166–8, 172–3, 176
    emulated 29–30, 163–6, 169–172
    as mascots 123, 160–1, 165–176
    stereotype of the savage 28–9, 160–3, 176
nativism 37, 45–6
Neal, Wes 57, 60–1
neurasthenia 22–3, 36
ninjutsu (martial art) 98
Nixon, Richard 153–4
nonbinary (gender identity) 127–9, 139

Obama, Barack 86, 160
O'Bannon, Ed 200–1
Olympic Games 14, 180–2, 184. See also IOC
    1932 Los Angeles 93
    1936 Berlin 49–52, 130–1
    1956 Melbourne 148
    1960 Rome 71
    1968 Mexico City 148
    1972 Munich 148
    1976 Montreal 149
    1988 Seoul 150
    1992 Barcelona 149–150
    1996 Atlanta 62, 86
    2012 London 117
    2016 Rio de Janeiro 120, 133
    2021 Tokyo 148
    2024 Paris 104
    and gender fraud 130–3
Omalu, Bennet 155–6
over-civilization 22–3, 28

Palmeiro, Rafael 184, 186
Parker, Ed 103
Patterson, Floyd 75–6
Pearl Harbor attack 51
performance enhancing drugs. See doping
Pepe, Maria 144–5

Phelps, Michael 132–3
Pollock, Syd 48–9
Pop Warner football 154–6
Price, Dani 210
Protestantism 20
Puckett, Adam 209

Rabbi Isaac Elchanan Theological Seminary (RIETS) 47–8
Ramadan (fasting) 16, 107–8, 117–121
Ratjen, Heinrich 130–1
recapitulation theory 28, 164
redskins 160
    Washington D.C. football team 160, 167, 172–6
    as racial slur 160, 173, 175–6
religion, definitions
    Christian prototype definition 6–7
    formal definition 4–5
    functional definition 3–4
    as a legal category 6–8
    substantive definition 5–6
religiously unaffiliated 136, 140–1
Rice, Tamir 157
Robinson, Jackie 49
Rock, Chris 188
Rodgers, Julie 134–5
Roosevelt, Franklin D. 51, 93
Roosevelt, Theodore 29, 36, 88, 92–3, 153

Salazar, Alberto 150–2
Sanchez, Linda 186–7
Sanders, Steve. See Steve Muhammad
Saperstein, Abe 48–9
Sceggel, Tim 206
Schilling, Curt 184, 186
Scouting USA. See BSA
segregation of sports
    by race 32–6, 143
    by sex 123, 143–158
September 11, 2001 attacks 70, 106–8, 110
Semenya, Caster 132–3
Seton, Earnest Thompson 29–30
Seton's Woodcraft Indians 29–30
Seven Years' War 163
sex 126–130, 137–8, 140–1. See also gender
Smith, Brian 206
Smith, Jerry 100–1
Smith, John 162
Snyder, Daniel 160, 173, 176
soccer (sport) 143, 156. See also FIFA, AYSO
social media 175, 195, 207–10
softball (sport) 135, 210. See also LLB/S

Sosa, Sammy 182, 184, 186
Souder, Mark 186–7
South Philadelphia Hebrew Association (SPHAs) 46–8
sport, definition of 15
sports ministry 54, 60–2
    on college campuses 66–9, 195, 206–10
    critique of 58–60, 66–9
    organizations (see AIA, FCA, CAC, Upward Sports)
    origins of 55–8
    and women 63–70
Sprinkle, Preston 67
Stephens, Helen 130–1
steroids. See under doping
Super Bowl. See also NFL
    1984 11–13
    1992 167
summer camp 29
Sweeney, John 187
swimming (sport) 111–13, 129, 132–3, 157

t-ball (sport) 147
taekwondo (martial art/sport) 88, 91, 104
tennis (sport) 121, 202–4. See also ITA
testosterone 126, 129, 132–3, 183
Teters, Charlene 168, 172
Thomas, Lia 128–130
Title IX 55, 62, 126, 144, 148, 202
Tom Brown's School Days 27–8
Tour de France 178, 180, 189–191
track and field (sport) 130–3, 150–2. See also IAAF
traumatic brain injury 155–6
transsexuality 127
    and sports 123, 126, 128–130, 133–4
Trevor Project 139
triathlon (sport) 114–15, 121. See also USA Triathlon
Trump, Donald 136, 202

Union Cycliste Internationale (UCI) 190
Upward Sports 157–8
urbanization 21–2, 33, 35–6
U.S. Anti-Doping Agency (USADA) 181, 190, 194
USA Triathlon 115
USA Weightlifting 113–14

veiling 16, 108–16
Vietnam War 59–60, 71, 77–86
volleyball (sport) 116

Walsh, David 178, 189
Walsh, Stella 130–1
Warner, Gary 59–61
Webster, Mike 155
weightlifting (sport) 57, 113–14. See also IWF, USA Weightlifting
white Protestantism 140, 143, 145, 163
whiteness 160, 166–7, 176, 208. See also nativism
Wild West shows 165
Wilken, Claudia 200–2
Williams, Donnie 88, 100–4
Winfrey, Oprah 178–9, 190–2
Women's National Basketball Association (WNBA) 62
World Athletics. See IAAF
World Anti-Doping Agency (WADA) 190
World Cup. See FIFA
World Series. See also MLB
    1919 41–4
    1991 167
    1994 cancellation 181–2
World War I 36, 49, 78, 153
World War II 51–2, 72, 78, 91, 154, 180, 197
    Japanese internment 88, 93–6, 104
    post-war occupation of Japan 97–9, 104

X, Malcolm 74–6, 84

Yearwood, Andraya 140
Yeshiva College. See RIETS
Yoshitsugu, Yamashita 92
Young Men's Christian Association (YMCA) 23–5, 29, 36, 39, 46, 104, 143
    Black YMCA 32–3
Young Men's Hebrew Association (YMHA) 37–40
Young Women's Christian Association (YWCA) 143
Young Women's Hebrew Association (YWHA) 40
youth sports 123, 125–6, 139. See also AYSO, LLB/S, Pop Warner
    for boys 153–7
    coaching 146–7, 150–2
    delay of puberty due to 148–150
    and gender 143–7, 157–8
    for girls 148–152

Zafar, Amaiya 116
Zülle, Alex 189